Attainment's

Life Skill Lessons

650 ready-to-use transition activities

5-minute lessons

**Coordinates with the
FUTR Tool Assessment and the PACT**

Ellen McPeek Glisan

Life Skill Lessons is a collection of 650 guided lesson plans that support life skill activities and align with math, science/health, social studies, and language arts curriculum areas. The lesson activities are part of the *Aligning Life Skills to Academics Program.*

Author: Ellen McPeek Glisan, Ph.D

Graphic Design: Jo Reynolds

Life Skill Lessons
ISBN 1-57861-596-8
©2006, 2008 Attainment Company, Inc.
All rights reserved.
Printed in the United States of America

Attainment Company, Inc.
P.O. Box 930160
Verona, Wisconsin 53593-0160 USA
1-800-327-4269
www.AttainmentCompany.com

Table of Contents

Introduction

Incorporating life skills into academic classes helps students understand the connection between school and their daily lives. Having such an understanding often helps students find school more meaningful and helps them see a bigger picture in which many daily-living functions take on a logical order. Students who are comfortable with this bigger picture are more likely to successfully manage their personal lives.

The **Life Skill Lessons** curriculum provides a method of inserting important life skills instruction into any academic curriculum with minimal interference. The 650 daily activities each take only a few minutes to complete, and cover different tasks, ideas, and skills that adults use in their daily lives.

As part of the *Aligning Life Skills to Academics Program,* these guided activity plans coordinate with the companion set of *Life Skill Worksheets,* which provides a variety of independent student activities. Both collections are aligned with math, social studies, science/health, and language arts curriculum areas. Curriculum alignment means that these activity plans and worksheets are optimized for integration with departmentalized academic programs. The 650 functional life skills addressed by the *Aligning Life Skills to Academics Program* smoothly integrate life skill activities into a subject-based academic curriculum through the concept of "functional academics." Both the activities and the worksheets focus on giving students an understanding of a specific skill as well as providing opportunities to practice the skills.

The Individuals with Disabilities Act (IDEA) requires that a student's Individual Educational Plan (IEP) include a coordinated set of transition activities. Life skill training is a key component in assuring that each student has a reasonable chance of a smooth movement from school to post-school activities. The *Life Skill Lessons* and the *Life Skill Worksheets* were created to help teachers and IEP teams address this broad set of student needs with outcome-oriented, process-specific objectives.

The 650 activity plans provided by **Life Skill Lessons** are divided into five subject areas:

Math	131 activities
Social Studies	141 activities
Science/Health	169 activities
Expressive Literacy	94 activities
Receptive Literacy	115 activities

To provide variety and to assure that different learning styles are addressed, activities utilize these diverse formats:

- Action
- Brainstorming
- Calculation
- Demonstration
- Discussion
- Drawing
- Graph or Chart
- Hands-On
- Oral Response
- Role Play
- Written

Activities are intended to instill a general awareness, not to offer complete training on any aspect of the skills nor to cover all aspects of the skills. When you think your students could benefit from additional lessons in connection with a particular skill, use additional activities and materials to expand as needed.

Ma 79: Reading charts, tables, and graphs

FUTR Tool: 18
PACT: yes

Supplies: An overhead or copies with a chart, table, and graph

Find a chart, a table, and a graph from a textbook, newspaper, or magazine. Either put all three items onto one overhead (or page to be copied) or make separate overheads (or pages to be copied). Show students the overhead (or pass out copies) and discuss how charts, tables, and graphs are alike and different and how to read each of them.

Objective: Student will study a chart, a table, and a graph and will discuss how they are alike and different as well as how to read each of them.

Subject: Math **Mode:** Demonstration **Training Zone:** [V] Observation	**Readiness Factor:** [2] Daily Living **Readiness Factor Category:** [g] Time and Order

One short activity is presented for each skill. The listing of needed activity supplies does not mention standard classroom equipment such as black or white board, chalk, wipe-off board markers, paper, pencils, or pens. In addition to subject areas and learning style formats, each *Life Skill Lessons* activity is assigned to one of 12 training zones and further described by readiness factors and categories.

Training Zones:

Organization [O]

Logic [L]

Responsibility [R]

Conscientiousness [C]

Flexibility [F]

Observation [V]

Socialization [Z]

Self-awareness [S]

Exploration [E]

Manipulation [M]

Analysis [A]

Conclusion [U]

Readiness Factors and sub-categories:

[1] Career Readiness
  [a] *Career Preparation* • [b] *Job Performance*

[2] Daily Living Readiness
  [c] *Finances* • [d] *Household Care and/or Chores* • [e] *Safety and Security*
  [f] *Shopping and Eating at Restaurants* • [g] *Time and Order* • [h] *Transportation/Travel/Worldliness*

[3] Personal/Social Readiness
  [i] *Relationships* • [j] *Leisure/Desires/Choices* • [k] *Community Involvement and Responsibility*
  [l] *Health, Diet, and Appearance*

Relationship to the FUTR Tool assessment system:

The *Life Skill Lessons* curriculum includes 180 activities that are addressed in the FUTR Tool (Forecasting and Understanding Transition Readiness) assessment plus 223 more that are used for the skills review checklists in the companion book *PACT* (PArents, Children and Teachers) *Life Skill Review*. 247 of the activities exist in this book only.

Activity plans from *Life Skill Lessons* are available as individual documents. Using the *Aligning Life Skills to Academics* document software, the activities may be saved as either Adobe PDF or Microsoft Word files. Use the MS-Word format to add special instructions or to customize the activity content.

System Requirements: Windows 2000 or higher / Mac OS 10.2 or higher / 32 MB RAM / Java Adobe Acrobat Reader for PDF (available on the CD) / Microsoft Word for MS-Word format

Lesson documents can be located by using the directory identifier codes, by typing in keywords from titles, or by choosing from a subject list.

Aligning Life Skills to Academics

File   Help

| Use Directory IDs | Use Keyword Search | Use Subject Lists | Sort Life Skill Lessons |

You can use the *Life Skill Lessons* subject and type categories to sort the activities.

Subject: **Math**
Training Zone: **[A] Analysis**
Learning Style: **Drawing**
Readiness Factor: **[2] Daily Living**
Readiness Factor Category: **[d] Household Care and/or Chores**

Select documents to be saved. Click Get Files to continue.   Documents: 2 (0)

(Ma 62) Measuring for a recipe
(Ma 130) Wrapping a gift

Life Skill Lesson: *Reading charts, tables, and graphs* (Ma 79)

Subject: **Math** / Training Zone: **[V] Observation**
Mode: **Demonstration** / Readiness Factor: **[2] Daily Living, [g] Time and Order**

Objective(s): *Student will study a chart, a table, and a graph and will discuss how they are alike and different as well as how to read each of them.*

Supplies: *An overhead or copies with a chart, table, and graph*

Find a chart, a table, and a graph from a textbook, newspaper, or magazine. Either put all three items onto one overhead (or page to be copied) or make separate overheads (or pages to be copied). Show students the overhead (or pass out copies) and discuss how charts, tables, and graphs are alike and different and how to read each of them.

Example: *Life Skill Lessons* **activity document**

The document software also includes the companion worksheets from *Aligning Life Skills to Academics.*

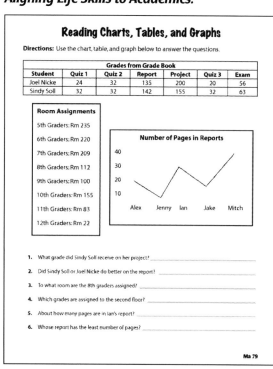

Example: *Aligning Life Skills to Academics* **worksheet document**

Math

Life Skill Lessons

Table of Contents: *Math*

Ma 1: **Allotting adequate time**

Supplies: None

Ask students to imagine this scenario: It is Saturday. You have to clean your room before you can go out with your friends. You know it will take an hour to clean your room. You want to leave with your friend at 3:00. Ask students when they should start cleaning the room.

Answer: Anytime before 2:00; Discuss that prompt action allows time to deal with unforeseen problems or distractions as well as for a relaxed pace.

Objective: Student will allot adequate time to complete tasks.

Subject: Math	**Readiness Factor:** [2] Daily Living
Mode: Discussion	**Readiness Factor Category:** [g] Time and Order
Training Zone: [O] Organization	

Ma 2: **Applying for a loan**

Supplies: None

Discuss these two common ways to get a loan:

1. Go to a bank or credit union and tell them you want to apply for a loan. They will ask you to fill out forms and tell you any other things they need you to do. Then, they will let you know if you qualify for the loan.
2. Ask a family member or friend if you can borrow money. Even though it is a family member or friend, plan to sign an agreement, pay on time, and pay interest.

Objective: Student will discuss common ways to get a loan.

Subject: Math	**Readiness Factor:** [2] Daily Living
Mode: Discussion	**Readiness Factor Category:** [c] Finances
Training Zone: [E] Exploration	

Ma 3: **Approximating measurements**

Supplies: Container that holds between six and ten cups, a book

Ask volunteers to approximate the measurements in each of the following situations:

a. Hold your hands about two feet apart and ask about how far apart your hands are.

b. Hold up a container and ask about how much water it holds.

c. Show students a book and ask about how much it weighs.

d. Ask about how far it is from the front of the classroom to the back of the classroom.

e. Ask about how tall you are.

f. Explain that Ali is planting her garden and the package of bean seeds says to plant one seed every inch. Ask students to show, with their forefingers and thumbs, how far apart to plant the seeds.

Answer: Either measure to confirm each answer or use your own approximations.

Objective: Student will approximate general measurements (length, weight, volume) with fairly good accuracy.

Subject: Math	**Readiness Factor:** [2] Daily Living
Mode: Oral Response	**Readiness Factor Category:** [d] Household Care and/or Chores
Training Zone: [F] Flexibility	

Ma 4: Arranging furniture so it is attractive and useful

FUTR Tool: no
PACT: no

Supplies: For each student: Piece of paper with a room layout, page of living room furniture that can be cut out and arranged in the room, scissors, tape

Give each student a piece of paper with a room layout. (Include shape of room, windows, doors, and other permanent things of choice such as a fireplace or built-in bookshelves.) Give each student a page of "living room furniture." (The living room furniture can be hand-drawn, from computer clip-art, etc.) Ask them to cut out the furniture and then arrange it in the room and tape it in place when they like their arrangements. Ask volunteers to share their arrangements. Discuss the benefits of the different arrangements.

Objective: Student will arrange furniture so it is attractive and useful.

Subject: Math	**Readiness Factor:** [2] Daily Living
Mode: Hands-On	**Readiness Factor Category:** [d] Household Care and/or Chores
Training Zone: [M] Manipulation	

Ma 5: Being punctual

FUTR Tool: 12
PACT: yes

Supplies: None

Ask volunteers to give examples of being punctual and being late for each of the following situations. Also, ask them to give the "best arrival" times.

a. You have a hair cut appointment at 10:00 a.m. [Punctual: between 9:45 and 10:00; Late: 10:01 or later; Best: between 9:55 and 9:59]

b. You are leaving on an airplane at 5:00 p.m. [Punctual: between 3:00 and 3:30; Late: 4:00 or later; Best: about two hours ahead of flight time]

c. You are meeting friends at a restaurant. Your reservation is for 7:00 p.m. [Punctual: 7:00 or before; Late: after 7:00; Best: between 6:55 and 6:59]

d. Your first class at school starts at 8:34 a.m. [Punctual: by 8:33; Late: after 8:34; Best: Varies]

Objective: Student will identify punctual and non-punctual times as well as "best" arrival time for appointments.

Subject: Math	**Readiness Factor:** [1] Career
Mode: Oral Response	**Readiness Factor Category:** [b] Job Performance
Training Zone: [C] Conscientiousness	

Ma 6: Budgeting

FUTR Tool: 32
PACT: yes

Supplies: None

Tell students to imagine they are short on money. Ask them to decide which of the choices below would be good ways to spend their money.

a. Eating at a nice restaurant [no]

b. Paying the water bill [yes]

c. Inviting a friend over for popcorn and a movie [yes]

d. Buying original art [no]

e. Getting new jeans because there is a new style you like [no]

f. Getting new tennis shoes because your old ones have fallen apart [yes]

Objective: Student will choose items that should be included in a tight budget.

Subject: Math	**Readiness Factor:** [2] Daily Living
Mode: Oral Response	**Readiness Factor Category:** [c] Finances
Training Zone: [A] Analysis	

Ma 7: Buying the best deal

Supplies: Some or all of these empty soda containers (or packages) with prices attached (large tags): 12 oz, 16 oz, 20 oz, 1 liter, 2 liter, 6-pack, 12-pack, case

Place the priced soda containers where students can easily see them. Ask students to list the items in order of the best deal per serving of soda. Allow students to use calculators if they have them. Point out that the one and two liter bottles also give ounces on the label and they will need to use the ounces so they can compare common units.

Objective: By comparing prices and sizes, student will decide which purchase is the best deal.

Subject: Math	**Readiness Factor:** [2] Daily Living
Mode: Calculation	**Readiness Factor Category:** [f] Shopping and Eating at Restaurants
Training Zone: [U] Conclusion	

Ma 8: Calculating quantities

Supplies: None

Ask students the following questions.

a. How much hamburger would you need to make hamburgers for eight people? [between two and four pounds]

b. How much soda would you need if you were having a party for ten people? [between 20 and 30 cans OR three large bottles]

c. Assume a person wears white socks everyday. How many pairs does he need? [about 7]

d. You can buy individual pencils, a package of three, a box of twelve, or a box of 24. How many does it make sense for you to buy at a time? [varies]

Objective: Student will use logic to calculate needed quantities.

Subject: Math	**Readiness Factor:** [2] Daily Living
Mode: Oral Response	**Readiness Factor Category:** [d] Household Care and/or Chores
Training Zone: [A] Analysis	

Ma 9: Checking to see what will fit in a new home

Supplies: None

Discuss that one way to tell what furniture will fit where when looking at a new home (and your furniture is still in your old home) is to measure the new home and measure the furniture. Explain that measuring lets you fairly easily figure out where things will and will not fit. Caution students that sometimes they will not be able to measure the new home right away. Tell them that they can get some general ideas by using their feet as measuring tools. Explain that they can walk heel-to-toe (no space in between) and count the "feet." Demonstrate this "human-foot-measure" for students by measuring a classroom wall. Count your steps aloud so students can easily see the process. (Make sure to count the first step as well as all the others.) Have students practice the measuring steps.

Objective: Student will use his feet to measure wall and furniture lengths.

Subject: Math	**Readiness Factor:** [2] Daily Living
Mode: Demonstration, Action	**Readiness Factor Category:** [d] Household Care and/or Chores
Training Zone: [V] Observation	

Ma 10: Choosing a lid that will fit based on shape

FUTR Tool: no
PACT: no

Supplies: Three different-sized boxes with removable lids, three other lids that do not fit the boxes

Place three boxes of different sizes and shapes where students can see them. Place six lids (three that fit the boxes and three of other shapes and sizes) where students can see them. Ask students to look at the boxes and lids and, without trying them, decide which lids fit which boxes. Then, let students try them to check their guesses.

Objective: Student will choose lids that fit based on shapes and sizes.

Subject: Math **Mode:** Hands-On **Training Zone:** [V] Observation	**Readiness Factor:** [2] Daily Living **Readiness Factor Category:** [d] Household Care and/or Chores

Ma 11: Choosing appropriate box sizes

FUTR Tool: no
PACT: yes

Supplies: Five different-sized boxes and ten items that can fit into the boxes (at least one item for each box)

Place the five boxes where students can see them. Choose one item and ask a volunteer to identify the box that would best hold the item. Have student check to see if the choice is correct. Repeat with each of the other items.

Discuss that, when choosing boxes, you should first make a size guess and then you should try it before planning to use the box.

Objective: Student will choose appropriate-sized boxes.

Subject: Math **Mode:** Hands-On **Training Zone:** [U] Conclusion	**Readiness Factor:** [2] Daily Living **Readiness Factor Category:** [d] Household Care and/or Chores

Ma 12: Choosing clothes that look good together

FUTR Tool: no
PACT: no

Supplies: None

Choose three students to come to the front of the room—one with a print shirt, one with a plaid or striped shirt, and one with a bright solid-colored shirt. As a group, choose clothing items from other students that match and items that clash with each of the shirts. (Make sure students understand that they are simply matching colors and prints, so they can match shirt to shirt.)

Objective: None

Subject: Math **Mode:** Action **Training Zone:** [V] Observation	**Readiness Factor:** [3] Personal/Social **Readiness Factor Category:** [l] Health, Diet, and Appearance

Ma 13: Choosing clothes that look nice on you

Supplies: None

Discuss that different people look good in different styles and colors. Suggest that students try different styles and colors to see which look best on them.

Also, point out that clothes that fit well usually look best. Tell students that clothes that are too big tend to make people look sloppy and heavier than they really are. Clothes that are too tight tend to make people look uncomfortable and heavier than they actually are.

Objective: Student will discuss different clothing choices.

Subject: Math	**Readiness Factor:** [3] Personal/Social
Mode: Discussion	**Readiness Factor Category:** [l] Health, Diet, and Appearance
Training Zone: [S] Self-Awareness	

Ma 14: Choosing measurement instruments

Supplies: Ruler, yardstick/meter stick, 2-quart pitcher, cup, tablespoon, bathroom scale, postal scale, science scale

Discuss with students that, when you want to measure something, it helps to know the measurement choices. Divide the class into small groups and pass out the measurement instruments. Ask each team to measure one thing with each of the instruments they have. Then, have teams rotate the instruments and repeat. If time allows, rotate and repeat until all students have used all items.

Objective: Student will use different measuring instruments.

Subject: Math	**Readiness Factor:** [2] Daily Living
Mode: Hands-On	**Readiness Factor Category:** [d] Household Care and/or Chores
Training Zone: [U] Conclusion	

Ma 15: Choosing the right kind of screwdriver

Supplies: Screwdrivers: 2 or 3 sizes of both phillips and slotted, several sizes of screws screwed into a piece of wood—use some phillips screws and some slotted screws

Place the screwdrivers and the piece of wood in the center of a table and have students gather around. Point out the different sizes of screwdrivers and the different shapes of the ends. Also, point out how the screwdrivers match the different screws. Then, point to the screws and ask volunteers to tell which screw drivers they would use with which screw.

Objective: Student will see the difference between phillips and slotted screwdrivers.

Subject: Math	**Readiness Factor:** [2] Daily Living
Mode: Demonstration	**Readiness Factor Category:** [d] Household Care and/or Chores
Training Zone: [V] Observation	

Ma 16: Collecting tax information and filing taxes

FUTR Tool: no
PACT: yes

Supplies: None

Discuss that people in the U.S. who work are supposed to pay income tax. Ask volunteers to name items that people need to gather together when doing their taxes. Make sure the list includes the following items:

- W-2 form
- Educational expenses
- Interest income
- Business expenses
- Other income
- Charitable contributions
- Medical expenses

Objective: Student will identify items to collect when preparing to do taxes.

Subject: Math **Mode:** Discussion **Training Zone:** [R] Responsibility	**Readiness Factor:** [2] Daily Living **Readiness Factor Category:** [c] Finances

Ma 17: Controlling credit card levels

FUTR Tool: 4
PACT: yes

Supplies: None

Ask students to brainstorm a list of positive reasons for using credit cards and a list of negative reasons for using credit cards. Discuss that the only way to control credit card levels is to pay off the balance at the end of each month and, if you can't, you are spending too much.

Answer: Some possible positive reasons: needed clothes, phone or on-line purchasing, travel expenses; Some negative reasons: unneeded clothes, wanted (not needed) items that you really cannot afford

Objective: Student will identify positive and negative uses for credit cards and will understand that he should pay credit card balances in full each month. Student will understand that not being able to pay a credit card bill at the end of the month is a sign that he is spending too much.

Subject: Math **Mode:** Brainstorming **Training Zone:** [L] Logic	**Readiness Factor:** [2] Daily Living **Readiness Factor Category:** [f] Shopping and Eating at Restaurants

Ma 18: Correlating room numbers and floors

FUTR Tool: no
PACT: no

Supplies: None

Discuss that, in large buildings with elevators, the beginning number(s) in the room or office number is (are) also the floor number. As examples, explain that Room 416 is on the 4th floor and Office 3321 is on the 33rd floor. Call out each of the following room or office numbers and ask volunteers to tell which floor each is on.

- Room 632 [6th]
- Suite 500 [5th]
- Office 6143 [61st]
- Apartment 608 [6th]
- Room 1831 [18th]

Objective: Student will correlate hotel rooms, offices, and apartment numbers with floors in a building.

Subject: Math **Mode:** Oral Response **Training Zone:** [A] Analysis	**Readiness Factor:** [2] Daily Living **Readiness Factor Category:** [h] Transportation/Travel/Worldliness

Ma 19: Counting from 1-30

FUTR Tool: no
PACT: yes

Supplies: None

Ask a volunteer to count aloud from 1–30. When student is finished, ask the whole class to count together aloud from 1–30. When group is finished, ask the whole class to count to 30 as a group, with just one person saying a number at a time. Tell students to be ready to say the next number when you point at them.

Answer: Watch for students who are not counting or not counting correctly. If necessary, repeat one or more of the activities for extra practice.

Objective: Student will correctly count orally from 1-30.

Subject: Math **Mode:** Oral Response **Training Zone:** [O] Organization	**Readiness Factor:** [2] Daily Living **Readiness Factor Category:** [g] Time and Order

Ma 20: Counting money

FUTR Tool: no
PACT: no

Supplies: Coins in the amounts below – either actual coins, realistic classroom coins, or coins on an overhead or on copies

Ask students to count the money in each of the groups below:

a. three pennies, two nickels, one dime, one half dollar [73¢]

b. three nickels, two dimes, three quarters [$1.10]

c. one nickel, three dimes, one quarter, one $1 bill, one $5 bill [$6.60]

d. four dimes, seven quarters, two $1 bills, two $5 bills [$14.15]

e. two nickels, two dimes, two quarters, two $10 bills, two $20 bills [$60.80]

Objective: Student will count coins and bills to get a total money amount.

Subject: Math **Mode:** Hands-On **Training Zone:** [M] Manipulation	**Readiness Factor:** [2] Daily Living **Readiness Factor Category:** [c] Finances

Ma 21: Counting ply

FUTR Tool: no
PACT: no

Supplies: String, rope, or yarn with different numbers of ply–One piece at least six inches long for each student

Hand each student a piece of string, rope, or yarn that has more than one ply (can unwrap into separate strings). Ask each student to find out how many ply her string has.

Objective: Student will count the ply in a piece of string, rope, or yarn.

Subject: Math **Mode:** Hands-On **Training Zone:** [V] Observation	**Readiness Factor:** [3] Personal/Social **Readiness Factor Category:** [j] Leisure/Desires/Choices

Ma 22: Counting using the skip method

Supplies: None

On paper, ask students to each make a row of Xs, 1/3s, circles standing for quarters, slash marks, and rectangles standing for dollars. On the board, show an example of each: XX, 1/3 1/3, OO, //, [ ][ ]

Have students trade papers with partners and count their partner's Xs by twos, 1/3s by threes, quarters by fours, slash marks by five, and dollar bills by tens. Have them circle their groupings as they count and write their totals at the ends of the rows.

Answer: Students will have different numbers of items to count. Make sure the Xs are circled in groups of twos, the 1/3s in groups of threes (discuss that three 1/3s equal a whole), quarters in groups of fours (discuss that four quarters equal one dollar), slash marks by fives (discuss that the fifth slash in each set can be made sideways to mark a group of five), dollar bills by tens (discuss that ten ones equal a $10 bill)

Objective: Student will skip count by twos, threes, fours, fives, and tens.

Subject: Math **Mode:** Written **Training Zone:** [O] Organization	**Readiness Factor:** [2] Daily Living **Readiness Factor Category:** [g] Time and Order

Ma 23: Creating a comparison shopping chart

Supplies: For each team of three or four students: One sheet of paper with a five-column, four row-grid that fills most of the page

Ask three volunteers with different brands of athletic shoes to each place one shoe where everyone can see it. Then, have the whole class gather in groups of three or four. Ask them to assume they want to buy new athletic shoes. Have students head the columns with some features they want to look for in shoes. (Examples: leather?, strong arch, design, colors, cost) Tell them to label the rows with the brand names of the three shoes. Then, have them fill in as many of the grid boxes as possible by looking at the shoes and talking to the shoe owners. Ask each group to choose a shoe and then share the final decision and reasons with the class. Discuss that, in this situation, the comparison charts will all be similar since everyone is looking at the same shoes. Point out that, in a real shopping situation, the shoes − or whatever is being purchased − will be based on individual choices. Explain that gathering the data into one chart makes it very easy to make logical comparisons.

Objective: Student will create a comparison shopping chart.

Subject: Math **Mode:** Role Play **Training Zone:** [O] Organization	**Readiness Factor:** [2] Daily Living **Readiness Factor Category:** [f] Shopping and Eating at Restaurants

Ma 24: Deciding if a temperature is too high

FUTR Tool: 35
PACT: yes

Supplies: None

Discuss that the temperature of a healthy human body stays within a small range. Ask a volunteer for the average human body temperature (98.6°) Write these temperatures on the board:

78°   84°   93°   94°   96°   98°   99°   100°   101°   102°   103°   104°

Ask volunteers to tell if each one is within the healthy range, too low, or too high. Discuss that most people who are sick have high temperatures, not low ones. Also discuss that 99.5° might be a sign of illness for one person while being within another person's upper range of OK. Likewise, 96° might be healthy for one person, but too low for another person.

Answer: Healthy range–96°, 98°, 99°; Too low – 94° and lower; Too high–over 100°

Objective: Student will determine if temperatures are normal or are a sign of illness.

Subject: Math **Mode:** Oral Response **Training Zone:** [U] Conclusion	**Readiness Factor:** [3] Personal/Social **Readiness Factor Category:** [l] Health, Diet, and Appearance

Ma 25: Deciding on level of tip

FUTR Tool: 34
PACT: yes

Supplies: None

Discuss that tipping is the method by which many waitstaff earn most of their wages. Point out that, when students go to a restaurant where they are waited on, they should leave a tip. Explain that, if the waitperson does a good job, the tip should be somewhere from 15% to 20%. Tell students that, when the waitperson does a poor job, it is acceptable to leave a lesser tip. Also, in buffet restaurants where the waitstaff only brings drinks, it is acceptable to leave a 5% or 10% tip.

Name different restaurants in your local area and describe a possible dining experience. For each, ask students what level of tip they would leave.

Objective: Student will determine level of tip based on service.

Subject: Math **Mode:** Oral Response **Training Zone:** [U] Conclusion	**Readiness Factor:** [2] Daily Living **Readiness Factor Category:** [f] Shopping and Eating at Restaurants

Ma 26: Determining miles from a mileage chart

FUTR Tool: no
PACT: no

Supplies: For each team: atlases with mileage charts (or use copies of a mileage chart)

Divide the class into teams and give each team an atlas. Have each team find the mileage chart that shows distances between major cities. Then, call out the following city pairs and have teams compete to be the first to call out the distance between the cities.

- Charleston, WV and Jackson, MS [809 miles]
- Tucson, AZ and Cleveland, OH [2057 miles]
- San Antonio, TX and Minneapolis, MN [1256 miles]
- Chicago, IL and Portland, OR [2122 miles]
- Orlando, FL and Buffalo, NY [1182 miles]

Objective: Student will use a mileage chart to find distances between major cities.

Subject: Math **Mode:** Hands-On **Training Zone:** [M] Manipulation	**Readiness Factor:** [2] Daily Living **Readiness Factor Category:** [h] Transportation/Travel/Worldliness

Ma 27: Differentiating between relative traits

FUTR Tool: no
PACT: no

Supplies: None

Discuss that some descriptions, such as brightness and smoothness, depend on the available options. Point out that, for example, a 5′ tall boy is very tall for a 3rd grader, but very short for a college student. Ask students to keep this idea in mind while writing the following explanations:

a. Choose someone you know who is tall and short, depending on how you look at it. Explain when the person is tall and when the person is short.

b. Identify two sources of bright light. Decide which is the brightest.

c. Choose a surface that is smooth. Then, identify a surface that is smoother.

Objective: Student will make choices that show the ability to differentiate between relative traits.

Subject: Math	**Readiness Factor:** [1] Career
Mode: Written	**Readiness Factor Category:** [b] Job Performance
Training Zone: [V] Observation	

Ma 28: Dividing into equal sections

FUTR Tool: no
PACT: yes

Supplies: For each student: A ruler and an 8x6 piece of paper

Ask students to use the rulers to divide the piece of paper into 12 equal sections. Invite students to share their finished products.

Answer:
(two methods)

• four divisions across the 8″ and three divisions down the 6″

• two divisions across the 8″ and six divisions down the 6″

Objective: Student will divide a piece of paper into 12 equal sections.

Subject: Math	**Readiness Factor:** [1] Career
Mode: Graph or Chart	**Readiness Factor Category:** [b] Job Performance
Training Zone: [A] Analysis	

Ma 29: Doing your banking

FUTR Tool: 7
PACT: yes

Supplies: A copy of a check register page for each student

Give each student a copy of a page from a check register. Walk them through entering these items in the register:

• A check for $56.83 to Center City Water Company to pay the water bill

• A paycheck deposit for $356.48

• A debit-card expenditure of $34.56 at a local grocery store

Objective: Student will enter expenditures and deposits in a check register.

Subject: Math	**Readiness Factor:** [2] Daily Living
Mode: Written	**Readiness Factor Category:** [c] Finances
Training Zone: [R] Responsibility	

Ma 30: Estimating to check expectations

FUTR Tool: 6
PACT: yes

Supplies: None

Tell students to imagine they have bought groceries that cost $14.95, and that they pay with a $20.00 bill. Ask them to tell, in whole dollars, about how much they should get back. [$5.00]

Repeat with these amounts:

a. Spend $21.32 and pay with two $10.00 bills and a $5.00 bill [$4.00]

b. Spend $11.78 and pay with a $10.00 bill and a $5.00 bill [$3.00[

c. Spend $5.55 and pay with six $1.00 bills [a few cents]

Objective: Student will estimate math calculations so she knows what to expect.

Subject: Math **Mode:** Oral Response **Training Zone:** [L] Logic	**Readiness Factor:** [2] Daily Living **Readiness Factor Category:** [e] Safety and Security

Ma 31: Estimating travel time

FUTR Tool: no
PACT: yes

Supplies: None

Discuss that when traveling between cities, a good generality is that sixty miles can be covered in one hour. Ask students to respond to the following scenarios:

About how far away is (name of a city or town that is about 60 miles away) and about how long does it take to drive there? Repeat scenario three more times with cities or towns that are about a half hour away, two hours away, and three hours away.

Discuss that, unlike driving on open roads, when driving in town, the time needed depends on the number of stop signs, the distance, and the time of day. Ask students to respond to these scenarios:

At 8:00 a.m., about how long would it take to go from the school to (name of a local business)? Repeat the question with 2:00 p.m and 5:00 p.m. Repeat all three questions with a second local business.

Objective: Student will estimate travel time both on open roads and in a local urban setting.

Subject: Math **Mode:** Oral Response **Training Zone:** [O] Organization	**Readiness Factor:** [2] Daily Living **Readiness Factor Category:** [h] Transportation/Travel/Worldliness

Ma 32: Evaluating purchasing power

FUTR Tool: no
PACT: yes

Supplies: None

Discuss that different people make different amounts of money and that we have to make choices based on what we can afford.

Write these amounts on the board:

$35 $95 $160 $300 $800 $2,000 $35,000

Ask students which one shows the cost of a warm coat. After they make their guesses, tell them that there are warm coats that sell for each of these prices. Point out that, for someone who makes $35,000 a year, it would obviously be crazy to try to pay $35,000 for a coat. Discuss that people have to decide the expense ranges that make sense for their own situations.

Objective: Student will understand the idea of determining ones purchasing power.

Subject: Math **Mode:** Discussion **Training Zone:** [A] Analysis	**Readiness Factor:** [2] Daily Living **Readiness Factor Category:** [f] Shopping and Eating at Restaurants

Ma 33: Exploring banking options

FUTR Tool: 27
PACT: yes

Supplies: Checkbook, debit card, online banking screen on a computer

Show students a checkbook, a debit card, and an online banking screen on a computer. Discuss the three different methods of using a checking account.

Discuss that most people also use banks to cash checks, save money, get loans, and set up automatic payments and withdrawals. Tell students how each of these services work.

Explain that the best way to learn about services offered by a bank is to sit down and talk with a banker.

Objective: Student will discuss banking options.

Subject: Math **Mode:** Discussion **Training Zone:** [E] Exploration	**Readiness Factor:** [2] Daily Living **Readiness Factor Category:** [c] Finances

Ma 34: Figuring ages

FUTR Tool: no
PACT: no

Supplies: None

Work this problem on the board:

Tobias was born in 1992. How old is he now? (current year) - 1992 = Tobias' age

Ask students to calculate these ages:

a. Karen was born in 2002. How old is she now?

b. Matt was born in 1977. How old is he now?

c. Tammy is 16-years old. In what year was she born?

d. Mitchell is 29 years old. In what year was he born?

e. Maya was born last month. In what year can she get her driver's license?

Objective: Working with birth years and ages, student will calculate ages and birth years.

Subject: Math **Mode:** Calculation **Training Zone:** [A] Analysis	**Readiness Factor:** [2] Daily Living **Readiness Factor Category:** [g] Time and Order

Ma 35: Figuring elapsed time

Supplies: A current calendar and a working clock

Ask volunteers these questions:

a. What time will it be in 35 minutes? (Allow students to look at clock)

b. What date will it be in two weeks? (Allow students to look at calendar)

c. What was the date two weeks ago? (Allow students to look at calendar)

d. About how long ago did (name something that happened about 30 minutes ago) take place?

e. How long until it is 7:30? (Allow students to look at clock)

Objective: Student will figure elapsed clock and calendar time.

Subject: Math **Mode:** Hands-On **Training Zone:** [M] Manipulation	**Readiness Factor:** [2] Daily Living **Readiness Factor Category:** [g] Time and Order

Ma 36: Figuring tips

Supplies: None

Discuss that, depending on the type and level of service, you should tip waitstaff and service people 5%, 10%, 15%, or 20%. Work the following problems on the board so students know how to figure the different percentages. Then, have them do some on their own.

Bill: $35.00

- 10%—Move the decimal point one place to the left: $3.50
- 20%—Double the 10% amount: 2 x 3.50 = $7.00
- 15%—Add 10% plus half of 10%: 3.50÷2 = 1.75; 3.50 + 1.75 = $5.25
- 5%—Divide 10% in half: 3.50÷2 = $1.75

Objective: Student will learn to figure tips in these amounts: 5%, 10%, 15%, and 20%.

Subject: Math **Mode:** Demonstration **Training Zone:** [A] Analysis	**Readiness Factor:** [2] Daily Living **Readiness Factor Category:** [f] Shopping and Eating at Restaurants

Ma 37: **Finding an address**

Supplies: None

Ask volunteers to answer the questions below. Sketch on the board as needed for clarification.

a. Many cities name their streets in groups to make it easier to find the streets. Which of these two streets do you think might be between Pennsylvania Street and Florida Street—Ohio Street or Stephenson Street? Name some local streets that are grouped by names.

b. Pretend you are looking for 705 S. Harlem. You turn left onto South Harlem Street and you see House #832, then #836. Are you going the right direction to find 705 S. Harlem?

c. Say you are looking for 55 Westwood. You come to 645 Westwood on one side of the street, then 638 Westwood on the other side. How many blocks do you have to drive before you will get to 55 Westwood? (5 or 6 blocks) Will 55 Westwood most likely be on the same side of the street as 603 Westwood or 600 Westwood? [603]

Objective: Student will understand about group street names and how houses are numbered.

Subject: Math **Mode:** Oral Response **Training Zone:** [A] Analysis	**Readiness Factor:** [2] Daily Living **Readiness Factor Category:** [h] Transportation/Travel/Worldliness

Ma 38: **Finding fun activities that are inexpensive or free**

Supplies: None

As a group, brainstorm a list of fun activities that are inexpensive or free. Ask a group of students to record the list as you brainstorm and to then create a poster to put up in the classroom.

Objective: Student will help create a list of fun activities that are inexpensive or free.

Subject: Math **Mode:** Brainstorming **Training Zone:** [Z] Socialization	**Readiness Factor:** [3] Personal/Social **Readiness Factor Category:** [j] Leisure/Desires/Choices

Ma 39: **Finding the desired newspaper page**

Supplies: Copy of local newspaper for every three students (Do not have to be alike nor current)

Ask students to find the following newspaper parts:

a. comics

b. editorials

c. national news summary

d. help-wanted ads

e. for-sale ads

f. sports

g. movie listings

h. obituaries

Objective: Student will locate requested parts of a newspaper.

Subject: Math **Mode:** Hands-On **Training Zone:** [U] Conclusion	**Readiness Factor:** [3] Personal/Social **Readiness Factor Category:** [j] Leisure/Desires/Choices

Ma 40: Finding your car in a parking lot

FUTR Tool: 17
PACT: yes

Supplies: None

As a group, brainstorm a list of ways to make sure you can find your car in a parking lot. Discuss both specific parking lots with which students are familiar and general parking lots.

Objective: Student will help make a list of ways to make sure he can find his car in a parking lot.

Subject: Math	**Readiness Factor:** [2] Daily Living
Mode: Brainstorming	**Readiness Factor Category:** [h] Transportation/Travel/Worldliness
Training Zone: [V] Observation	

Ma 41: Folding laundry

FUTR Tool: no
PACT: no

Supplies: Clean laundry items such as these: T-shirt, towel, pair of jeans, pair of socks, sweatshirt

Discuss that one way to keep your clothes looking tidy is to fold everything as soon as it comes out of the dryer or off the clothes line.

Show students how to fold each of the laundry items. Then, let them take turns folding the different items.

Objective: Student will fold laundry items.

Subject: Math	**Readiness Factor:** [2] Daily Living
Mode: Hands-On	**Readiness Factor Category:** [d] Household Care and/or Chores
Training Zone: [M] Manipulation	

Ma 42: Having good attendance

FUTR Tool: 10
PACT: yes

Supplies: None

Discuss that good attendance is important at school, at work, and in organizations you join. Ask volunteers for examples of good and bad attendance for each of the three situations.

Answer:
(one possible set of answers)

• *School:* Good attendance—missing no more than one day every two or three months; Bad attendance—missing one or more days every month

• *Work:* Good attendance—same as school

• *Organization:* Rarely missing a meeting or any activity you have agreed to participate in

Objective: Student will give examples of good and bad attendance at work, school, and in organizations.

Subject: Math	**Readiness Factor:** [1] Career
Mode: Oral Response	**Readiness Factor Category:** [b] Job Performance
Training Zone: [C] Conscientiousness	

Ma 43: Identifying basic object characteristics such as size, color, and shape

FUTR Tool: no
PACT: no

Supplies: None

Have students look around the room and each choose one item. Have them write the name, size, color, and shape of their items as well as any other specific descriptive factors they think are important. Tell students to try to describe the item clearly enough that others will be able to guess what it is.

Collect the papers and choose one at a time. Read the size, color, shape, and other descriptive factors and have the class guess the item. Tell students that they are not to guess if they think it is their item that has been pulled.

Objective: Student will describe an item clearly enough that others can guess what it is.

Subject: Math	**Readiness Factor:** [1] Career
Mode: Written	**Readiness Factor Category:** [b] Job Performance
Training Zone: [A] Analysis	

Ma 44: Identifying coins and bills

FUTR Tool: no
PACT: yes

Supplies: Coins in the amounts below–either actual coins, realistic classroom coins, or coins on an overhead or on copies

Show students the coins below and ask them to give the name and amount of each.

- penny–1¢
- nickel–5¢
- dime–10¢
- quarter–25¢
- half-dollar (50¢ piece)–50¢

- $1 bill–$1
- $5 bill–$5
- $10 bill–$10
- $20 bill–$20

Objective: Student will identify coins and bills by name and amount.

Subject: Math	**Readiness Factor:** [2] Daily Living
Mode: Hands-On	**Readiness Factor Category:** [c] Finances
Training Zone: [V] Observation	

Ma 45: Identifying interest and principal

FUTR Tool: no
PACT: yes

Supplies: Copies or an overhead of a loan payment receipt

Make a copy of a loan payment receipt that shows principal and interest for both the last payment and for year-to-date. If needed, use a black marker to cover up personal information on the copy. Then, either create an overhead or make copies to pass out. Explain that principal is actual money paid back on the loan and that interest is money paid to the loaner of the money as payment for loaning the money. Discuss the following related issues: 1) Which numbers show principal and which show interest for both current payment and for year-to-date? 2) How can you tell principal and interest apart? 3) How can you tell current payment and year-to-date numbers apart?

Objective: Student will identify principal and interest on a loan receipt.

Subject: Math	**Readiness Factor:** [2] Daily Living
Mode: Hands-On	**Readiness Factor Category:** [c] Finances
Training Zone: [R] Responsibility	

Ma 46: Identifying months by numbers

Supplies: None

As a group, say the months and their numbers in order. (Example: 1–January, 2–February, etc.) Then, call out months and ask volunteers to give the numbers. Begin with the first three and last three months and call each out several times. When students are good at those six months, work on the middle six months. Finally, work on 12 months randomly. Periodically, repeat the saying of all 12 months and their numbers in order.

Objective: Student will identify the months by their order numbers.

Subject: Math **Mode:** Oral Response **Training Zone:** [L] Logic	**Readiness Factor:** [2] Daily Living **Readiness Factor Category:** [g] Time and Order

Ma 47: Judging comparative sizes

FUTR Tool: no
PACT: no

Supplies: None

Discuss that sizes are often relative to each other. Explain that, for example, a watermelon that looks large does not look so large when a larger watermelon shows up.

Ask students to use these word sets in written sentences.

a. large, larger, largest

b. small, smaller, smallest

c. wide, wider, widest

d. tall, taller, tallest

e. old, older, oldest

Objective: Student will use comparative words in sentences.

Subject: Math **Mode:** Written **Training Zone:** [V] Observation	**Readiness Factor:** [1] Career **Readiness Factor Category:** [b] Job Performance

Ma 48: Judging mailing time

FUTR Tool: no
PACT: yes

Supplies: Six envelopes and stamps

Discuss that the amount of time it takes for mail delivery depends on how far away, and sometimes how remote, the destination is. Ask students to use this activity to experiment with mailing distances:

As a group, choose six known people to which you can send mail, who live in the areas listed below, and who will agree to call you when the letters arrive. For each, have the group predict the mailing time. Then, write a letter to each asking him or her to let you know the exact date the mailing arrives. Compare the actual time to the predicted times.

- within your local area
- nearby city within your state
- large city in a state next to you
- very small town or rural area in the state next to you
- large city that is at least 1000 miles away
- very small town or rural area that is at least 1000 miles away

Objective: Student will find out how long it takes to mail to different parts of the country.

Subject: Math **Mode:** Written **Training Zone:** [U] Conclusion	**Readiness Factor:** [2] Daily Living **Readiness Factor Category:** [g] Time and Order

Ma 49: Knowing months in order and number of days in month

FUTR Tool: no
PACT: no

Supplies: None

Review the two memory clues below. Ask volunteers to recite them by heart. Then, randomly ask students to identify the number of days in different months and to name the month that follows a certain month.

Jan fed Mark's ape.
Mable judged Julie's autograph.
Seth oiled Noah's decorations.

30 days hath September, April, June, and November
All the rest have 31, except for February which usually has 28.

Objective: Using memory clues and practice, student will remember the order of the months and number of days in each month.

Subject: Math **Mode:** Oral Response **Training Zone:** [O] Organization	**Readiness Factor:** [2] Daily Living **Readiness Factor Category:** [g] Time and Order

Ma 50: Knowing the days of the week in order

FUTR Tool: no
PACT: no

Supplies: None

Ask volunteers to name the days of the week in order beginning with the day you call out. Randomly call out different days of the week or use this list:

Sunday   Wednesday   Monday   Friday   Thursday   Tuesday   Saturday

Make sure to call each day of the week at least a couple of times.

Objective: Student will say the days of the week in order.

Subject: Math **Mode:** Oral Response **Training Zone:** [O] Organization	**Readiness Factor:** [2] Daily Living **Readiness Factor Category:** [g] Time and Order

Ma 51: Knowing where to find other area codes

FUTR Tool: 26
PACT: yes

Supplies: An online computer, a phone, and a phone book

Divide the class into three teams. Have the teams race to see who can get the area code for (choose a city that is far from where you live). Assign the teams each one of these procedures to follow:

a. Look on the Internet

b. Call directory assistance

c. Look in the phone book

Whether or not they are first or last, have all teams complete the hunt before quitting. Ask all three teams to share the process they went through.

Objective: Student will use the Internet, directory assistance, or a phone book to get an area code.

Subject: Math **Mode:** Action **Training Zone:** [E] Exploration	**Readiness Factor:** [2] Daily Living **Readiness Factor Category:** [h] Transportation/Travel/Worldliness

Ma 52: Knowing where to find other zip codes

FUTR Tool: no
PACT: yes

Supplies: An online computer, a phone, and a phone book

Divide the class into three teams. Have the teams race to see who can get the zip code for (choose a city that is far from where you live). Assign the teams each one of these procedures to follow:

a. Look on the Internet   b. Call the post office   c. Look in the phone book

Whether or not they are first or last, have all teams complete the hunt before quitting. Ask all three teams to share the process they went through.

Objective: Student will use the Internet, post office, or a phone book to get a zip code.

Subject: Math	**Readiness Factor:** [2] Daily Living
Mode: Action	**Readiness Factor Category:** [h] Transportation/Travel/Worldliness
Training Zone: [E] Exploration	

Ma 53: Knowing your area code and phone number

FUTR Tool: 22
PACT: yes

Supplies: None

Discuss that all U.S. phone numbers have a seven-digit local number and a three-digit area code. Explain that the seven numbers are all that are needed when calling locally. Ask students to write their seven-digit local phone numbers.

Explain that, when you fill out forms or give your phone number to someone who is not local, you need to write or say your phone number with the area code. Ask them to write their phone numbers with the area code.

Objective: Student will write her phone number with and without the area code.

Subject: Math	**Readiness Factor:** [2] Daily Living
Mode: Written	**Readiness Factor Category:** [e] Safety and Security
Training Zone: [S] Self-Awareness	

Ma 54: Knowing your clothing and shoe sizes

FUTR Tool: 24
PACT: yes

Supplies: None

Discuss with students that, once they are done growing, their clothes and shoe sizes will not change very often, if at all. Give students this homework assignment:

List the sizes that fit you for each of the items below. In some cases (ie: t-shirts), a size category such as "medium" or "medium or large" is fine. In other cases (ie:shoes), list a specific size.

- t-shirt
- sweat suit or jogging suit
- blouse or button-down shirt
- blue jeans
- tennis shoes
- long-sleeved sweater
- dress (girls only)
- dress shoes
- underwear
- dress pants
- jean shorts
- bra (girls only)

Objective: Student will list the sizes he wears in clothes and shoes.

Subject: Math	**Readiness Factor:** [2] Daily Living
Mode: Action	**Readiness Factor Category:** [f] Shopping and Eating at Restaurants
Training Zone: [S] Self-Awareness	

Ma 55: **Knowing your height and weight**

FUTR Tool: 23
PACT: yes

Supplies: Height measuring strip and scale

Discuss that there are times when you have to give your height and weight on a form, and that, even if you didn't ever have to provide this information, it is a good idea to know your own height and weight. Using a strip of calculator paper and a marker, create a height measuring strip on the classroom wall. Check each student's height and weight. Since weight tends to be a sensitive issue, make sure the weighing sessions are private. As each student finishes, ask him to repeat his height and weight so you know for sure he got it.

Objective: Student will state his height and weight.

Subject: Math	**Readiness Factor:** [3] Personal/Social
Mode: Action	**Readiness Factor Category:** [l] Health, Diet, and Appearance
Training Zone: [S] Self-Awareness	

Ma 56: **Making a bed**

FUTR Tool: no
PACT: no

Supplies: None

As a group, brainstorm the steps involved in making a bed from the no-sheet state. Make sure the list includes the following steps:

a. Put the bottom sheet on

b. Put the top sheet on so that the head end goes right to the end of the mattress and the foot end is tucked under the mattress

c. Put the blanket on so that the head end goes right to the end of the mattress and the foot end is tucked under the mattress

d. Put the pillow(s) on the head end of the mattress.

Objective: Student will help make a list of steps to follow when making a bed.

Subject: Math	**Readiness Factor:** [2] Daily Living
Mode: Brainstorming	**Readiness Factor Category:** [d] Household Care and/or Chores
Training Zone: [M] Manipulation	

Ma 57: **Making a savings plan**

FUTR Tool: no
PACT: no

Supplies: None

Discuss that it is a good plan to save some money each month. Point out that even a small amount, such as $5.00, is a good plan if that is what you can afford. Divide the class into teams of three to five students. Assign each team one of the income and expense lists below. Explain that some of the lists are for individuals and some are for families. Ask teams to make plans that allow for some fun and as much savings as possible. Have teams share their final plans.

Income	$20,000	$30,000	$40,000	$45,000	$50,000
Rent	$500/mo.	$600/mo.	$750/mo.	$900/mo.	$1200/mo.
Utilities	$100/mo.	$100/mo.	$150/mo.	$150/mo.	$200/mo.
Food	$120/mo.	$150/mo.	$250/mo.	$300/mo.	$250/mo.

Objective: Student will help to make a savings plan based on income and expenses.

Subject: Math	**Readiness Factor:** [2] Daily Living
Mode: Role Play	**Readiness Factor Category:** [c] Finances
Training Zone: [R] Responsibility	

Ma 58: **Making accurate reservations**

FUTR Tool: no
PACT: yes

Supplies: None

Discuss that the best way to be sure you make an accurate reservation is to make sure you know the related details before calling. As a group, brainstorm reservation situations and necessary details for each. Include ideas such as those listed below:

1. Hotel reservation: number of people, dates, smoking or not, number of beds

2. Restaurant reservation: number of people, date, time

3. Trip reservation: number of people, amount of deposit, date, destination

Objective: Student will help brainstorm reservation details.

Subject: Math **Mode:** Brainstorming **Training Zone:** [C] Conscientiousness	**Readiness Factor:** [3] Personal/Social **Readiness Factor Category:** [j] Leisure/Desires/Choices

Ma 59: **Making change**

FUTR Tool: 28
PACT: yes

Supplies: Classroom money for each student

Give students classroom money and have them make "purchases" from each other and make sure their "change" is correct. Suggest they imagine transactions such as those below.

a. Akika bought a candy bar for 65¢. She paid for it with a $1 bill. How much change should she have gotten? [35¢]

b. Terri bought a CD for $10.50. She paid for it with a $20.00 bill. How much change should she have gotten? [$9.50]

c. Jerome bought some knee pads for $15.00. He paid for them with a $20 bill. How much change should she have gotten? [$5.00]

Objective: Student will role play making money transactions.

Subject: Math **Mode:** Role Play **Training Zone:** [M] Manipulation	**Readiness Factor:** [2] Daily Living **Readiness Factor Category:** [c] Finances

Ma 60: **Making payment choices**

FUTR Tool: no
PACT: no

Supplies: None

Discuss that sometimes when you make payments, you have some options. For example:

a. You can usually pay a few dollars over the payment amount, and it will make a big difference in how soon the payments will be finished. If you are ever making payments, find out if they are set up that way and, if so, decide how much extra you can afford.

b. Some loans can be paid a little each month, or a large sum once a year. You would have to decide if you are good enough at saving money to save all year to make the big payment at the end.

c. A large loan, such as for a house, can be set up for 30 years. For just a little more each month, you might be able to pay it off in 20 years. Make sure you know which option is best for you.

Objective: Student will discuss some loan payment choices.

Subject: Math **Mode:** Discussion **Training Zone:** [U] Conclusion	**Readiness Factor:** [2] Daily Living **Readiness Factor Category:** [c] Finances

Ma 61: **Making sure you wake up on time**

FUTR Tool: no
PACT: yes

Supplies: None

Ask students to brainstorm a list of ways to make sure to wake up on time for a job that starts at 6:00 a.m. Write the ideas on the board as they are given. When finished, ask each student to choose the two ways that would work best for him or her. Invite students to share their final choices.

Objective: Student will describe one or more ways for waking up on time.

Subject: Math **Mode:** Brainstorming **Training Zone:** [R] Responsibility	**Readiness Factor:** [1] Career **Readiness Factor Category:** [b] Job Performance

Ma 62: **Measuring for a recipe**

FUTR Tool: no
PACT: yes

Supplies: Several measuring cups, several small plastic tubs or bowls 3/4 full of water

Divide students into teams of three to five students. Give each team a measuring cup and a plastic tub or bowl with water. Ask teams to measure out the following amounts of water (Make sure each student takes at least two turns,):

3 1/2 cups	2 1/4 cups	3/4 cup	1 cup	1 1/4 cups	2 1/3 cups
1/2 cup	2/3 cups	1/4 cup	1 3/4 cups	1/3 cup	2 cups

Objective: Student will measure amounts typically used in following recipes.

Subject: Math **Mode:** Action **Training Zone:** [M] Manipulation	**Readiness Factor:** [2] Daily Living **Readiness Factor Category:** [d] Household Care and/or Chores

Ma 63: **Measuring for curtains, frames, etc.**

FUTR Tool: no
PACT: no

Supplies: Pages from a catalog showing curtain sizes for different styles of curtains. Pieces of paper cut to 3x5, 4x6, 5x8, and 8x10 (one piece per student)

Choose a window in the classroom (or elsewhere in the school) and have students measure it. Then divide the class into teams and give each team a catalog page and ask members to choose the curtain size that would best fit the window.

Discuss that picture frames come in some basic sizes such as these (write them on the board): 3x5, 4x6, 5x8, 8x10. Pass out the cut pieces of paper. Tell students to imagine that each piece of paper is a photo. Ask them to measure their "photos" and decide which size frames they need.

Objective: Student will measure for curtains and picture frames.

Subject: Math **Mode:** Hands-On **Training Zone:** [M] Manipulation	**Readiness Factor:** [2] Daily Living **Readiness Factor Category:** [d] Household Care and/or Chores

Ma 64: Mending clothes

FUTR Tool: no
PACT: no

Supplies: For each student: Needle, thread, and two small pieces of fabric

Discuss that the best way to mend most clothing is to use a sewing machine, but that lots of rips can be fixed by hand—and that you can do that anywhere as long as you have a needle and thread. Give each student two small squares of fabric, a needle, and some thread. Walk them through threading the needle, and using a running stitch to sew the two pieces of fabric together. Point out that overlapping stitches are stronger than end-to-end stitches. Draw these two sketches on the board to show students the difference between the two ways to sew:

— — — — —   end-to-end stitches   ‑—‑—‑—‑—‑—   overlapping stitches

Objective: Student will hand-sew a seam that could be used for mending.

Subject: Math	**Readiness Factor:** [2] Daily Living
Mode: Hands-On	**Readiness Factor Category:** [d] Household Care and/or Chores
Training Zone: [M] Manipulation	

Ma 65: Mixing proper amounts

FUTR Tool: no
PACT: no

Supplies: Copies (or an overhead) of mixing directions from a cleaning product that is designed to mix with water

Discuss that some cleaning solutions are designed to be mixed with water before using them. Pass out the cleaning product directions (or show the overhead). Ask students to figure out how much solution and water to use if they want to (name a task such as "clean three classrooms").

Tell students to imagine a water/vinegar solution for cleaning tile. If the mixture is to have one cup of vinegar for every four cups of water, how much vinegar should you add to a gallon (16 cups) of water? [4 cups]

Objective: Student will calculate a proper cleaning solution mixture.

Subject: Math	**Readiness Factor:** [2] Daily Living
Mode: Calculation	**Readiness Factor Category:** [d] Household Care and/or Chores
Training Zone: [V] Observation	

Ma 66: Monitoring miles per gallon

FUTR Tool: no
PACT: no

Supplies: None

Discuss that it is easy to figure out a fairly accurate miles-per-gallon for a vehicle as long as the gas tank is filled each time gas is gotten, because the "new" gas serves as a measure of the "used" gas.

Ask students to figure these miles per gallons (Let them use calculators if they have them.):

a. Beginning odometer reading (BOR): 34,622; Ending odometer reading (EOR): 34,838; Amount of gas used: 14 gallons [15.4 mpg]

b. BOR: 104,371; EOR: 104,998; Amount of gas: 21 gallons [29.9 mpg]

c. BOR: 223,423; EOR: 223,657; Amount of gas: 10 gallons [23.4 mpg]

Discuss which of the three vehicles are most cost-effective from a gas point of view. [b]

Objective: Student will calculate miles per gallon.

Subject: Math	**Readiness Factor:** [2] Daily Living
Mode: Calculation	**Readiness Factor Category:** [h] Transportation/Travel/Worldliness
Training Zone: [V] Observation	

Ma 67: Ordering at a restaurant on a budget

FUTR Tool: no
PACT: yes

Supplies: Several menus from a casual sit-down local restaurant.

Divide the class into several small teams. Discuss that eating out can be expensive, but that careful selections allow a person to eat within a tight budget. Point out that ways to keep a bill down include drinking water, eating hors d'oeuvres, sharing meals, and choosing a-la-carte items. Tell each team they have $6.48 to spend. Tell them to use the money to find something to order for a meal. Make sure they realize that, since they are only buying a meal for one, sharing meals will not be a possibility in this situation. Also, tell them that they should plan on a $1 tip and 65¢ in tax.

Ask each team to share their final selections with the class.

Objective: Student will order a meal on a $6.48 budget.

Subject: Math	**Readiness Factor:** [2] Daily Living
Mode: Role Play	**Readiness Factor Category:** [f] Shopping and Eating at Restaurants
Training Zone: [F] Flexibility	

Ma 68: Ordering at a restaurant when someone else is paying

FUTR Tool: no
PACT: yes

Supplies: Several menus from a local restaurant

Discuss that, when someone else is paying the bill at a restaurant, it is best to order a medium- or low-priced item unless the person who is paying orders first. In that case, it is best to order something in a similar price range as the dish the "payer" orders.

Divide the class into several teams. Give each team a menu. Tell teams that they are going to role play being people ordering at a restaurant and that you are going to be the "payer." Explain that each team will function as one person at the restaurant table. Role play a few rounds of ordering, making sure to touch on these scenarios: Payer orders first and orders a low-priced item; Payer orders first and orders a high-priced item; Payer asks someone else to order first and then orders last.

Objective: Student will make tactful choices when ordering at a restaurant while someone else is paying.

Subject: Math	**Readiness Factor:** [2] Daily Living
Mode: Role Play	**Readiness Factor Category:** [f] Shopping and Eating at Restaurants
Training Zone: [F] Flexibility	

Ma 69: Packing for a trip

FUTR Tool: 5
PACT: yes

Supplies: None

Divide students into teams of three to five each. Ask teams to imagine that they are packing for a week-long camping vacation. Tell them to assume that the weather will probably be between 70° and 80° F in the daytime and between 50° and 60° F during the night. Have them draw sketches of the types of items they will pack and place numbers next to the sketches to tell how many of each item they will pack. Ask them to share and discuss their final plans.

Answer/examples:

Objective: Student will decide what to pack for a week-long camping trip.

Subject: Math	**Readiness Factor:** [2] Daily Living
Mode: Drawing	**Readiness Factor Category:** [h] Transportation/Travel/Worldliness
Training Zone: [L] Logic	

Ma 70: Planning around daylight savings time

Supplies: None

Discuss that daylight savings time was put into effect so that the light of day would better coincide with the time when people are out of the house for daytime activities. Also, explain that some states and areas use daylight savings time and some do not—and your state/area (does, does not).

If your area observes daylight savings time, remind students that the clocks are turned ahead one hour in the spring and turned back one hour in the fall. (Spring ahead, Fall back) Ask volunteers to answer these questions:

a. It is 9:00 on the second Sunday of March (as of 2007). Where should you set the clock for daylight savings time? [10:00]

b. It is 7:30 on the first Sunday of November (as of 2007). Where should you set the clock for daylight savings time? [6:30]

Objective: Student will know how to set the clock for daylight savings time.

Subject: Math	**Readiness Factor:** [2] Daily Living
Mode: Oral Response	**Readiness Factor Category:** [g] Time and Order
Training Zone: [F] Flexibility	

Ma 71: Planning around time zones

Supplies: None

Ask students to state the local time they should call so that people in the following states receive phone calls at the listed times.

- California—8:00 a.m. (Pacific Time)
- Wisconsin—8:00 a.m. (Central Time)
- New York—8:00 a.m. (Eastern Time)
- Colorado—8:00 a.m. (Mountain Time)
- Oregon—7:00 p.m. (Pacific Time)
- Oklahoma—7:00 p.m. (Central Time)
- South Carolina—7:00 p.m. (Eastern Time)
- New Mexico—7:00 p.m. (Mountain Time)

Objective: Student will calculate times in different times zones.

Subject: Math	**Readiness Factor:** [2] Daily Living
Mode: Calculation	**Readiness Factor Category:** [g] Time and Order
Training Zone: [F] Flexibility	

Ma 72: Planning to remember birthdays of friends and relatives

Supplies: None

Discuss methods of remembering birthdays of friends and relatives. [Some possibilities: Use a calendar, Keep a list that you check at the beginning of each month] Discuss that, when planning to send a card, it is important to "remember" the date enough ahead to allow time for sending the card.

Ask students to imagine that Kaydra is sending a birthday card to Brandon who lives in another state. Tell them that Brandon's birthday is on Friday the 12th. Ask them when Kaydra should mail the card. (Either Monday, Tuesday, or Wednesday—but Wednesday might be too late for the card to arrive on time)

Objective: Student will state a way of remembering others' birthdays and when to send a card so it arrives on time.

Subject: Math	**Readiness Factor:** [3] Personal/Social
Mode: Oral Response	**Readiness Factor Category:** [i] Relationships
Training Zone: [Z] Socialization	

Ma 73: **Projecting needed time for an activity**

FUTR Tool: no
PACT: no

Supplies: None

Discuss that it helps to plan out your time if you have think about how long different activities will take. As a group, brainstorm a list of daily activities such as cooking a meal, watching a movie, or packing a suitcase for a trip. Once the list is made, decide about how much time each activity requires.

Objective: Student will help decide about how much time typical daily activities require.

Subject: Math **Mode:** Brainstorming **Training Zone:** [O] Organization	**Readiness Factor:** [2] Daily Living **Readiness Factor Category:** [g] Time and Order

Ma 74: **Providing quality work**

FUTR Tool: 11
PACT: yes

Supplies: None

Discuss that employs who do quality work are usually the most successful. Ask volunteers to describe examples of quality work in each of the following situations.

- waitress
- nurse
- mechanic
- store check-out clerk
- bus driver
- painter
- toll booth worker
- factory line worker

Objective: Student will describe quality work in different jobs.

Subject: Math **Mode:** Oral Response **Training Zone:** [C] Conscientiousness	**Readiness Factor:** [1] Career **Readiness Factor Category:** [b] Job Performance

Ma 75: **Putting names in a cell phone address book**

FUTR Tool: 30
PACT: yes

Supplies: None

Draw a phone number pad on the board. (First row: 1, 2, 3 with ABC under the 2 and DEF under the 3; Second row: 4, 5, 6 with GHI under the 4, JKL under the 5, and MNO under the 6; Third row: 7, 8, 9 with PQRS under the 7, TUV under the 8, and WXYZ under the 9. Fourth row: star, 0, pound sign) Discuss that one thing cell phones have in common is that the keypad numbers are paired with the same letters. Also, point out that, to enter names into the address book, cell phones require that the number be pushed once to indicate the first letter, twice quickly to choose the second letter, three times quickly to choose the third letter, and four times quickly to choose the fourth letter (when there is a fourth letter). Ask students to go to the number pad on the board and show how they would enter their own names. Ask them to say aloud how many times they are pushing each button.

Objective: Student will role play entering his name into a cell phone directory.

Subject: Math **Mode:** Role Play **Training Zone:** [M] Manipulation	**Readiness Factor:** [2] Daily Living **Readiness Factor Category:** [h] Transportation/Travel/Worldliness

Ma 76: Putting things in order

FUTR Tool: 2
PACT: yes

Supplies: Copies of the items listed below—cut as indicated and placed in separate envelopes.

List:

• A table of contents with numbered units or chapters with each unit or chapter in a separate strip.

• A page from a dictionary with each word and its definition in a separate strip.

• A sports schedule that lists the months and days of each game with each game cut into a separate strip.

Pass out the envelopes to individuals or teams of two or three students. Have students re-assemble the pieces into sequential order.

Objective: Student will put pieces back in order according to numbers, letters, and dates.

Subject: Math **Mode:** Hands-On **Training Zone:** [O] Organization	**Readiness Factor:** [2] Daily Living **Readiness Factor Category:** [g] Time and Order

Ma 77: Reading and writing dates

FUTR Tool: no
PACT: yes

Supplies: None

Write these dates on the board to show different date formats:

7/15/05	7-15-05	7.15.05	July 15, 2005
Jul.15, '05	15 July '05		

If desired, also alert them to the European format, but don't have them practice it: 15/7/05 or 15.7.05 or 15.07.05

Discuss each of the formats. On their own paper, ask students to write today's date using the different formats.

Objective: Student will write the current date in a variety of different formats.

Subject: Math **Mode:** Written **Training Zone:** [L] Logic	**Readiness Factor:** [2] Daily Living **Readiness Factor Category:** [g] Time and Order

Ma 78: Reading and writing numbers

FUTR Tool: no
PACT: no

Supplies: None

Write the following numbers on the board and ask students to read the numbers aloud as a group.

49	872	24,684	841,904

Ask students to write these numbers as you read them:

25	362	2,461	233,651

Objective: Student will read and write numbers.

Subject: Math **Mode:** Oral Response **Training Zone:** [M] Manipulation	**Readiness Factor:** [1] Career **Readiness Factor Category:** [b] Job Performance

Ma 79: Reading charts, tables, and graphs

FUTR Tool: 18
PACT: yes

Supplies: An overhead or copies with a chart, table, and graph

Find a chart, a table, and a graph from a textbook, newspaper, or magazine. Either put all three items onto one overhead (or page to be copied) or make separate overheads (or pages to be copied). Show students the overhead (or pass out copies) and discuss how charts, tables, and graphs are alike and different and how to read each of them.

Objective: Student will study a chart, a table, and a graph and will discuss how they are alike and different as well as how to read each of them.

Subject: Math **Mode:** Demonstration **Training Zone:** [V] Observation	**Readiness Factor:** [2] Daily Living **Readiness Factor Category:** [g] Time and Order

Ma 80: Reading Roman numerals

FUTR Tool: no
PACT: yes

Supplies: None

Write this Roman numeral key on the board:

I=1   V=5   X=10   L=50   C=100   D=500   M=1000

Ask volunteers to write the cardinal numerals that match each of the following Roman numerals. (Write each on the board.)

XIV [14]   VIII [8]   CXC [190]   LXIX [69]   MMV [2005]   MDCLXVI [1666]

Ask volunteers to write Roman numerals to match each of the following cardinal numerals:

47 [XLVII]   2008 [MMVIII]   29 [XXIX]   532 [DXXXII]   70 [LXX]

Objective: Student will write and decode Roman numerals.

Subject: Math **Mode:** Calculation **Training Zone:** [L] Logic	**Readiness Factor:** [1] Career **Readiness Factor Category:** [b] Job Performance

Ma 81: Reading the speedometer and gas gauge

FUTR Tool: 16
PACT: yes

Supplies: None

Give students this homework assignment: Draw a speedometer and a gas gauge from a car.
Have students compare the speedometers and gas gauges from different cars.
Talk about the speed limits on local streets, main roads, and high ways. Have students mark the different speeds on their drawings.

On their gas gauges, ask students to mark the point where they need to get gas and the point at which the tank is half full.

Objective: Student will read a speedometer and a gas gauge.

Subject: Math **Mode:** Drawing **Training Zone:** [V] Observation	**Readiness Factor:** [2] Daily Living **Readiness Factor Category:** [h] Transportation/Travel/Worldliness

Ma 82: Recognizing letter and legal sizes

FUTR Tool: no
PACT: no

Supplies: For each student—one piece of letter-sized paper and one piece of legal-sized paper

Give each student one piece of letter-size paper and one piece of legal-size paper. Ask students to fold the legal-sized paper so that it is the same size as the letter paper. Have them firmly crease their folds so they can tear the excesses off. On the excess pieces, have them write, "This is how much larger legal-sized paper is than letter-sized paper."

Ask a volunteer to explain how a legal-sized filing cabinet is different than a letter-sized filing cabinet. [Legal-sized cabinet is wider]

Objective: Student will identify the difference between legal- and letter-sizes.

Subject: Math	**Readiness Factor:** [1] Career
Mode: Hands-On	**Readiness Factor Category:** [b] Job Performance
Training Zone: [V] Observation	

Ma 83: Recognizing standard measurements

FUTR Tool: no
PACT: yes

Supplies: None

Discuss that some things, such as doors, ceilings, and pieces of wood, have standard sizes. Ask volunteers to answer the following questions about standard measurements:

a. Will a three-foot-square box easily slide through a standard door? [Yes, standard door is 32" wide]

b. Will a 7'2" basketball player have to duck to go through a standard door or to stand under a standard ceiling in an older house? [Yes and No, standard door is 7' high; standard ceiling is 8' high]

c. What is a 2 x 4 and what are the measurements of an 8-foot 2 x 4? [A standard piece of wood; An 8-foot 2 x 4 is 8' long, about 4" wide, and about 2" high]

Objective: Student will recognize standard measurements and how they relate to daily life.

Subject: Math	**Readiness Factor:** [2] Daily Living
Mode: Oral Response	**Readiness Factor Category:** [f] Shopping and Eating at Restaurants
Training Zone: [V] Observation	

Ma 84: Scheduling errands

FUTR Tool: no
PACT: yes

Supplies: None

Point out that people are busy and that running errands often requires scheduling. Discuss how students and/or their families work the following errands into their busy lives.

- Getting hair cuts
- Getting gas
- Getting groceries
- Going to the dry cleaners
- Going to the post office
- Taking the dog to the vet
- Going to the bank
- Getting new shoes
- Dropping some books off at a friend's house

Objective: Student will schedule errands.

Subject: Math	**Readiness Factor:** [2] Daily Living
Mode: Discussion	**Readiness Factor Category:** [g] Time and Order
Training Zone: [O] Organization	

Ma 85: Scoring sports

FUTR Tool: 21
PACT: yes

Supplies: None

Ask a volunteer to choose a sport and go to the board to show and tell how scoring works for that sport. As a group, discuss the scoring procedures to make sure all students understand. Repeat with additional volunteers and other sports.

Objective: Student will discuss scoring procedures for different sports.

Subject: Math **Mode:** Discussion **Training Zone:** [Z] Socialization	**Readiness Factor:** [3] Personal/Social **Readiness Factor Category:** [j] Leisure/Desires/Choices

Ma 86: Setting the alarm on a clock

FUTR Tool: no
PACT: no

Supplies: Typical alarm clock

Divide the class into teams of three or four students. Give the alarm clock to the first team and ask the team to set the alarm so that it sounds in five minutes. When the alarm sounds, ask the second team to set it so that it sounds in five more minutes. Repeat until each team has set the alarm.

Objective: Student will set an alarm clock to ring at a predetermined time.

Subject: Math **Mode:** Hands-On **Training Zone:** [M] Manipulation	**Readiness Factor:** [2] Daily Living **Readiness Factor Category:** [g] Time and Order

Ma 87: Setting the time on a clock

FUTR Tool: no
PACT: no

Supplies: Typical alarm clock, typical wall clock

Bring a typical alarm clock and a typical wall clock to school. Divide the class into teams of three or four students. Assign each team a time that is different from times the other teams have. Ask teams to take turns setting the two clocks, making sure that each team sets each clock to its assigned time. Tell them to have their settings checked by you before passing the clocks onto other teams.

Objective: Student will set an alarm clock and a wall clock to a predetermined time.

Subject: Math **Mode:** Hands-On **Training Zone:** [M] Manipulation	**Readiness Factor:** [2] Daily Living **Readiness Factor Category:** [g] Time and Order

Ma 88: Sewing by hand

FUTR Tool: no
PACT: yes

Supplies: These sewing supplies for each student: needle, thread, button, patch of fabric

Ask students to each sew a button onto a piece of fabric. Make sure they know how to knot the thread, both to start and to end. Make sure they go back and forth sufficient times to securely fasten the button.

Objective: Student will sew a button onto a piece of fabric.

Subject: Math **Mode:** Hands-On **Training Zone:** [M] Manipulation	**Readiness Factor:** [2] Daily Living **Readiness Factor Category:** [d] Household Care and/or Chores

Ma 89: Shopping for clothes

FUTR Tool: no
PACT: yes

Supplies: None

Discuss different local shopping options. As a group, rank the options in order from most to least expensive. For each option, identify these components:

1. Benefits of shopping there

2. How to get there

3. The types of things sold

4. The hours of operation.

Objective: Student will discuss details relating to different local shopping options.

Subject: Math **Mode:** Discussion **Training Zone:** [A] Analysis	**Readiness Factor:** [2] Daily Living **Readiness Factor Category:** [f] Shopping and Eating at Restaurants

Ma 90: Sizing recipes

FUTR Tool: no
PACT: yes

Supplies: For each student: a copy of a recipe with about 10 ingredients, some being in amounts other than "1"

Give students copies of the recipe. Ask them to make three columns on a piece of paper and write the following headings for the columns:

1. Original recipe

2. Doubled recipe

3. Tripled recipe

Have them make enough rows across the columns to give each ingredient a row. Ask them to label the rows with the recipe ingredients and then fill in the chart.

Objective: Student will double and triple a recipe.

Subject: Math **Mode:** Calculation **Training Zone:** [F] Flexibility	**Readiness Factor:** [2] Daily Living **Readiness Factor Category:** [d] Household Care and/or Chores

Ma 91: Telling time

FUTR Tool: no
PACT: yes

Supplies: None

Ask students these questions:

How many minutes are in an hour? [60]   How many hours are in a day? [24]

What time is it right now? (Repeat this question periodically to address a variety of times and to give multiple students a chance to answer.)

Objective: Student will know the minutes in an hour and hours in a day and will be able to tell time.

Subject: Math	**Readiness Factor:** [2] Daily Living
Mode: Oral Response	**Readiness Factor Category:** [g] Time and Order
Training Zone: [V] Observation	

Ma 92: Translating a phone number from words to numbers

FUTR Tool: no
PACT: yes

Supplies: None

Draw a phone number pad on the board. (First row: 1, 2, 3 with ABC under the 2 and DEF under the 3; Second row: 4, 5, 6 with GHI under the 4, JKL under the 5, and MNO under the 6; Third row: 7, 8, 9 with PQRS under the 7, TUV under the 8, and WXYZ under the 9. Fourth row: star, 0, pound sign) Discuss that to help people remember them, some phone numbers are written as words or as word puzzles. Write the four "phone numbers" below on the board. Ask students to decode them and to guess who might have such license plates.

• FLY FISH (359-3474–maybe a person who likes to fish)

• TIN ROOF (846-7663–maybe a roofing company)

• TALL MAN (825-5626–maybe a guy who is very tall)

• BOX SHIP (269-7447–maybe a shipping company)

Objective: Student will decode phone numbers that are given in letters.

Subject: Math	**Readiness Factor:** [3] Personal/Social
Mode: Discussion	**Readiness Factor Category:** [k] Community Involvement and Responsibility
Training Zone: [L] Logic	

Ma 93: Translating sales percents into dollars

FUTR Tool: no
PACT: no

Supplies: None

Discuss that some stores have sales by giving a certain percent discount, such as 30% off. Write the following prices and discounts on the board and ask students to figure out the discounted prices. Accept estimations or let students use calculators. If students use calculators, point out that an easy method is to multiply the original price by the non-discounted percentage. In other words, for a 25% discount, multiply by 75%.

• Sweater: $44.98 with a 25% discount [$33.74]

• Jeans: $58.75 with a 50% discount [$29.38]

• Jacket: $127.00 with a 15% discount [$107.95]

Objective: Student will calculate sales discounts from percents.

Subject: Math	**Readiness Factor:** [2] Daily Living
Mode: Calculation	**Readiness Factor Category:** [f] Shopping and Eating at Restaurants
Training Zone: [A] Analysis	

Ma 94: Understanding A.M. and P.M.

FUTR Tool: no
PACT: no

Supplies: None

Discuss that "a.m." refers to the time from midnight until noon, including midnight and that "p.m." refers to the time from noon until midnight, including noon. Ask students to discuss things they have done over the past week and to give times with each activity. Tell them to include "a.m." or "p.m." with each time.

Objective: Student will know when to use a.m. and p.m.

Subject: Math	**Readiness Factor:** [2] Daily Living
Mode: Discussion	**Readiness Factor Category:** [g] Time and Order
Training Zone: [V] Observation	

Ma 95: Understanding costs of owning a car

FUTR Tool: no
PACT: no

Supplies: None

As a group, brainstorm costs involved with owning a car. Make sure to include the following ideas:

• car payments

• gas

• oil changes

• cleanings

• tune-ups

• insurance

Objective: Student will help make a list of costs involved with owning a car.

Subject: Math	**Readiness Factor:** [2] Daily Living
Mode: Brainstorming	**Readiness Factor Category:** [h] Transportation/Travel/Worldliness
Training Zone: [V] Observation	

Ma 96: Understanding costs of personal hygiene products

FUTR Tool: no
PACT: no

Supplies: For each student: Copy of hygiene list with two empty columns

Check the current costs of the personal hygiene products listed below to use as an approximate answer key. Then, make a copy of the list with two empty columns to the right and copy the chart for each student. In the first column, ask students to write the amount they think each item costs. Ask them to take the sheets to a grocery or department store (or go there as a group) and fill in actual costs to compare to their guesses.

Hygiene Products:

toilet paper (4 rolls)	toothpaste	deodorant
tissue	shampoo	feminine products
mouthwash	bar soap	squirt hand soap

Objective: Student will guess and then verify the costs of various hygiene products.

Subject: Math	**Readiness Factor:** [2] Daily Living
Mode: Action	**Readiness Factor Category:** [c] Finances
Training Zone: [V] Observation	

Ma 97: **Understanding counterclockwise**

FUTR Tool: no
PACT: no

Supplies: None

Ask students to form a large circle around the classroom. Then, ask them to follow your orders. Give these orders repeatedly and randomly:

• Move counterclockwise

• Stand still

• Move clockwise

Objective: Student will move clockwise and counterclockwise upon command.

Subject: Math	**Readiness Factor:** [2] Daily Living
Mode: Action	**Readiness Factor Category:** [g] Time and Order
Training Zone: [O] Organization	

Ma 98: **Understanding credit history**

FUTR Tool: no
PACT: no

Supplies: None

Explain to students that as soon as they start having bills in their own names, they will begin to build credit histories. Tell them that, if they pay their bills on time, their credit histories will be good, but if they pay bills late, their credit histories will be bad. Also, point out that buying things on credit—and paying for them as scheduled—will help to build a good credit history. Make sure they understand that a good credit history is very helpful for adults—especially when they want to make financial deals such as buying a car, renting an apartment, or buying a house.

Objective: Student will discuss the importance of a good credit history and how to have a good credit history.

Subject: Math	**Readiness Factor:** [2] Daily Living
Mode: Discussion	**Readiness Factor Category:** [c] Finances
Training Zone: [A] Analysis	

Ma 99: **Understanding household meters and gauges**

FUTR Tool: no
PACT: yes

Supplies: Two or three gauges such as on an electric blanket, slow cooker, electric skillet, toaster, computer volume and/or meters such as on a computer printer, timer, cell phone

Have students experiment with setting gauges at different levels. Discuss situations where each level would be appropriate. [Example: A toaster can be set to dark if toasting something frozen and thick or if being used by someone who likes dark toast.]

Have students read the different meters and discuss which levels call for action. [Example: A low-battery sign on a cell phone indicates you should plug the phone in.]

Objective: Student will set gauges and read meters.

Subject: Math	**Readiness Factor:** [2] Daily Living
Mode: Hands-On	**Readiness Factor Category:** [d] Household Care and/or Chores
Training Zone: [V] Observation	

Ma 100: Understanding how to use credit

FUTR Tool: no
PACT: no

Supplies: None

Explain that credit is the process of buying something without actually having the money. Tell students that two typical forms of credit include using a credit card and buying something on lay-away. Explain that when you use credit, you need to know how and when you will be able to pay it off.

Discuss that credit can be a helpful tool if used properly. Explain that "properly" means to use it in situations such as when you already have the money, but do not have it with you, or when you know for sure that you will have the money soon. Point out that credit can be very damaging if used improperly, such as when you do not have the money and have no idea how or when you will be able to get the money.

Objective: Student will discuss how to properly use credit.

Subject: Math **Mode:** Discussion **Training Zone:** [A] Analysis	**Readiness Factor:** [2] Daily Living **Readiness Factor Category:** [f] Shopping and Eating at Restaurants

Ma 101: Understanding interest rates

FUTR Tool: no
PACT: no

Supplies: Know the current interest rates for saving accounts, Certificates of Deposit, car loans, and house loans.

Explain the following points: Interest is money that people pay so they can borrow money. For example, if you borrow $200 and pay it back at the rate of $10 per week, you would need 20 weeks to pay it back if you didn't have to pay interest. But, if you were paying 5% simple interest, you would only pay back $9.50 each week because the other 50¢ would be interest. So, instead of taking 20 weeks to pay the money back, you would need 21 weeks.

Also, explain that, when you have money in a bank savings plan, the bank pays you interest.

Discuss current interest rates for savings accounts, Certificates of Deposit, car loans, and house loans.

Objective: Student will discuss current interest rates for loans and savings plans.

Subject: Math **Mode:** Discussion **Training Zone:** [A] Analysis	**Readiness Factor:** [2] Daily Living **Readiness Factor Category:** [c] Finances

Ma 102: Understanding logical sequences

FUTR Tool: 3
PACT: yes

Supplies: None

Write the information below on the board. Read items 1–4 to students and ask volunteers to fill in the blanks with information from the box.

> **40, 12, Aug, 24, flies, 80, Mar**

1. 10, 20, 30, _____ , 50, 60, 70, ___ , 90, 100
2. ants, bees, crickets, _____ , spiders
3. Jan, Feb, _____ , Apr, May, Jun, Jul, _____ , Sep, Oct, Nov, Dec
4. March 8, 2004; March _____ , 2004; March _____ , 2004

Objective: Student identifies logical sequences of numbers, letters, and dates.

Subject: Math **Mode:** Oral Response **Training Zone:** [O] Organization	**Readiness Factor:** [2] Daily Living **Readiness Factor Category:** [g] Time and Order

Ma 103: Understanding measurement equivalents

FUTR Tool: no
PACT: yes

Supplies: None

Ask volunteers to supply numbers for each of the following:

a. inches in a foot [12]

b. feet in a yard [3]

c. inches in a yard [36]

d. quarts in a gallon [4]

e. cups in a quart [4]

f. things in a dozen [12]

g. things in a gross [144]

Objective: Student will know common measurement equivalents.

Subject: Math	**Readiness Factor:** [1] Career
Mode: Oral Response	**Readiness Factor Category:** [b] Job Performance
Training Zone: [V] Observation	

Ma 104: Understanding net and gross pay

FUTR Tool: 31
PACT: yes

Supplies: None

Ask students these questions:

a. If you worked for five hours and made $8.00 per hour, would you end up with $40 to spend? [No, because the $40 is gross pay before payroll deductions are taken out.]

b. What is an automatic deduction? [Amount that is taken out of each paycheck before you receive the paycheck.]

c. Give an example of an automatic deduction that you can choose to have and one that you are required to have. [Choose: Some possibilities – savings account, rent, loan; Required: Some possibilities – income tax, social security, court-ordered fine such as from non-payment of income tax, court-ordered payment such as child support]

Objective: Student will address factors affecting net and gross pay.

Subject: Math	**Readiness Factor:** [2] Daily Living
Mode: Oral Response	**Readiness Factor Category:** [c] Finances
Training Zone: [A] Analysis	

Ma 105: Understanding quantity relationships

FUTR Tool: no
PACT: yes

Supplies: Ask volunteers to bring the empty containers listed below.

Empty container list:

- 2-liter soda bottle, 2-quart pitcher, one-cup measure, one-gallon zipper bag, one-pound butter box, one-quart zipper bag, 12-ounce water bottle, approx. 170 gram hair product container, approx. 236 ml. hair product container

Have students place the containers in size order. Discuss the relationship between each of the following: liter, quart, pound (of butter), gallon, ounce (of water), gram (hair product), and milliliter. Point out that volume measurements are always the same size (Example: A liter of soda and a liter of soup take the same space), but weight measurements vary in size (Example: an ounce of soda would likely take up more space than an ounce of soup since soup pieces would logically be heavier).

Objective: Student will explore the relationship between different-size containers.

Subject: Math	**Readiness Factor:** [3] Personal/Social
Mode: Hands-On	**Readiness Factor Category:** [i] Relationships
Training Zone: [L] Logic	

Ma 106: **Understanding ratios**

Supplies: None

Write these ratios on the board: 3 : 5   5 : 7   10 : 15 3/8   7/15   7/10

Ask volunteers to choose a ratio to match each of the following situations:

a. Out of every seven cookies they baked, Allison and Donnie ate five. [5 : 7]

b. Nina was late for seven of the ten classes. [7/10]

c. The Huskies played five games. They won three and lost two. [3 : 5 – wins and total]

d. Teams A and B are competing. On Team A, Carol has 3 years of experience and Nan has 7 years. On Team B, Dana has 7 years of experience and Maya has 8 years. [10 : 15]

e. Kyle had eight textbooks this year. He still has to turn five of them in. [3/8]

f. Emily is 15 years old. She has been a competitive swimmer for the last seven years. [7/15]

Objective: Student will match ratios to realistic situations.

Subject: Math	**Readiness Factor:** [2] Daily Living
Mode: Oral Response	**Readiness Factor Category:** [g] Time and Order
Training Zone: [L] Logic	

Ma 107: **Understanding sports statistics**

Supplies: In a newspaper or online, find statistics for at least two different sports. Make a copy for each student.

From your local newspaper, cut out sports statistic charts for two different sports (or have students find them and cut them out). (Choose whatever sports are in season.) Make copies of the charts and pass them out.

Discuss the meanings of the different columns and numbers. If you do not understand some of the abbreviations, research using methods such as the following: ask fans of the sport for help, go online and look for information about the sport, ask a coach at your school for explanations.

Objective: Student will discuss the meanings of columns in sports statistics charts.

Subject: Math	**Readiness Factor:** [3] Personal/Social
Mode: Graph or Chart	**Readiness Factor Category:** [j] Leisure/Desires/Choices
Training Zone: [A] Analysis	

Ma 108: Understanding Types of Taxes

Supplies: None

Write these three terms on the board:

• income tax   • property tax   • sales tax

Give the following examples and ask students to match each to one of the tax terms on the board.

a. You buy things in a department store, and the cost is more than the total of the items. [sales]

b. You buy a house, and you have to pay yearly taxes based on the cost of the house. [property]

c. You buy a computer, and the bill is $150 more than the cost of the computer. [sales]

d. You get your payroll check, and state and federal taxes have been taken out. [income]

e. You hire a house painter. He adds the hourly charges and then adds another amount. [sales]

Objective: Student will differentiate between types of taxes.

Subject: Math	**Readiness Factor:** [2] Daily Living
Mode: Oral Response	**Readiness Factor Category:** [c] Finances
Training Zone: [E] Exploration	

Ma 109: Understanding years and decades

FUTR Tool: no
PACT: yes

Supplies: None

Discuss that a year is 365 days long and a decade is 10 years long. Also, explain that decades go from 0 to 9 as in 1990 to 1999.

Write the following years on the board and ask volunteers to write the beginning and ending years in the decade to which each year belongs.

• 1961 [1960–1969]   • 1842 [1840–1849]   • 2029 [2020–2029]

• 2005 [2000–2009]   • 1783 [1780–1789]   • 1950 [1950–1959]

Objective: Student will identify decades that include specific years.

Subject: Math	**Readiness Factor:** [2] Daily Living
Mode: Written	**Readiness Factor Category:** [g] Time and Order
Training Zone: [E] Exploration	

Ma 110: Using a calculator

FUTR Tool: 29
PACT: yes

Supplies: A calculator for each student or one for every two students

Ask students to work the following problems on a calculator.

a. Add 98 and 33 [131]   c. Multiply 8 x 321 [2568]   e. Add 93¢ and 64¢ [$1.57]

b. Subtract 32 from 84 [52]   d. Divide 476 by 4 [119]   f. Find 5% of $24.60 [$1.23]

Objective: Student will use a calculator to solve simple math problems.

Subject: Math	**Readiness Factor:** [2] Daily Living
Mode: Hands-On	**Readiness Factor Category:** [c] Finances
Training Zone: [M] Manipulation	

Ma 111: Using a calendar as a reminder to pay bills

FUTR Tool: 8
PACT: yes

Supplies: None

Draw a one-month calendar on the board. Ask volunteers to write bill-payment reminders on the calendar for the following bills:

- Electric bill — $75.00 — due on the 4th
- Rent — $650 — due on the 12th
- Cell phone bill — $42.74 — due on the 8th
- Water bill — $26.95 — due on the 18th

Answer: Make sure students mark bills for payment early enough to allow for mailing (about five days ahead of due dates).

Objective: Student will make notes on a calendar as reminders to pay bills on time.

Subject: Math **Mode:** Role Play **Training Zone:** [R] Responsibility	**Readiness Factor:** [2] Daily Living **Readiness Factor Category:** [c] Finances

Ma 112: Using a debit card wisely

FUTR Tool: no
PACT: yes

Supplies: None

Discuss that, when you keep money in a bank, a debit card is a way of using it. Explain that the amounts of purchases made with a debit card are subtracted from the money the person has in the bank. Tell students that debit cards are used instead of cash and checks. Point out that using a debit card is safer than using cash, because a lost or stolen debit card can be easily replaced with no money lost. Also, point out that a debit card is only good for the amount of money in the bank account to which it is attached.

Objective: Student will discuss debit card procedures and benefits.

Subject: Math **Mode:** Discussion **Training Zone:** [R] Responsibility	**Readiness Factor:** [2] Daily Living **Readiness Factor Category:** [c] Finances

Ma 113: Using a grid to arrange furniture

FUTR Tool: no
PACT: no

Supplies: For each team: one large posterboard, one yard stick, one pencil, one black marker

Have teams use the yardstick and a pencil to cover the posterboards with a grid with 1″ squares. Measure the classroom to determine a ratio of distance in the room to 1″ so that the posterboards can be used as to-scale drawings of the room. Have each team use the arrived-at ratio, to make a room rearrangement plan. Ask teams to share their plans with the class.

Objective: Student will use a grid to rearrange furniture.

Subject: Math **Mode:** Graph or Chart **Training Zone:** [M] Manipulation	**Readiness Factor:** [2] Daily Living **Readiness Factor Category:** [d] Household Care and/or Chores

Ma 114: **Using a microwave**

Supplies: None

As a group, brainstorm a list of container types that can and cannot be used in microwaves. Make sure to include these container types:

• Can be used: glass, plastic, paper plates; Cannot be used: metal, tin foil, styrofoam

Discuss that people should cover most things that are cooked in a microwave. Brainstorm a list of things that can be used as a cover in a microwave. Make sure to include these covering possibilities:

• Paper towels, plastic lids, glass lids, paper plates.

Objective: Student will help list container types and covering possibilities that are microwave safe.

Subject: Math	**Readiness Factor:** [2] Daily Living
Mode: Brainstorming	**Readiness Factor Category:** [d] Household Care and/or Chores
Training Zone: [M] Manipulation	

Ma 115: **Using a padlock**

FUTR Tool: no
PACT: yes

Supplies: A padlock with its combination

Write the padlock combination on the board and explain how to use it. Then, pass the padlock around so that each student can take a turn working the combination.

Objective: Student will use a combination to open a padlock.

Subject: Math	**Readiness Factor:** [2] Daily Living
Mode: Hands-On	**Readiness Factor Category:** [e] Safety and Security
Training Zone: [M] Manipulation	

Ma 116: **Using an oven**

FUTR Tool: no
PACT: yes

Supplies: None

Discuss that some ovens have dials and others have computerized buttons. For homework, ask students to draw the dials or buttons on their ovens at home. Also, if they do not already know how their ovens work, tell them to ask their parents. Then, have them explain how their ovens work.

Objective: Student will draw oven dials and/or buttons like those on his family's oven and will explain how the dials and/or buttons work.

Subject: Math	**Readiness Factor:** [2] Daily Living
Mode: Drawing	**Readiness Factor Category:** [d] Household Care and/or Chores
Training Zone: [M] Manipulation	

Ma 117: **Using an oven timer**

FUTR Tool: no
PACT: yes

Supplies: None

Discuss that ovens have one of two types of timers: a mechanical timer or a computerized timer.

Explain that mechanical timers are set by turning a dial to the number of desired minutes. Point out that, when setting a mechanical timer to minutes less than 20, the dial must first be turned past the 20 and then brought back to the desired number.

Tell students that computerized timers are set by pushing a button which digitally shows the numbers as you go and you stop pushing when you reach the desired number of minutes.

Objective: Student will discuss how oven timers work.

Subject: Math **Mode:** Discussion **Training Zone:** [M] Manipulation	**Readiness Factor:** [2] Daily Living **Readiness Factor Category:** [g] Time and Order

Ma 118: **Using burners**

FUTR Tool: no
PACT: no

Supplies: None

For homework, ask students to each make a drawing of their oven tops. Tell them that they can size it to fit on a piece of paper, but to make a blow-up of one of the dials or of the computerized buttons. On their drawings, ask students to mark settings that would be appropriate for each of the following:

• boiling water (high)
• frying an egg (medium)
• cooking green beans (high until boils, then low)

Objective: Student will identify burner settings for specific cooking challenges.

Subject: Math **Mode:** Drawing **Training Zone:** [M] Manipulation	**Readiness Factor:** [2] Daily Living **Readiness Factor Category:** [d] Household Care and/or Chores

Ma 119: **Using counting words**

FUTR Tool: no
PACT: no

Supplies: None

One at a time, ask volunteers to use the words below in sentences.

once	last	next	single	more	triplets
few	several	second	twice	triple	quadruplets
first	middle	biggest	none	double	twins
many	oldest	most			

Objective: Student will use counting words in sentences.

Subject: Math **Mode:** Oral Response **Training Zone:** [O] Organization	**Readiness Factor:** [2] Daily Living **Readiness Factor Category:** [g] Time and Order

Ma 120: Using non-traditional measuring devices

FUTR Tool: no
PACT: no

Supplies: An 8 1/2" x 11" piece of paper

Discuss that, when measuring length, non-traditional measuring devices can replace rulers and yardsticks. Show students what you mean with the following demonstration:

Explain that you want to know the width of your desk, but you do not have a ruler. Take a piece of paper and tell them that you know it is 11" long and 8 1/2" wide, so you can use the paper to get a pretty close measurement of the width of the desk. Measure the desk with the paper and guess at the total width.

Have students each choose one item in the room to measure using a piece of paper.

Objective: Student will use a piece of paper to measure a distance or length of an item.

Subject: Math **Mode:** Action **Training Zone:** [L] Logic	**Readiness Factor:** [2] Daily Living **Readiness Factor Category:** [c] Finances

Ma 121: Using prescription medication properly

FUTR Tool: 9
PACT: yes

Supplies: None

Divide the class into teams of three or four students. Ask each team to decide on a timing plan for taking one of the following medications:

a. Take two pills twice a day

b. Take one pill four times per day

c. Take two pills with meals, Take one pill between meals and at bedtime

d. Take three times a day

e. Take five times a day

f. Take four times a day with food

Objective: Student will make a plan for taking prescription medication.

Subject: Math **Mode:** Oral Response **Training Zone:** [R] Responsibility	**Readiness Factor:** [3] Personal/Social **Readiness Factor Category:** [l] Health, Diet, and Appearance

Ma 122: Using rulers, yard sticks, and meter sticks

FUTR Tool: no
PACT: yes

Supplies: A ruler, a yard stick, a meter stick

Divide the class into three teams. Give the ruler to one team, the yard stick to another team, and the meter stick to the third team. Ask each team to measure the length of the classroom. Compare the three measurements and discuss how they relate. Have teams trade measuring tools and measure the height of the classroom door. Compare measurements again. Have teams trade for the tool they have not yet used and then measure the width of the writing board. Compare the measurements again.

Objective: Student will use a rule, a yard stick, and a meter stick.

Subject: Math **Mode:** Action **Training Zone:** [M] Manipulation	**Readiness Factor:** [2] Daily Living **Readiness Factor Category:** [b] Job Performance

Ma 123: Using shapes

FUTR Tool: no
PACT: yes

Supplies: None

Discuss that drawing circles and rectangles freehand can be difficult and that it is easy to trace around items to get nice shapes.

Ask students to find something in the room that they can use to draw a circle.

Ask students to find something in the room that they can use to draw a rectangle or square.

Ask students what shape pans they could use to make a birthday cake that looks like a

a. snowman. [two or three round ones]

b. computer with a keyboard. [one square and one rectangular]

c. favorite book. [one rectangular]

d. a group of three balloons with the strings in a box. [three round and one square or rectangular]

Objective: Student will trace items to get perfect shape and will identify shapes that can be used to create pictures.

Subject: Math	**Readiness Factor:** [2] Daily Living
Mode: Action	**Readiness Factor Category:** [d] Household Care and/or Chores
Training Zone: [E] Exploration	

Ma 124: Using tallies

FUTR Tool: no
PACT: no

Supplies: A pen or pencil; a favorite poem, joke, or one-page story

On the board, show students how to use tallies to keep tack of the count of something. Make sure they understand how to draw four tally lines and cross them to make five. Then, ask students to use tallies for the following activities:

a. Keep track of the number of times I tap my pen (or pencil) on the desk.

b. Keep track of the number of times you hear the word "the" as I read the (poem, joke, or story).

Compare student tally counts to the actual count.

Objective: Student will use tallies to count.

Subject: Math	**Readiness Factor:** [2] Daily Living
Mode: Written	**Readiness Factor Category:** [g] Time and Order
Training Zone: [O] Organization	

Ma 125: Using tax tables

FUTR Tool: no
PACT: no

Supplies: Copies of a tax table from the Internet or the government tax booklet (table does not have to be current one)

Give students copies of a tax table. Choose an income amount that can be found on the table. Ask students to find the tax owed. Repeat with several other income amounts that are on the page.

Objective: Student will find taxes owed from a government tax table.

Subject: Math	**Readiness Factor:** [2] Daily Living
Mode: Hands-On	**Readiness Factor Category:** [c] Finances
Training Zone: [M] Manipulation	

Ma 126: **Watching for good shopping deals**

FUTR Tool: no
PACT: no

Supplies: Several sales flyers from different stores

Discuss that watching sales flyers is one way to know about good shopping deals. Divide the class into teams and give each team a sales flyer. Ask them to find an item on the flyer that is a good deal and share both the original price and the sale price with the class.

Explain that another way to know about good shopping deals is to pay attention in stores. Ask volunteers to share different ways they have seen sales advertised in stores. [Examples: small sign on edge of shelf next to price of item, large sign by item or at top of shelf, separate display with a sign, sign at front of store that indicates a store-wide sale, surprise discount at register]

Objective: Student will study sales flyer and will discuss in-store sales advertising.

Subject: Math	**Readiness Factor:** [2] Daily Living
Mode: Hands-On	**Readiness Factor Category:** [f] Shopping and Eating at Restaurants
Training Zone: [E] Exploration	

Ma 127: **Watching refrigerator and freezer temperatures**

FUTR Tool: no
PACT: yes

Supplies: None

Discuss that refrigerators are usually kept around 35° or 40° F (a little above freezing) and freezers are usually kept somewhere between 0° and 10° F (well below freezing). Ask volunteers to answer these questions:

a. If your refrigerator is set at 40°, and your milk has ice on it, to what should you adjust the temperature? (Turn it to 41° or 42°)

b. If your refrigerator is set to 40° and your milk does not taste cold, how should you adjust the temperature? (Turn it to 39° or 38°)

c. If your freezer is set at 10° and your ice cream is too soft, how should you adjust your temperature? (Turn it to 9° or 8°)

d. If your freezer is set at 10° and your ice cream is too hard, how should you adjust your temperature? (Turn it to 11° or 12°)

Objective: Student will determine how to adjust refrigerator and freezer temperatures.

Subject: Math	**Readiness Factor:** [2] Daily Living
Mode: Oral Response	**Readiness Factor Category:** [e] Safety and Security
Training Zone: [R] Responsibility	

Ma 128: Working at a rate that shows effort

FUTR Tool: 13
PACT: yes

Supplies: None

Explain that "effort" refers to how hard you try and that, when you do your best, you are putting out your best effort. Discuss that everything you do requires effort on your part. Ask students to make a list of things they did yesterday and next to each, rate themselves from 1–5 as to how much effort they put into it, with 5 being top effort. (Some activities they might include: getting up on time, brushing their teeth, eating breakfast, getting to school on time, taking part in class, talking with friends, eating a good lunch, making good use of time after school, doing homework, talking with family members, helping out at home, getting to bed on time)

Discuss that effort levels can be raised with ongoing self-determination.

Objective: Student will rate the effort she gives to typical daily activities.

Subject: Math **Mode:** Written **Training Zone:** [F] Flexibility	**Readiness Factor:** [1] Career **Readiness Factor Category:** [b] Job Performance

Ma 129: Working with a bus schedule

FUTR Tool: 15
PACT: yes

Supplies: A copy of a regional or local bus schedule for each student

Using the bus schedule, ask hypothetical questions about someone wanting to use the bus.

Examples:

If you are leaving from school, what time would you need to be at the closest bus station if you wanted to get to the Main Street stop by 3:30?

What connections would you have to make to go from school to the Foster Hotel?

Objective: Student will use a bus schedule to plan transportation.

Subject: Math **Mode:** Hands-On **Training Zone:** [F] Flexibility	**Readiness Factor:** [2] Daily Living **Readiness Factor Category:** [h] Transportation/Travel/Worldliness

Ma 130: Wrapping a gift

FUTR Tool: no
PACT: no

Supplies: Enough newspaper for each student to use some for wrapping paper, a box for each student to wrap, tape

Using an empty box and a sheet of newspaper, demonstrate how to wrap a gift. Discuss that, for most gift situations, newspaper is not the appropriate gift wrap, but that it works well for demonstrating and practicing. Pass out the newspapers and boxes and ask each student to wrap a "gift."

Objective: Student will gift-wrap a box.

Subject: Math **Mode:** Action **Training Zone:** [M] Manipulation	**Readiness Factor:** [2] Daily Living **Readiness Factor Category:** [d] Household Care and/or Chores

Ma 131: **Writing money amounts in numbers and words**

Supplies: None

On the board, give students an example of how money amounts are written in words on a check:

Forty-five and 34/100----------------------

Explain that the "forty-five" is the whole dollars and the 34/100 is the way 34¢ is written. Point out that cents are written as an amount over 100 since there are 100 cents in a dollar.

Ask students to write the following money amounts in words:

a. $14.16   b. $29.23   c. $152.79

d. $50.00   e. $61.50   f. $10.01

Objective: Student will write money amounts in words.

Subject: Math **Mode:** Written **Training Zone:** [M] Manipulation	**Readiness Factor:** [2] Daily Living **Readiness Factor Category:** [c] Finances

Social Studies

Life Skill Lessons

Table of Contents: *Social Studies*

Ss 1: Adjusting behavior for different situations

FUTR Tool: no
PACT: yes

Supplies: None

Ask volunteers to give examples of times when it would be OK to do each of the following actions and times when it would not be OK.

a. Laugh aloud

b. Argue with your sibling

c. Go barefoot

d. Talk on a cell phone

e. Invite a friend to join you

f. Refuse to carry something for someone

g. Eat while you talk

Objective: Student will identify situations where certain behaviors are OK and situations where the same behaviors are not OK.

Subject: Social Studies	**Readiness Factor:** [3] Personal/Social
Mode: Oral Response	**Readiness Factor Category:** [k] Community Involvement and
Training Zone: [C] Conscientiousness	Responsibility

Ss 2: Apologizing when you hurt or inconvenience others

FUTR Tool: no
PACT: no

Supplies: None

Discuss that apologies do not always make problems go away, but they are definitely a step in the right direction. Discuss how to accept apologies as well as how to give them. For a week, look for opportunities for apologies either to or from students. Following each apology, discuss how the apology helped the situation

Objective: Student will give and accept apologies.

Subject: Social Studies	**Readiness Factor:** [3] Personal/Social
Mode: Oral Response	**Readiness Factor Category:** [i] Relationships
Training Zone: [F] Flexibility	

Ss 3: Asking a person for a date

FUTR Tool: no
PACT: no

Supplies: None

Discuss that asking a person for a date is often difficult and stressful. Point out that one way to make it easier is to practice so you are comfortable with what you will say. Ask volunteers to role play asking dates to attend the following events:

a. a dance

b. a movie

c. a dinner out

d. a party

Objective: Student will role play asking a person for a date.

Subject: Social Studies	**Readiness Factor:** [3] Personal/Social
Mode: Role Play	**Readiness Factor Category:** [i] Relationships
Training Zone: [Z] Socialization	

Ss 4: Assembling a first aid kit

FUTR Tool: no
PACT: no

Supplies: None

Ask students to draw the items they would include in a first aid kit. If they need ideas, suggest they include items such as the following: bandaids, bandages, disinfectant cream, tweezers, over-the-counter pain medication, thermometer, cough drops, and tissue.

Objective: Student will draw the contents of a first aid kit.

Subject: Social Studies **Mode:** Drawing **Training Zone:** [M] Manipulation	**Readiness Factor:** [2] Daily Living **Readiness Factor Category:** [e] Safety and Security

Ss 5: Becoming familiar with a new community

FUTR Tool: no
PACT: yes

Supplies: None

As a group, brainstorm places of business that families want to find when they move into a new community.

Answer: Some possibilities—grocery store, place for hair cuts, dry cleaner, department store, assorted restaurants, drug store, bank, library, gym, doctor, dentist, hospital, church, gas station

Objective: Student will help make a list of places of business that families need to find in a new community.

Subject: Social Studies **Mode:** Brainstorming **Training Zone:** [E] Exploration	**Readiness Factor:** [3] Personal/Social **Readiness Factor Category:** [k] Community Involvement and Responsibility

Ss 6: Behaving appropriately for the weather

FUTR Tool: 71
PACT: yes

Supplies: None

Make a chart on the board. Across the top, write these headings: Drive, Take a walk, Run, Use an umbrella, Go out without a coat, and Open your windows for fresh air.
Down the side, list these weather conditions:

• heavy fog
• heavy rain
• very hot temperatures
• high winds
• heavy snow
• very cold temperatures

As a group, write yes or no to tell whether each activity would be safe in the given weather condition.

Objective: Student will help create a chart showing appropriate behaviors for different weather conditions.

Subject: Social Studies **Mode:** Graph or Chart **Training Zone:** [U] Conclusion	**Readiness Factor:** [2] Daily Living **Readiness Factor Category:** [e] Safety and Security

Ss 7: Being honest

FUTR Tool: no
PACT: no

Supplies: None

Discuss that honesty is not always easy, but it is always the best choice. Ask students to complete these sentences in writing:

a. If I am not honest with my friends, ...

b. When I tell my parents a lie, they eventually ....

c. When I am dishonest, I feel....

d. When I am honest in a difficult situation, I feel...

Ask volunteers to share some of their responses.

Objective: Student will complete open-ended sentences having to do with honesty.

Subject: Social Studies	**Readiness Factor:** [3] Personal/Social
Mode: Written	**Readiness Factor Category:** [k] Community Involvement and
Training Zone: [C] Conscientiousness	Responsibility

Ss 8: Being part of a team

FUTR Tool: 49
PACT: yes

Supplies: None

Discuss that, when you are part of a team, you should put the success of the team ahead of your own success. As a group, brainstorm examples of putting team success ahead of your own.

Some possible responses: Even though she wants to shoot, a basketball player passes the ball to the player who has been shooting the best in the game; Even though a person on a committee likes his idea best, he can see that others like a different idea, so he drops his own idea and begins to build on the favored idea; When the teachers tells Jim the idea for his part of the team project was great, Jim says thanks, but then points out how his idea is part of the whole team idea.

Objective: Student will help think of some examples of putting team success ahead of personal success.

Subject: Social Studies	**Readiness Factor:** [3] Personal/Social
Mode: Brainstorming	**Readiness Factor Category:** [i] Relationships
Training Zone: [F] Flexibility	

Ss 9: Being responsible at work

FUTR Tool: 44
PACT: yes

Supplies: None

Discuss that being responsible means doing your fair share and doing what you think is right. Divide the class into four groups. Ask each group to role play being responsible and not being responsible related to the following work situations:

a. Getting to work on time

b. Tidying up at the end of the day

c. Doing personal tasks while at work

d. Having a good attitude

Objective: Student will role play an example of being responsible at work.

Subject: Social Studies	**Readiness Factor:** [1] Career
Mode: Role Play	**Readiness Factor Category:** [b] Job Performance
Training Zone: [R] Responsibility	

Ss 10: **Being sensitive to others**

Supplies: None

Discuss that being sensitive to others refers to paying attention to others' emotions and reactions and changing what you do or say to help others feel better. Ask volunteers to role play being sensitive as they respond to the following situations:

a. You are hungry and your mother is making dinner. Suddenly, she slips, the dinner spills onto the floor and burns her leg. While she is taking care of her leg, she tells you that she knows you are hungry and feels badly for ruining the dinner. What will you say to her?

b. You get your test back and you have a good grade. You say, "This test was so easy." Then, you notice that your friend has a bad grade. What will you do or say?

c. You have some nice new shoes. You know your cousin has been wanting new shoes, but didn't get any. Your cousin says, "How do you rate getting those shoes?" What will you say?

Objective: Student will role play responding in a sensitive way to others.

Subject: Social Studies	**Readiness Factor:** [3] Personal/Social
Mode: Role Play	**Readiness Factor Category:** [i] Relationships
Training Zone: [Z] Socialization	

Ss 11: **Calling 911**

Supplies: None

Discuss that calling 911 is the best way to get help in an emergency. As a group, brainstorm examples of emergencies. Make sure the list includes situations such as the following: someone is hurt, there is a fire in the house, two cars have crashed and it looks as if people are hurt, someone has collapsed and needs help. Caution students against frivolously making 911 calls that take up valuable operator time.

Have students take turns using the emergencies on the list to role play 911 calls. Make sure they include these pieces of information: name of caller, name of insured person, address, phone number, description of situation.

Objective: Student will help make lists of 911-type emergencies and will role play 911 calls.

Subject: Social Studies	**Readiness Factor:** [2] Daily Living
Mode: Role Play	**Readiness Factor Category:** [e] Safety and Security
Training Zone: [R] Responsibility	

Ss 12: **Carrying money safely**

Supplies: A few money-carrying containers such as purses, wallets, and pouches

Show students safe and unsafe ways to carry money.
Some safe possibilities: Front pocket, Small pouch around neck and under shirt

Some unsafe possibilities: A loose hanging purse [can easily be grabbed or handle cut], wallet in back pocket [easy for a pick pocket]

Objective: Student will see some safe and unsafe ways to carry money.

Subject: Social Studies	**Readiness Factor:** [2] Daily Living
Mode: Demonstration	**Readiness Factor Category:** [e] Safety and Security
Training Zone: [U] Conclusion	

Ss 13: **Choosing an apartment**

FUTR Tool: no
PACT: yes

Supplies: None

Discuss that since people have different needs, an apartment that is right for one person is not right for another. As a group, think of reasons to choose each of the following apartments.

a. An apartment with only one bedroom

b. An apartment with a pool

c. An apartment with a garage

d. An apartment close to downtown

e. An apartment with three bedrooms

f. An apartment with a large living room

g. An apartment with large closets

Objective: Student will identify reasons to choose different apartments.

Subject: Social Studies **Mode:** Brainstorming **Training Zone:** [L] Logic	**Readiness Factor:** [2] Daily Living **Readiness Factor Category:** [f] Shopping and Eating at Restaurants

Ss 14: **Choosing people to ask for references**

FUTR Tool: 72
PACT: yes

Supplies: None

Discuss that the best references are people who are not related to you, who know you fairly well, who can speak to your ability to perform well on a job, and who you believe will speak well of you. Explain that, if you have had jobs, you should think of your bosses or other people in authority at your places of work as possible references. Explain that other reference possibilities include people in authority such as teachers, club advisors, and ministers.

Ask each student to make a list of at least ten people they could consider asking for references. Then, have them choose three out of the ten. Finally, have them find addresses and phone numbers for the final three choices. Tell them that, before they actually use someone as a reference, they need to talk with the person and make sure the person is agreeable to giving you a good reference.

Objective: Student will decide on three people to use as references.

Subject: Social Studies **Mode:** Written **Training Zone:** [U] Conclusion	**Readiness Factor:** [3] Personal/Social **Readiness Factor Category:** [j] Leisure/Desires/Choices

Ss 15: **Choosing the best route**

FUTR Tool: 37
PACT: yes

Supplies: Five road maps

Discuss that, when deciding on the best route between two points on a map, you need to think about components such as distance, heavy traffic, time of day, size of roads, number of stop signs, and speed limits.

Divide the class into five teams and give each team a road map. Ask them to choose a route between two locations. (Name two locations that show on the map and that could have more than one logical route between them.) Then, have the teams share their plans and explain whey they think it is best. If all teams do not choose the same plan, choose a "best plan" as a group.

Objective: Student will use a map to help choose the best route between two named locations.

Subject: Social Studies **Mode:** Hands-On **Training Zone:** [O] Organization	**Readiness Factor:** [2] Daily Living **Readiness Factor Category:** [g] Time and Order

Ss 16: **Choosing to have fresh breath**

FUTR Tool: no
PACT: no

Supplies: None

Discuss that some things we eat give us bad breath. Also discuss that there are ways to freshen breath so it doesn't smell bad.
Brainstorm a list of foods and drinks that often leave people with bad breath. (Examples: garlic, wine, pork rinds, onions)
Brainstorm a list of ways to freshen one's breath. [Examples: brushing, using mouthwash, chewing gum, sucking on a mint, eating a food that doesn't cause bad breath]

Caution that some people have medical reasons for having bad breath, and if you always have bad breath, you should talk to a doctor about it.

Objective: Student will help identify foods that cause bad breath and ways to freshen breath.

Subject: Social Studies **Mode:** Brainstorming **Training Zone:** [S] Self-Awareness	**Readiness Factor:** [3] Personal/Social **Readiness Factor Category:** [I] Health, Diet, and Appearance

Ss 17: **Comparing leases, floorplans, etc.**

FUTR Tool: no
PACT: no

Supplies: Posterboard for each team

Tell your students that apartments vary a lot, so they will have to look at the floor plans, common activity areas, lease requirements, rental amounts, and location to compare possible apartments.

Divide the class into teams of three or four students and give each team a piece of posterboard. Ask each team to create an imaginary apartment (or use a real apartment with which they are familiar) and present the floor plans, common activity areas, lease requirements, rental amounts, and location on a poster. Have teams share their posters.

Objective: Student will help to create a poster showcasing a real or imaginary apartment.

Subject: Social Studies **Mode:** Drawing **Training Zone:** [A] Analysis	**Readiness Factor:** [2] Daily Living **Readiness Factor Category:** [f] Shopping and Eating at Restaurants

Ss 18: **Crossing the street safely**

FUTR Tool: no
PACT: yes

Supplies: None

Create a two-columned chart on the board. Title the chart Crossing the Street. Title the left column "Safe" and the right column "Unsafe." As a group, identify safe and unsafe actions when crossing a street.

Some safe examples: Look both ways, wait until no cars are coming, cross in the crosswalk, cross with a light, stay alert

Some unsafe examples: Talk with friends while you are crossing, cross away from crosswalks, run to beat cars that are coming, cross when the light says "Do Not Walk," wait for a car to pass and then start walking without looking in the other direction again

Objective: Student will help make a chart showing safe and unsafe street-crossing choices.

Subject: Social Studies **Mode:** Graph or Chart **Training Zone:** [A] Analysis	**Readiness Factor:** [2] Daily Living **Readiness Factor Category:** [e] Safety and Security

Ss 19: Dealing with conflict

FUTR Tool: 55
PACT: yes

Supplies: None

Discuss that conflict rarely goes away on its own, so it is important to address it. Ask students to write endings for these sentences:

• If someone is mean to me and I don't even know why....

• If my parents tell me I can't do something, and I do not think they are being fair...

• If a friend says something unkind about me and I hear it later....

• If I am really upset with a friend....

• If someone I do not know says some nasty things to me at a ball game....

• If a teacher embarrasses me in class...

Objective: Student will complete open-ended sentences having to do with conflict.

Subject: Social Studies **Mode:** Written **Training Zone:** [Z] Socialization	**Readiness Factor:** [3] Personal/Social **Readiness Factor Category:** [i] Relationships

Ss 20: Dealing with job issues

FUTR Tool: 56
PACT: yes

Supplies: None

Ask volunteers to respond to the following situations. Discuss the responses as a group.

a. Why is it in your best interest to be nice to customers who come to the place where you work?

b. Natasha doesn't like her boss very well. She thinks her boss wastes time and has bad ideas. What do you think Natasha should do about her situation?

c. David's boss told him he works too sloppily. David doesn't think he is sloppy. What should David do?

d. Is it a good idea to share your personal secrets with everyone at work? Why or why not?

e. Imagine you get sick at work and need to go home. What should you say and to whom?

Objective: Student will discuss common job issues.

Subject: Social Studies **Mode:** Discussion **Training Zone:** [Z] Socialization	**Readiness Factor:** [1] Career **Readiness Factor Category:** [b] Job Performance

Ss 21: Differentiating between obvious male and female names

FUTR Tool: no
PACT: no

Supplies: None

Call out the following names (as well as others that are popular in your area) and ask volunteers to identify each as male or female. If a name can be either male or female, tell students to say "both."

Ann	Paul	Chris	Pat	Dixie	Connie
Chloe	Juan	Demetri	Derek	Mathew	Whitney
Morgan	Randy	Kelsey	Shauna	Alexander	Eric
Miquel	Ryan	Tyler	Erin	Elsa	Anisha

Objective: Student will identify names as male, female, or both.

Subject: Social Studies **Mode:** Oral Response **Training Zone:** [A] Analysis	**Readiness Factor:** [2] Daily Living **Readiness Factor Category:** [h] Transportation/Travel/Worldliness

Ss 22: **Discussing current events**

FUTR Tool: 68
PACT: yes

Supplies: Current newspaper

Discuss each of the major headlines in a current newspaper. Explain to your students that, if they at least pay attention to the major headlines each day, they will have a general understanding of some main current events. Also, discuss that listening to the news on radio or television at least once a day is another way to have a general understanding of main current events.

Objective: Student will discuss current events based on major newspaper headlines.

Subject: Social Studies **Mode:** Discussion **Training Zone:** [A] Analysis	**Readiness Factor:** [2] Daily Living **Readiness Factor Category:** [h] Transportation/Travel/Worldliness

Ss 23: **Drawing directions**

FUTR Tool: 65
PACT: yes

Supplies: None

Ask students to draw directions from the school to their homes. Tell them to make sure to include all major roads or streets and all needed roads or streets. Have them label each street they include on their maps.

Objective: Student will draw directions from school to his home.

Subject: Social Studies **Mode:** Drawing **Training Zone:** [M] Manipulation	**Readiness Factor:** [2] Daily Living **Readiness Factor Category:** [h] Transportation/Travel/Worldliness

Ss 24: **Evaluating your own attitude**

FUTR Tool: no
PACT: yes

Supplies: None

Discuss that it is common to get upset with someone and then blame that person for the problem. Encourage students to always think about whether or not their own attitudes are making a situation more of a problem. Ask volunteers to share examples of when they were upset with someone and then realized that they themselves could adjust a little and make the situation better.

Objective: Student will discuss how her own attitude can sometimes improve problem situations.

Subject: Social Studies **Mode:** Discussion **Training Zone:** [S] Self-Awareness	**Readiness Factor:** [3] Personal/Social **Readiness Factor Category:** [l] Health, Diet, and Appearance

Ss 25: Explaining why hitchhiking is not safe

FUTR Tool: no
PACT: yes

Supplies: None

As a group, brainstorm reasons why hitchhiking is not safe. Make sure the list includes the following ideas:

• The person who picks you up could be evil and intent on hurting you.

• The person who picks you up could be involved in unlawful activities and you would then be involved by association.

• The person who picks you up could drop you off somewhere that is not safe.

• You could be hit by a car

• You could have problems with extreme temperatures.

Objective: Student will will help make a list of reasons hitchhiking is not safe.

Subject: Social Studies **Mode:** Brainstorming **Training Zone:** [U] Conclusion	**Readiness Factor:** [2] Daily Living **Readiness Factor Category:** [e] Safety and Security

Ss 26: Finding weather reports for varying locations

FUTR Tool: no
PACT: yes

Supplies: Several daily newspaper weather maps; A video tape of a national weather forecast

Divide the class into teams of three or four students. Give each team a daily newspaper weather map. Ask each team to study the weather map and tell the class which parts of the country are forecasted to have precipitation.

Assign each team a state in the U.S. and tell them you want them to watch the weather forecast video and check the weather for their assigned states. Show the class the weather forecast video. Discuss that weather forecasts are educated guesses that might or might not come true.

Objective: Student will interpret weather reports.

Subject: Social Studies **Mode:** Hands-On **Training Zone:** [E] Exploration	**Readiness Factor:** [2] Daily Living **Readiness Factor Category:** [h] Transportation/Travel/Worldliness

Ss 27: Following neighborhood guidelines

FUTR Tool: no
PACT: yes

Supplies: None

Discuss typical neighborhood guidelines and rules such as the following:

a. Due to the presence of underground wires and pipes, do not dig in your yard without a permit.

b. Keep all pets inside, fenced in, or on a leash.

c. Clean up all pet waste.

d. Campers, boats, and semi-trucks cannot be parked in front of a house for over 24 hours at a time.

e. Permits are required for all building projects.

f. Approval is required for paint color choices.

g. Yards must be mowed regularly.

Objective: Student will discuss typical neighborhood guidelines.

Subject: Social Studies **Mode:** Discussion **Training Zone:** [F] Flexibility	**Readiness Factor:** [3] Personal/Social **Readiness Factor Category:** [k] Community Involvement and Responsibility

Ss 28: Following through

FUTR Tool: 46
PACT: yes

Supplies: None

Discuss that "following through" means to complete what you have planned or started. Ask students to raise their hands if they know how to play golf well enough to explain the scoring process (or if they know a favorite TV show well enough to tell the class about it). Then, ask one of them to explain how to score golf (or to tell about a favorite TV show). Point out that saying you know how to score golf (or that you can tell about a TV show) is an example of making a statement. Explain that, in this situation, actually telling how to score golf (or telling about the TV show) is an example of following through.

Ask volunteers to share a time when they started or planned something and followed through OR didn't want to follow through.

Objective: Student will participate in a follow-through demonstration and will discuss the concept of following through.

Subject: Social Studies **Mode:** Demonstration **Training Zone:** [C] Conscientiousness	**Readiness Factor:** [3] Personal/Social **Readiness Factor Category:** [i] Relationships

Ss 29: Getting a birth certificate

FUTR Tool: no
PACT: yes

Supplies: Computer with online access

Discuss that birth certificates are available from the courthouse in the county where you were born. Make a list of the different birth counties (and states) for your students. As a group, go online and find and print the instructions for each different location. Compare the different directions.

Objective: Student will go online to find instructions for getting a birth certificate in the county where he was born.

Subject: Social Studies **Mode:** Action **Training Zone:** [R] Responsibility	**Readiness Factor:** [2] Daily Living **Readiness Factor Category:** [e] Safety and Security

Ss 30: Getting along with a roommate

FUTR Tool: no
PACT: no

Supplies: None

Discuss that many people, especially college students and young adults, have roommates. Explain that when people live close together, they often have problems. Talk about some possible problems and how to work through them.

Make sure to include some of these possible problems: leaving dirty dishes, eating food that isn't yours, making too much noise, choosing TV channels without consensus, deciding who will clean, not paying rent, not paying fair share of utilities, paying late, using things that are not yours, taking things that are not yours.

Objective: Student will discuss possible roommate problems.

Subject: Social Studies **Mode:** Discussion **Training Zone:** [Z] Socialization	**Readiness Factor:** [3] Personal/Social **Readiness Factor Category:** [i] Relationships

Ss 31: Getting along with others

Supplies: None

Create a chart on the board with these headings: Could help people get along, Will probably make sense when think about it later, Is the way you would want someone to react to you. Down the side, enter abbreviations for the situations below. Then, write yes or no in each box.

a. Tess is angry with her friend, so she yells "I don't know why I hang around with someone as fat and ugly as you anyhow."

b. Jo is so angry with Lou that she wants to hit her, but she turns and walks away instead.

c. Malik is upset with a teacher, so he scribbles on the school wall with a black marker.

d. Dennis is upset with his mother, so he refuses to talk to her.

e. Paige is feeling a little edgy, so she trips Kyle as he walks by her desk.

Objective: Student will help make a chart to study the results of human behavior.

Subject: Social Studies	**Readiness Factor:** [3] Personal/Social
Mode: Graph or Chart	**Readiness Factor Category:** [i] Relationships
Training Zone: [F] Flexibility	

Ss 32: Getting ready to go to bed

FUTR Tool: no
PACT: yes

Supplies: None

As a group, brainstorm steps involved in going to bed at night. Make sure to include ideas such as the following: turn the TV off, make sure the doors are locked, set the house alarm, wash your face, brush your teeth, go to the bathroom, set the alarm clock, turn the night light on, and turn the lights off. Discuss that not everyone performs all the same steps and not everyone does the things in the same order. Then, in order, have each student make a list of the steps he or she follows.

Objective: Student will help make a master list of general steps people might follow when getting ready for bed and will then make an ordered personal list of the steps she actually goes through.

Subject: Social Studies	**Readiness Factor:** [2] Daily Living
Mode: Brainstorming, Written	**Readiness Factor Category:** [d] Household Care and/or Chores
Training Zone: [U] Conclusion	

Ss 33: Giving directions to a driver

FUTR Tool: no
PACT: yes

Supplies: None

Ask volunteers to answer these questions:

a. If you are giving directions to someone from out of town, why shouldn't you tell them to turn left on the corner where the big blue truck is parked? [Might not be there]

b. When would it be OK to tell someone that they will know it is your house because they will see a green blanket on the clothes line? [When you know they will come while the blanket is still there.]

c. What would be an example of a good landmark to use when giving directions? [buildings, signs]

Ask each student to give oral directions from school to home using at least one landmark.

Objective: Student will give directions to her house using at least one landmark.

Subject: Social Studies	**Readiness Factor:** [2] Daily Living
Mode: Oral Response	**Readiness Factor Category:** [h] Transportation/Travel/Worldliness
Training Zone: [F] Flexibility	

Ss 34: **Handling peer pressure**

FUTR Tool: 57
PACT: yes

Supplies: None

Divide the class into groups of four or five students. Ask each group to role play responding to peer pressure in one of the following situations:

a. Your friend wants you to quietly talk on your cell phone after you are in bed even though your parents have said no phone calls after 10:00.

b. Some of your friends are mean to a kid in your class who has few friends. You don't think he deserves to be picked on, but you don't want your friends turning on you.

c. Your friend came over to study for tomorrow's test, but he wants to watch your favorite TV show instead. He says the test is really not that important.

d. You and some friends get some fast food on the way home from school. The driver throws his paper trash out the window and says, "Don't make a mess in my car, guys."

Objective: Student will role play a response to peer pressure.

Subject: Social Studies **Mode:** Role Play **Training Zone:** [Z] Socialization	**Readiness Factor:** [3] Personal/Social **Readiness Factor Category:** [i] Relationships

Ss 35: **Having a working knowledge of the 50 states**

FUTR Tool: no
PACT: yes

Supplies: None

Divide the class into teams of four to six students. Ask state-related questions such as those below and have teams compete to see who can answer first most often.

a. How many states are in the U.S. [50]

b. Name a large state. [TX, AK, CA, MT, AZ, NM, CO, OR, WY, NV]

c. Name a small state [MA, DE, MD, CT, RI, NJ, NH, VT]

d. Name a state on the West Coast. [AK, WA, OR, CA]

e. Name a state that borders Canada. [WA, ID, MT, ND, MN, MI, NY, VT, NH, ME]

f. Name a state that borders Illinois. [WI, IA, MO, KY, IN]

Objective: Student will answer questions about the 50 states.

Subject: Social Studies **Mode:** Oral Response **Training Zone:** [E] Exploration	**Readiness Factor:** [2] Daily Living **Readiness Factor Category:** [h] Transportation/Travel/Worldliness

Ss 36: Identifying actions that are criminal

Supplies: None

Ask students to number from a to h on a piece of paper, and then write T or F for these statements:

a. Shoplifting is not a big deal and will not go on a person's record. [F]

b. Walking across someone's yard might not be nice, but it is not necessarily a criminal act. [T]

c. Breaking windows in an empty building doesn't hurt anyone and is not illegal. [F]

d. It is not against the law to take food at the grocery store if you are really hungry. [F]

e. There is no law against refusing to help a neighbor who is ill. [T]

f. In most states, it is legal to take your pet dog into a restaurant with you. [F]

g. All customers can park anywhere in a restaurant parking lot—even the handicapped spots. [F]

h. It is OK to drive faster than the speed limit as long as you are a good driver. [F]

Objective: Student will determine whether specific actions are criminal or not.

Subject: Social Studies **Mode:** Written **Training Zone:** [U] Conclusion	**Readiness Factor:** [2] Daily Living **Readiness Factor Category:** [e] Safety and Security

Ss 37: Identifying cities

Supplies: None

Ask volunteers to respond to the following requests:

a. Name a city you would like to visit.

b. Name one of the five largest cities in the U.S. [New York, Los Angeles, Chicago, Houston, Philadelphia]

c. Name any city in Michigan.

d. Name any city in Colorado.

e. Name any city in France.

f. Name any city in England.

Objective: Student will name cities that match specific requests.

Subject: Social Studies **Mode:** Oral Response **Training Zone:** [E] Exploration	**Readiness Factor:** [2] Daily Living **Readiness Factor Category:** [h] Transportation/Travel/Worldliness

Ss 38: Identifying directions (North, South, East, West)

FUTR Tool: 61
PACT: yes

Supplies: Classroom map or map in a textbook

Discuss that we sometimes have to orient ourselves in a new location so that we know where the directions are. Point out a landmark in the room that can serve as "north." Then, make sure students understand that east is to the right of north, west is to the left, and south is directly opposite of north. Ask students as a group to point to each direction: North, South, East, West.

Show students a classroom map or have students open to a map in a textbook. Point to each of the directions north, south, east, and west and ask students to identify each as you point.

Ask different students to answer this question: What direction do you live from the school?

Objective: Student will point in cardinal directions as requested.

Subject: Social Studies **Mode:** Action **Training Zone:** [E] Exploration	**Readiness Factor:** [2] Daily Living **Readiness Factor Category:** [h] Transportation/Travel/Worldliness

Ss 39: Identifying ethnic foods

FUTR Tool: no
PACT: yes

Supplies: Stack of old magazines with food pictures, one posterboard for each team, tape, markers

Divide the class into teams and assign each team an ethnic food to look for such as Mexican, Italian, German, and Chinese. Ask each team to find pictures in the magazines and create a collage showing examples of the assigned type of ethnic food. Have teams share their collages.

Objective: Student will help to make a collage showing a specific type of ethnic food.

Subject: Social Studies **Mode:** Action **Training Zone:** [V] Observation	**Readiness Factor:** [2] Daily Living **Readiness Factor Category:** [f] Shopping and Eating at Restaurants

Ss 40: Identifying foreign countries on a map

FUTR Tool: no
PACT: yes

Supplies: Map or globe

Using a map or globe, call out countries and ask volunteers to find them. Include countries such as Brazil, Mexico, Canada, France, Switzerland, Australia, Denmark, Argentina, Scotland, Greece, China, Japan, and Thailand.

Objective: Student will find identified countries on a map or globe.

Subject: Social Studies **Mode:** Action **Training Zone:** [E] Exploration	**Readiness Factor:** [2] Daily Living **Readiness Factor Category:** [h] Transportation/Travel/Worldliness

Ss 41: Identifying jobs that are well-matched to personal strengths

FUTR Tool: no
PACT: no

Supplies: None

Ask each student to draw a square in the middle of a piece of paper. At each corner, have them place another square. In each of the four corner squares, ask them to write one thing they can do well. Then, working as a group, identify jobs that will match each student's skills and have students write those jobs in their center squares.

Sample layout:

Objective: Student will make a visual showing some of his skills and a job that requires those skills.

Subject: Social Studies	Readiness Factor: [1] Career
Mode: Drawing	Readiness Factor Category: [a] Career Preparation
Training Zone: [A] Analysis	

Ss 42: Identifying nearby cities

FUTR Tool: no
PACT: no

Supplies: None

On the board, draw a dot representing your city or town. Then, place dots around it in the general location of a dozen or so nearby cities, but do not add the city names. Add major roads if doing so will make your map easier to follow. Ask your students to study the map and add names to the nearby-cities' dots.

Objective: Student will identify nearby cities on a rough local map.

Subject: Social Studies	Readiness Factor: [2] Daily Living
Mode: Action	Readiness Factor Category: [h] Transportation/Travel/Worldliness
Training Zone: [S] Self-Awareness	

Ss 43: Identifying realistic job possibilities

FUTR Tool: 40
PACT: yes

Supplies: Newspaper job ad pages for each student (do not need to be current and only need if doing second activity)

Do one of the following:

Write a list of jobs on the board that you know are periodically available locally. Have students choose those that they think they would be able to do.

Have students try to find job ads that they could apply for as students and that they have the skills to do.

Objective: Student will choose jobs that are realistic possibilities.

Subject: Social Studies	Readiness Factor: [1] Career
Mode: Hands-On	Readiness Factor Category: [a] Career Preparation
Training Zone: [L] Logic	

Ss 44: Interacting in the community

Supplies: None

Discuss situations where you can take part in the community, such as going to a park, eating at a restaurant, going to a school event, taking part in a fund raiser, getting a hair cut, talking to friends you encounter in a store, and reading the local news.

Ask volunteers to answer these questions:

a. Whom should you call if your sink is plugged? [plumber]

b. Whom should you call if you want to buy or sell a house? [realtor]

c. Where should you go if you want to have a picnic? [park]

d. Where can you keep your dog while you are out of town? [kennel]

Objective: Student will discuss opportunities for taking part in the community and will identify community solutions for common needs.

Subject: Social Studies **Mode:** Oral Response **Training Zone:** [Z] Socialization	**Readiness Factor:** [3] Personal/Social **Readiness Factor Category:** [k] Community Involvement and Responsibility

Ss 45: Keeping commitments

Supplies: None

Discuss that commitments are things you tell others you will do and you should only make commitments you are able to keep. Explain that commitments can be small things like "I will be home for dinner at 6:30," or larger things like "I will pick up, vacuum, and dust my room before Sunday."

Explain that, as people mature, they usually get better at knowing how to make commitments they are able to keep. Ask each student to think of one commitment they have made and kept and one that they made and did not keep.

Objective: Student will share a commitment he has kept and one he has not kept.

Subject: Social Studies **Mode:** Oral Response **Training Zone:** [C] Conscientiousness	**Readiness Factor:** [3] Personal/Social **Readiness Factor Category:** [k] Community Involvement and Responsibility

Ss 46: Keeping hands in appropriate places when in public

Supplies: None

Discuss that the behaviors listed below are not appropriate in public:

a. picking your nose

b. itching your crotch

c. touching your private parts

d. playing with your tongue

e. playing with your feet

f. feeling your under arms

g. putting your fingers in your mouth

Objective: Student will discuss behaviors that are not appropriate in public.

Subject: Social Studies **Mode:** Discussion **Training Zone:** [V] Observation	**Readiness Factor:** [3] Personal/Social **Readiness Factor Category:** [l] Health, Diet, and Appearance

Ss 47: Knowing and following driving rules

FUTR Tool: 48
PACT: yes

Supplies: None

Ask volunteers to answer the following questions:

a. Everyone knows that drinking and driving is against the law. But, is it OK to smoke marijuana and drive? [No, it is against the law to drive while under the influence of any substance.]

b. Assume you are stopped for speeding. What is the worst that can happen if you are polite vs. if you swear at and try to hit the officer? [Polite: get a ticket; Impolite: ticket plus other charges]

c. Describe the appearance and meaning of some signs that drivers must obey.

Objective: Student will discuss some driving rules.

Subject: Social Studies **Mode:** Oral Response **Training Zone:** [C] Conscientiousness	**Readiness Factor:** [2] Daily Living **Readiness Factor Category:** [e] Safety and Security

Ss 48: Knowing family relationships

FUTR Tool: 38
PACT: yes

Supplies: None

Ask students to draw family trees with their names on the trunks. Have them add their parents', grandparents', and great-grandparents names on the branches. Tell them to put their fathers' parents and grandparents on the left and their mothers' parents and grandparents on the right. For students who are not sure of all the needed names, ask them to draw the tree and then to take it home and finish it with the help of their parents.

Objective: Student will draw a family tree that includes self, parents, grandparents, and great-grandparents.

Subject: Social Studies **Mode:** Drawing **Training Zone:** [O] Organization	**Readiness Factor:** [3] Personal/Social **Readiness Factor Category:** [i] Relationships

Ss 49: Knowing holiday dates and traditions

FUTR Tool: no
PACT: no

Supplies: A current calendar

Ask volunteers to find these special days on a calendar: New Year's Day, Valentine's Day, Presidents' Day, St. Patrick's Day, Memorial Day, 4th of July, Labor Day, Halloween, Thanksgiving, Christmas. Discuss related family traditions and whether or not each special day is also a school holiday.

Answer:

School holidays—New Year's Day, Presidents' Day, Memorial Day, 4th of July, Labor Day, Thanksgiving, Christmas

Not school holidays—Valentine's Day, St. Patrick's Day, Halloween

Objective: Student will find holiday dates on a calendar and discuss related family traditions.

Subject: Social Studies **Mode:** Action **Training Zone:** [V] Observation	**Readiness Factor:** [2] Daily Living **Readiness Factor Category:** [g] Time and Order

Ss 50: Knowing how current events relate to you

FUTR Tool: no
PACT: no

Supplies: None

Choose a current news topic that relates to your students in some way. Discuss the current event and then ask students to discuss how the current event relates to them

Ask volunteers to share other current events that relate to them. Have them tell about the current event and then specifically explain how it relates to them.

Discuss reasons students should pay attention to current events. Make sure to include ideas such as to know what is going on, to know when a specific activity is taking place, to know situations to be careful of, to know when something happens that causes others to need you.

Objective: Student will discuss current events and how they relate to him.

Subject: Social Studies **Mode:** Oral Response **Training Zone:** [S] Self-Awareness	**Readiness Factor:** [2] Daily Living **Readiness Factor Category:** [h] Transportation/Travel/Worldliness

Ss 51: Knowing languages spoken in different countries

FUTR Tool: no
PACT: yes

Supplies: None

Make a chart on the board with these three headings: Country, Language, "Hello." Under the "Country" heading, write these countries: U.S.A., France, Germany, England, Spain, and Italy. As a group, fill in the rest of the chart.

Answer:		
U.S.A.	English	Hello
France	French	Bonjour
Germany	German	hallo
England	English	Hello
Italy	Italian	ciao
Spain	Spanish	hola

Objective: Student will help complete a chart matching languages to countries.

Subject: Social Studies **Mode:** Graph or Chart **Training Zone:** [E] Exploration	**Readiness Factor:** [2] Daily Living **Readiness Factor Category:** [h] Transportation/Travel/Worldliness

Ss 52: **Knowing left and right**

Supplies: None

Ask students to stand by their desks and do the following actions:

- Wave their left hands
- Tug their right ears
- Tap their left feet
- Bend their right arms

- Pat their left legs
- Open and close their right hands
- Bend their bodies to the right
- Look to the left

Objective: Student will do right- and left-oriented actions on demand.

Subject: Social Studies **Mode:** Action **Training Zone:** [S] Self-Awareness	**Readiness Factor:** [2] Daily Living **Readiness Factor Category:** [g] Time and Order

Ss 53: **Knowing people at school**

Supplies: None

Write the following list on the board and ask students to add names next to the titles.

- Math teachers
- Deans
- English teachers
- Counselors
- Science teachers
- Coaches

- Social Studies teachers
- Principal
- Physical Education teachers
- Office Staff
- Foreign language teachers
- School nurse

Objective: Student will help identify school employees.

Subject: Social Studies **Mode:** Oral Response **Training Zone:** [Z] Socialization	**Readiness Factor:** [3] Personal/Social **Readiness Factor Category:** [k] Community Involvement and Responsibility

Ss 54: **Knowing personal choices**

Supplies: Drawing paper, markers, crayons, old magazines for cutting up

Ask volunteers to name a favorite color, food, and TV program. Give students each a piece of drawing paper. Have them draw a circle in the center and write Some of (Name)'s Favorite Things in the circle and draw short lines out from the edge of the circle to mark places for adding favorite things. Ask them to either draw or cut out pictures to show some of their favorite things. Tell them to only include one thing from a category, such as only one favorite food, one favorite TV program, etc.

Objective: Student will create a graphic showing some of her favorite things.

Subject: Social Studies **Mode:** Drawing **Training Zone:** [S] Self-Awareness	**Readiness Factor:** [3] Personal/Social **Readiness Factor Category:** [j] Leisure/Desires/Choices

Ss 55: **Knowing personal facts**

Supplies: None

Discuss that personal facts are details about yourself, your family, and your city or town. Ask students to create a form with blanks for the following details. Then, have them exchange papers with a partner and fill out each other's forms.

Name: First, Middle, Last	Street address	City
State	Zip	County
Birth Date: Month, Day, Year	Place of birth: City, State	Phone #
Cell phone #	Sex: M or F	Height
Weight	Marital status: S, D, M, W	Hair color
Eye color	Age	Food allergies
Exercise habits	Name of physician	Name of school
Country of residence	Citizenship	Mother's maiden name

Objective: Student will create and fill in a personal information form.

Subject: Social Studies **Mode:** Drawing **Training Zone:** [S] Self-Awareness	**Readiness Factor:** [3] Personal/Social **Readiness Factor Category:** [l] Health, Diet, and Appearance

Ss 56: **Knowing recent U.S. Presidents**

Supplies: None

Ask volunteers to answer these questions:

a. Who is president of the U.S. right now?

b. Not counting President (insert name of current U.S. President), name two people who have been president during your lifetime.

c. Which of these people have been president of the U.S.: George Bush, Brad Pitt, or Tim Duncan? [George Bush]

d. Which of these people have been president of the U.S.: Jesse Jackson, Bill Clinton, or Bill Gates? [Bill Clinton]

Objective: Student will name the current and some recent U.S. Presidents.

Subject: Social Studies **Mode:** Oral Response **Training Zone:** [V] Observation	**Readiness Factor:** [2] Daily Living **Readiness Factor Category:** [h] Transportation/Travel/Worldliness

Ss 57: Knowing the area where you live

FUTR Tool: 59
PACT: yes

Supplies: None

Ask volunteers to provide the following information about your local area:

a. Four main streets

b. Number and names of high schools

c. Where the downtown area is located

d. Four local businesses that employ more than 20 people

e. Four products that are made locally

f. Location of the County Courthouse

g. Location of the closest airport

h. Name of the state capital

Objective: Student will identify assorted locations in the local area.

Subject: Social Studies	**Readiness Factor:** [2] Daily Living
Mode: Oral Response	**Readiness Factor Category:** [h] Transportation/Travel/Worldliness
Training Zone: [S] Self-Awareness	

Ss 58: Knowing what you will do after high school

FUTR Tool: no
PACT: no

Supplies: None

Write these three questions on the board:

• Where will you live after high school?

• Where will you get money after high school?

• What will you do for fun after high school?

As a group, brainstorm some possible answers for each question and write the answers on the board. Then, ask students to think about answers that fit their individual situations. (Either those on the board or others) Have them each write a one- or two-sentence personal answer for each of the questions.

Objective: Student will help make a list of possible after-high-school plans and then will write a personal after-high-school plan.

Subject: Social Studies	**Readiness Factor:** [1] Career
Mode: Brainstorming, Written	**Readiness Factor Category:** [a] Career Preparation
Training Zone: [S] Self-Awareness	

Ss 59: Knowing when and how to use travelers checks

FUTR Tool: no
PACT: no

Supplies: None

Explain that travelers checks are sort of like special money that thieves cannot use and that can be replaced if stolen. Point out that travelers checks are designed for vacations and can be gotten at a bank. Tell students that, between credit cards and travelers checks, people can go on long vacations without ever carrying any large amount of money that they have to worry about having stolen. Explain that, as a rule, travelers checks are only for vacations that are at least a week long and to a place where you would have difficulty getting along without the cash.

Ask volunteers to describe a vacation where it would be logical to take travelers checks.

Objective: Student will discuss how travelers checks work and when to use them.

Subject: Social Studies	**Readiness Factor:** [2] Daily Living
Mode: Discussion	**Readiness Factor Category:** [h] Transportation/Travel/Worldliness
Training Zone: [U] Conclusion	

Ss 60: Knowing your legal rights

FUTR Tool: 43
PACT: yes

Supplies: None

Ask volunteers to answer the following questions:

a. At what age is a person considered an adult in your state? [Varies—could be 18 for most things, 21 for drinking alcohol, 25 for driving rented vehicles]

b. Can you legally say what you think about the U.S. government without being arrested? [yes]

c. If Joe dislikes Louise, can he say mean untrue things about her without worrying about getting in trouble with the law? [No, he could be brought to court for libel]

d. What would happen if you were accused of a crime and needed a lawyer, but could not afford one? [The court would appoint a lawyer for you at no charge.]

e. In the U.S., can you be sent to jail for years while you wait to go on trial? [no]

f. What is an appeal and when is it helpful? [A chance to ask for another trial; Could reverse a guilty conviction]

Objective: Student will answer questions about citizens' legal rights in the U.S.

Subject: Social Studies **Mode:** Oral Response **Training Zone:** [R] Responsibility	**Readiness Factor:** [2] Daily Living **Readiness Factor Category:** [e] Safety and Security

Ss 61: Knowing your mother's maiden name

FUTR Tool: no
PACT: yes

Supplies: None

Explain that a maiden name is a girl's last name before she gets married. Also, explain that your mother's maiden name is often used as a secret code to prove that you are who you say you are, so it is important to know it and know how to spell it—but that you shouldn't share it with strangers.

Ask students to take turns writing their mothers' maiden names on the board. For students who do not know the names or are not sure how to spell them, have them check after school and write the names tomorrow.

Objective: Student will write his mother's maiden name on the board.

Subject: Social Studies **Mode:** Written **Training Zone:** [V] Observation	**Readiness Factor:** [3] Personal/Social **Readiness Factor Category:** [i] Relationships

Ss 62: Knowing your neighbors

FUTR Tool: no
PACT: yes

Supplies: None

Have students draw maps of their neighborhoods using this procedure:

1. In the middle of a piece of paper, draw a rectangle to represent your house or apartment.

2. Draw rectangles representing your neighbors' houses. Place these rectangles so they are laid out in relation to your "house" similarly to how they actually are on your street or road.

3. Add your neighbors' names to the different neighbor rectangles.

Objective: Student will draw a layout showing her home and her neighbors' homes.

Subject: Social Studies **Mode:** Drawing **Training Zone:** [Z] Socialization	**Readiness Factor:** [3] Personal/Social **Readiness Factor Category:** [k] Community Involvement and Responsibility

78   Life Skill Lessons

Ss 63: Listing pros and cons

FUTR Tool: 42
PACT: yes

Supplies: None

Ask students to draw a line down the center of a piece of paper. Have them label their left columns "Pros" and their right columns "Cons." Then have them each choose one of the topics below (or other approved topics) and fill in the chart. Tell them to try to have at least three ideas on each side. When they are finished, ask volunteers to share their lists.

- Should I stop watching TV on school nights?
- Should I tell my parents that I will start preparing dinner on my own one night a week?
- Should I join a club or organization at school?
- Should I bring sack lunches instead of buying food in the school cafeteria?

Objective: Student will choose a topic and make pro and con lists.

Subject: Social Studies **Mode:** Written **Training Zone:** [L] Logic	**Readiness Factor:** [3] Personal/Social **Readiness Factor Category:** [j] Leisure/Desires/Choices

Ss 64: Maintaining quality work for eight hours

FUTR Tool: no
PACT: no

Supplies: None

Discuss that when you are at work, you are to keep working the whole time except for planned breaks. Make sure students realize that the company is paying for your time and, if you are not fully working, it is like stealing time from the company. As a group, brainstorm a list of ideas that can help a person to put in a full day of quality work. Make sure the list includes some of these ideas: get a good night's sleep, get up early enough to easily get to work on time, make sure you know what you are to do each day, tell friends and relatives not to call you at work unless it is necessary, tell friends and relatives not to expect to hear from you during the day, make sure you keep your lunch hours and breaks at the allowed length.

Objective: Student will help to make a list of ideas that can help a person have a full day of quality work.

Subject: Social Studies **Mode:** Brainstorming **Training Zone:** [C] Conscientiousness	**Readiness Factor:** [1] Career **Readiness Factor Category:** [a] Career Preparation

Ss 65: Making and carrying out plans

FUTR Tool: no
PACT: no

Supplies: None

Explain that many things work out better if you plan them in advance and then follow your plan. Point out that, when making plans, it is logical to make them realistic so you can follow them. Ask students to each take a piece of paper and make a plan for what they will do after school tonight. Remind them to be realistic and ask them, for tomorrow, to plan to share how well they carried out their plans.

Objective: Student will make a plan and carry it out.

Subject: Social Studies **Mode:** Action **Training Zone:** [O] Organization	**Readiness Factor:** [3] Personal/Social **Readiness Factor Category:** [j] Leisure/Desires/Choices

Ss 66: **Making assumptions**

Supplies: None

Discuss that assumptions are guesses based on facts. Ask volunteers to make assumptions to answer the following questions. Then, discuss the facts used in each assumption.

a. Amy was playing on the swingset. She fell off and cut herself on the muddy rock. Do you think it was a clean cut or a dirty one? [Probably dirty since the rock was muddy]

b. Kellie woke up during the storm Wednesday night and saw that the clock on the microwave was not set. Why do you think it wasn't set? [Storm probably knocked the electricity out]

c. Dino went down to the pond to go ice skating and found three baby ducks swimming out in the middle where there was no ice. What should the swimming ducks have told Dino about ice skating? [Since the ice is melting in the middle, it is probably not safe for skating today]

Objective: Student will make assumptions and discuss the facts that support the assumptions.

Subject: Social Studies	**Readiness Factor:** [2] Daily Living
Mode: Oral Response	**Readiness Factor Category:** [h] Transportation/Travel/Worldliness
Training Zone: [L] Logic	

Ss 67: **Making decisions**

Supplies: None

Discuss that making decisions requires logic and an awareness of yourself and others. Divide the class into teams of three or four students. Tell each team to assume they are going to make a decision about how to remodel some part of the school. Tell them that they are to use logic and an awareness of themselves and others. Have all teams share their ideas and explain how they used logic and awareness in their plans.

Objective: Student will help role play making a decision.

Subject: Social Studies	**Readiness Factor:** [1] Career
Mode: Role Play	**Readiness Factor Category:** [b] Job Performance
Training Zone: [L] Logic	

Ss 68: **Making friends**

Supplies: None

Discuss why the following points are important when making friends:

a. Choose friends who like to do the same kinds of things you do.

b. Try to have at least some friends who are in some of your classes.

c. Choose friends whose parents allow them the same kinds of freedoms you have.

d. Try to have some friends who live close to you.

e. Work to keep friends with whom you can talk easily.

f. Work to keep friends who agree to do things with you when you ask them.

g. Work to keep friends with whom you are comfortable and can be yourself.

Objective: Student will discuss choices to consider when making friends.

Subject: Social Studies	**Readiness Factor:** [3] Personal/Social
Mode: Discussion	**Readiness Factor Category:** [i] Relationships
Training Zone: [Z] Socialization	

Ss 69: **Making leisure choices**

Supplies: None

With your students, brainstorm a long list of leisure activities. Ask each student to choose the five activities that sound the most fun and make an individual list. Then, ask students to share their individual lists. Discuss the differences in peoples' leisure choices.

Objective: Student will help make a master list of leisure choices and will then choose the five that interest her the most.

Subject: Social Studies **Mode:** Brainstorming, Written **Training Zone:** [Z] Socialization	**Readiness Factor:** [3] Personal/Social **Readiness Factor Category:** [j] Leisure/Desires/Choices

Ss 70: **Making safe choices when out at night**

Supplies: None

Point out that most crime happens at night, so people need to take extra safety precautions at night. Ask students to write endings for these sentences:

a. To safely walk to your car in a parking lot at night....

b. When walking somewhere at night...

c. If you see some people who are fighting...

d. When you are picking a place to park at night...

e. If you get a flat tire at night...

f. If you think you want to go with some friends to get pizza at 2:00 a.m.....

Objective: Student will complete open-ended sentences about making safe choices at night.

Subject: Social Studies **Mode:** Written **Training Zone:** [U] Conclusion	**Readiness Factor:** [2] Daily Living **Readiness Factor Category:** [h] Transportation/Travel/Worldliness

Ss 71: **Making travel decisions based on typical climate**

Supplies: None

As a group, identify two or three locations where people travel because of seasonal climates. Discuss the times of the year when the season would typically be right for the planned activities. [Examples: Florida beaches during spring and summer, Colorado ski slopes during winter and spring]

Objective: Student will discuss climate issues for different vacation spots.

Subject: Social Studies **Mode:** Discussion **Training Zone:** [U] Conclusion	**Readiness Factor:** [2] Daily Living **Readiness Factor Category:** [h] Transportation/Travel/Worldliness

Ss 72: **Naming elected officials**

Supplies: None

Ask your student to name these elected officials:

- U.S. President
- Governor of your state
- Your Representative to the U.S. House

- Your senators to the U.S. Senate
- Your senator and representative to the state congress
- Your mayor

If your students do not know the names, provide the names for them. Have them write the names on paper and study the list. Wait a few days and quiz them again.

Objective: Student will name people who hold prominent elected positions.

Subject: Social Studies **Mode:** Oral Response **Training Zone:** [S] Self-Awareness	**Readiness Factor:** [2] Daily Living **Readiness Factor Category:** [h] Transportation/Travel/Worldliness

Ss 73: **Naming major local intersections**

Supplies: None

Discuss that intersections are named using the streets that intersect—for example, the intersection where Empire Street crosses West Street is known as the Intersection at Empire and West Streets. Ask volunteers to identify several of the busiest intersections in your area using this naming procedure.

Objective: Student will discuss how intersections are named and will name major intersections in his local area.

Subject: Social Studies **Mode:** Discussion **Training Zone:** [U] Conclusion	**Readiness Factor:** [2] Daily Living **Readiness Factor Category:** [h] Transportation/Travel/Worldliness

Ss 74: **Packing to move**

Supplies: None

Point out that packing to move is a hard job, but that there are steps a person can take to make the job go smoothly and to make the end result better. Discuss the following "smooth moving" tips:

a. If you do not have boxes from a moving company, get a large supply from a grocery store or some other source of free empty boxes. When gathering, start at least a week ahead of time.

b. Get a big marker for labeling boxes, and keep it in your pocket so you can always find it.

c. Label each box with initials that tell where you want to put it in your new home, such as BR, KIT, etc.

d. Pack boxes tightly and full, but make sure you can fold the flaps so the boxes stack easily.

e. Stack filled boxes out of the way, preferably close to the door.

f. Use paper or clothing to wrap breakable items for protection.

g. Fill bigger boxes with lighter things so the boxes do not get so heavy.

h. Stay organized by packing one whole room before moving onto the next.

i. Accept help from friends and relatives.

Objective: Student will discuss tips to help packing to move go more easily.

Subject: Social Studies **Mode:** Discussion **Training Zone:** [M] Manipulation	**Readiness Factor:** [2] Daily Living **Readiness Factor Category:** [h] Transportation/Travel/Worldliness

Ss 75: Parenting

Supplies: None

Discuss that parents must give a lot of time to their children and must make many decisions for their children. Ask volunteers to role play being parents and children (and other people as needed) in the following situations. Tell them to include both the situations and the reactions to them.

a. 17-year-old Dale has several friends over and they are being so loud that the neighbors have called and complained. [One parent idea: Tell Dale to quiet down or the friend must leave]

b. 6-year-old Byron and 7-year-old Tatyana are getting bored on a long car trip and they start to bicker. [One parent idea: Come up with a fun activity such as a license plate game]

c. 10-year-old Ginny wants to wear makeup to school. [One parent idea: Allow for some play time with makeup, but insist that it not be worn to school at 10-years-old.]

Objective: Student will role play child and parent interactions.

Subject: Social Studies **Mode:** Role Play **Training Zone:** [R] Responsibility	**Readiness Factor:** [3] Personal/Social **Readiness Factor Category:** [i] Relationships

Ss 76: Planning a picnic

Supplies: None

Divide the class into teams of three or four students. Ask each team to make a written plan for a picnic. Make sure they include the detail listed below. Ask each team to share its plan.

a. Where and when (date and time) will the picnic be held?

b. Who is invited?

c. What will you eat?

d. What will you drink?

e. What will you sit on?

f. What will you carry the food in?

g. What will you do if the weather is bad?

h. Will you have activities other than eating? Is so, what?

Objective: Student will help plan a picnic.

Subject: Social Studies **Mode:** Written **Training Zone:** [Z] Socialization	**Readiness Factor:** [3] Personal/Social **Readiness Factor Category:** [l] Health, Diet, and Appearance

Ss 77: Planning a vacation

Supplies: None

Divide the class into teams of four or five students. Give each team one of the budget amounts (per person): $200, $500, $1000, $1500, $2000, $3000, $4000. Ask each team to plan a vacation that sounds fun and is within the budget. For the sake of time, tell students that you will provide "teacher guesstimates" for expenses such as transportation, hotels, and meals. (For the guesstimates, use your best guesses.)

Objective: Student will work with a team to plan a fun vacation within a budget.

Subject: Social Studies **Mode:** Role Play **Training Zone:** [O] Organization	**Readiness Factor:** [2] Daily Living **Readiness Factor Category:** [g] Time and Order

Ss 78: Preparing to get married

FUTR Tool: no
PACT: no

Supplies: None

Discuss that there are different aspects concerning preparing to get married. Go over the following ideas:

a. Spend time talking about serious issues so you know the two of you are compatible. If possible, attend an engagement weekend so you have help talking about the issues.

b. Make a budget for your new lives together so you know you can afford your plan.

c. Decide how you want your wedding day to be and who you will ask to share it with you.

d. Figure out how you will pay for your wedding day. Try to avoid starting out with a large wedding debt.

Objective: Student will discuss ideas related to getting married.

Subject: Social Studies **Mode:** Discussion **Training Zone:** [R] Responsibility	**Readiness Factor:** [3] Personal/Social **Readiness Factor Category:** [k] Community Involvement and Responsibility

Ss 79: Protecting your identity

FUTR Tool: no
PACT: no

Supplies: None

Discuss that identity theft is a crime that causes a lot of frustration for the victim and that you can take some steps to try to protect yourself from becoming such a victim. As a group, brainstorm ways to protect yourself from identity theft. Make sure to include these ideas:

a. Do not give your social security number unless you know you are giving it safely. This includes in-person, over the phone, or on the Internet.

b. Do not carry your social security card in your wallet or purse.

c. If you are throwing away papers with personal information other than just your name and address, cut it up or shred it.

d. Use locks for protection. Make sure your car, house, and mail box are all locked.

e. Only download or open e-mailed computer files from people you know and trust.

Objective: Student will identify theft-protection tips.

Subject: Social Studies **Mode:** Discussion **Training Zone:** [S] Self-Awareness	**Readiness Factor:** [2] Daily Living **Readiness Factor Category:** [e] Safety and Security

Ss 80: Providing identification

FUTR Tool: no
PACT: no

Supplies: None

Discuss with your students that they will often have times when they need to have identification. Explain that, most of the time, an ID needs to have a picture on it. Point out that one common picture ID is a driver's license, but that the state also provides picture IDs for non-drivers. Also, if your school requires students to have picture IDs, make sure they know that they can probably also use their school IDs for non-school purposes.

As a group, brainstorm situations where IDs are required and reasons why picture IDs are often required.

Objective: Student will discuss typical IDs and situations where they are required.

Subject: Social Studies **Mode:** Discussion **Training Zone:** [R] Responsibility	**Readiness Factor:** [2] Daily Living **Readiness Factor Category:** [e] Safety and Security

Ss 81: Putting utilities in your name

FUTR Tool: no
PACT: yes

Supplies: None

Ask volunteers to explain the term "utility bills." [Basic household bills including gas, electricity, water, cable TV (in some situations), Phone/Internet hookup (in some situations)] Discuss that when you move to a new location, you are responsible for calling the utility company and asking to have the bills put into your name. Explain that when people move out of a house or apartment, they cancel their service at that location, so when you move into a new place, there is no service until you call to set up service. Also, explain that, most utility services will require a deposit when you start up service. Explain that gas, water, and electricity are simple turn on/turn offs, but when you sign up for cable TV and Internet service, you have choices to make.

Objective: Student will discuss issues concerning putting utilities in her name.

Subject: Social Studies **Mode:** Discussion **Training Zone:** [O] Organization	**Readiness Factor:** [2] Daily Living **Readiness Factor Category:** [d] Household Care and/or Chores

Ss 82: Reacting to strangers

FUTR Tool: no
PACT: yes

Supplies: None

Discuss that very young children are taught to stay away from strangers, but that teenagers and adults are more able to take care of themselves, so they can speak to strangers in safe situations such as in a store, at the doctor's office, at a community meeting, or at a school function. Explain that, even though older people can safely speak to strangers in public places, they should still follow these rules: Do not go anywhere with a stranger. Do not eat or drink anything a stranger gives you. Do not give a stranger your phone number nor address. Do not tell private information to a stranger.

Objective: Student will discuss safe and logical reactions to strangers.

Subject: Social Studies **Mode:** Discussion **Training Zone:** [A] Analysis	**Readiness Factor:** [2] Daily Living **Readiness Factor Category:** [e] Safety and Security

Ss 83: Reading a map

FUTR Tool: no
PACT: yes

Supplies: An assortment of local maps

Explain that, when reading a map, you have to first orient yourself so you understand where north is on the map and in relation to where you are. Point out that most maps are set up so that the upright reading position has north at the top, but that every now and then, a map is set up differently. Pass out maps to the students. Ask them to find "north" on the map and to face their bodies towards the north.

On maps that include the school area, have students find (on the map) the street that runs in front of the school and have them actually point in the direction of the street from their desks.

Objective: Student will orient north on a map with north from within the classroom.

Subject: Social Studies **Mode:** Action **Training Zone:** [O] Organization	**Readiness Factor:** [2] Daily Living **Readiness Factor Category:** [h] Transportation/Travel/Worldliness

Ss 84: Reading a map while in the car

FUTR Tool: no
PACT: yes

Supplies: A road map

Discuss that when reading a map in a car, someone other than the driver should read the map. Explain that, when you are driving alone, you should stop the car to read the map. Tell them that, in most situations, you can pull over without going out of your way too much. Point out that, even if you have to take an unnecessary exit to be able to stop safely, it is best to take the extra time than to endanger yourself by trying to read a map while driving.

Have students take turns demonstrating the dangers of driving while reading a map by doing this role play:

Arrange the classroom so that there is a clear path from one corner of the room to the opposite corner, but make the path curvy so that a person walking straight will bump into desks or chairs. Give student a local map and choose a non-main street from the map, give the map to the student, and have student "drive" through the path while looking for the street. Discuss that it is not possible to read a map while safely giving full attention to driving.

Objective: Student will role play the dangers of reading a map while driving.

Subject: Social Studies **Mode:** Role Play **Training Zone:** [M] Manipulation	**Readiness Factor:** [2] Daily Living **Readiness Factor Category:** [h] Transportation/Travel/Worldliness

Ss 85: Recognizing area types

FUTR Tool: no
PACT: yes

Supplies: A stack of old magazines, drawing paper, markers

Divide the class into eight teams. Assign each team one of the types of areas listed below. Ask each team to draw (or find) one or more visual example of the assigned type of area.

- rural
- Urban
- inner city
- suburban
- small town
- large town
- small city
- large city

Discuss that some of the distinctions, such as between a large town and a small city, are very subjective and might even overlap.

Objective: Student will differentiate between different area types.

Subject: Social Studies **Mode:** Drawing **Training Zone:** [O] Organization	**Readiness Factor:** [2] Daily Living **Readiness Factor Category:** [h] Transportation/Travel/Worldliness

Ss 86: Recognizing areas of town or city by street categories

FUTR Tool: no
PACT: no

Supplies: None

Discuss that many cities and towns have street clusters that are helpful when locating a street. For example, a city might have an area where Maple, Oak, Chestnut, Cherry, Pine, and Walnut are all close together. As a group, identify street clusters in your area or a nearby area. For each cluster, give a name to the cluster (such as "Trees" for the above example).

Objective: Student will help identify local street clusters that are grouped by related names.

Subject: Social Studies **Mode:** Discussion **Training Zone:** [A] Analysis	**Readiness Factor:** [2] Daily Living **Readiness Factor Category:** [h] Transportation/Travel/Worldliness

Ss 87: Recognizing colors in your world

Supplies: None

Divide the class into four teams. Ask teams to look around the room and at classmate clothing to find as many different colors as they can. Have each team list the colors they see along with a clue to help them remember where they saw the color. Tell them to use color shade variations such as olive green, forest green, lime green, grass green, and sea green instead of just "green." Have each team present its color list.

Discuss that the core colors are red, blue, and yellow (actually, magenta, cyan, and yellow—but red, blue, and yellow are close enough for a general discussion) and that all other colors are created by mixing different amounts of the core colors.

Objective: Student will identify colors that are visible in the classroom.

Subject: Social Studies **Mode:** Action **Training Zone:** [V] Observation	**Readiness Factor:** [2] Daily Living **Readiness Factor Category:** [g] Time and Order

Ss 88: Recognizing famous people

FUTR Tool: no
PACT: yes

Supplies: Pictures of four famous people

One at a time, show students four famous-people pictures and ask volunteers to name each person.

Choose a famous person in each of the categories below. (Do not use the any of the people used above.) Call out each name and ask students to identify why the person is famous.

- Professional ball player
- Actor or actress
- Governor or President
- Writer

Objective: Student will identify some famous people from pictures and will explain why certain people are famous.

Subject: Social Studies **Mode:** Oral Response **Training Zone:** [V] Observation	**Readiness Factor:** [2] Daily Living **Readiness Factor Category:** [h] Transportation/Travel/Worldliness

Ss 89: Recognizing geographical differences

FUTR Tool: 54
PACT: yes

Supplies: None

Divide the class into four teams. Assign one of the groups below to each of the teams. Ask each team to prepare a short presentation explaining the differences between the geographical features in the group.

a. oceans, ponds, lakes, rivers

b. canyons, valleys, lowlands

c. hills, foothills, mountains, plateaus

d. forests, deserts, meadows

Objective: Student will identify differences between some geographical features.

Subject: Social Studies **Mode:** Oral Response **Training Zone:** [V] Observation	**Readiness Factor:** [2] Daily Living **Readiness Factor Category:** [h] Transportation/Travel/Worldliness

Ss 90: Recognizing house styles

FUTR Tool: no
PACT: yes

Supplies: None

Ask students to make simple drawings showing each of these types of houses:

- ranch
- two story
- split level
- tri-level
- story-and-a-half
- duplex
- three story

Objective: Student will draw different house styles.

Subject: Social Studies Mode: Drawing Training Zone: [V] Observation	Readiness Factor: [2] Daily Living Readiness Factor Category: [h] Transportation/Travel/Worldliness

Ss 91: Respecting cultural diversity

FUTR Tool: no
PACT: no

Supplies: A bag of jelly beans

Pass a bag of jelly beans around and ask each student to take one, and hold it. Discuss that the world is made up of people from different cultural backgrounds and that from the point of view of each person, his or her cultural background is natural and everyone else is a little different. Point out that, from this point of view, we are all a little different to lots of other people and that the best tactic is to respect and accept everyone's differences. Point out that, like a bag of jelly beans, the world is more colorful and interesting because of the differences. And, like a bag of jelly beans, there is no one right color or one color that everyone sees as the most or least desirable. Ask students to share the colors of jelly beans they chose and then eat their jelly beans if desired.

Objective: Student will choose a jelly bean and then discuss how a bag of jelly beans relates to cultural diversity.

Subject: Social Studies Mode: Hands-On Training Zone: [U] Conclusion	Readiness Factor: [3] Personal/Social Readiness Factor Category: [k] Community Involvement and Responsibility

Ss 92: Respecting individuals with physical/mental challenges

FUTR Tool: no
PACT: no

Supplies: None

Discuss that people have different levels of abilities, and that we are all better at some things than at other things. Point out that you only appear challenged when asked to do something you do not do well. Ask students to answer these questions:

- Would you like to sing a song in front of the class?
- Could you fix a car that won't start?
- Can you smile at and be happy to see everyone you meet?
- Would you enjoy writing a 12-page story?
- Could you run three times around a football field without stopping?
- Can you sit and listen to someone talk for an hour without getting antsy?

Encourage students to think of what others can do, not what they cannot do.

Objective: Student will discuss individual differences and focus on what people can do, not what they cannot do.

Subject: Social Studies Mode: Discussion Training Zone: [U] Conclusion	Readiness Factor: [3] Personal/Social Readiness Factor Category: [k] Community Involvement and Responsibility

Ss 93: **Respecting others' privacy**

Supplies: None

As a group, brainstorm examples of respecting others' privacy. Make sure to include ideas such as not eavesdropping; not reading others' e-mails, notes, diaries; not looking in others' drawers and closets; and not insisting that someone share information he doesn't want to share.

Objective: Student will help brainstorm examples of respecting others' privacy.

Subject: Social Studies **Mode:** Brainstorming **Training Zone:** [F] Flexibility	**Readiness Factor:** [3] Personal/Social **Readiness Factor Category:** [i] Relationships

Ss 94: **Respecting others' property**

Supplies: None

Divide the class into four teams. Ask each team to brainstorm one of the following ideas and then share the results with the class.

a. Examples of property disrespect that are illegal and can send someone to prison

b. Examples of property disrespect that are not illegal, but that can harm a relationship

c. Examples or property disrespect that are just plain mean.

d. Examples of property disrespect that have no purpose and ruin how something looks

Objective: Student will help brainstorm specific examples of property disrespect.

Subject: Social Studies **Mode:** Brainstorming **Training Zone:** [C] Conscientiousness	**Readiness Factor:** [3] Personal/Social **Readiness Factor Category:** [k] Community Involvement and Responsibility

Ss 95: **Searching for service providers**

Supplies: None

Discuss that a good way to find professional services such as a doctor, lawyer, hair dresser, dentist, painter, window washer, repairman, or dry cleaner is to ask friends and relatives who they use. Ask students to each choose one type of professional and ask around to find out who friends and relatives are using. Then, have them all report back to the class.

Objective: Student will find a service provider by asking friends and relatives for suggestions.

Subject: Social Studies **Mode:** Action **Training Zone:** [A] Analysis	**Readiness Factor:** [3] Personal/Social **Readiness Factor Category:** [k] Community Involvement and Responsibility

Ss 96: Serving on a jury

Supplies: None

Explain that a jury is a group of 12 people who are asked to decide the guilt or innocence of a person on trial. Explain that serving on a jury is both a duty and a privilege, but that it is not always convenient, fun, nor easy.

- As a group, make a list of reasons why serving on a jury is not always convenient.
- As a group, make a list of reasons why serving on a jury might not be fun.
- As a group, identify some situations where serving on a jury might not be easy.

Objective: Student will help make lists of reasons or situations where serving on a jury is not convenient, fun, or easy.

Subject: Social Studies	**Readiness Factor:** [3] Personal/Social
Mode: Brainstorming	**Readiness Factor Category:** [k] Community Involvement and
Training Zone: [R] Responsibility	Responsibility

Ss 97: Showing a positive attitude

Supplies: None

Discuss with students that their attitudes are the main things that determine how their days will go. Point out that, if you have a positive attitude, you will see the good in each day, and will be relatively happy. Explain that, on the other hand, if you have negative attitudes, you will probably be too busy complaining and being displeased to feel happy. Ask students to take special steps to show particularly positive attitudes for the rest of the day. Look for opportunities to point out positive attitudes.

Objective: Student will discuss positive attitudes and then try to show a positive attitude for a day.

Subject: Social Studies	**Readiness Factor:** [1] Career
Mode: Action	**Readiness Factor Category:** [b] Job Performance
Training Zone: [Z] Socialization	

Ss 98: Showing country loyalty

Supplies: None

Discuss the fine line between expressing a negative opinion about your country in a non-patriotic (example: There is nothing good about this stupid country.) versus patriotic (example: Even if it is not perfect, I believe I live in a great country.) way. Discuss why we are lucky to live in the United States.

Discuss that people who come from other countries to live in the U.S. often feel loyalty to their original countries. Explain that it is both natural and healthy to feel great loyalty to one's birth country.

Brainstorm examples of showing country loyalty and examples of not being loyal to one's country.

Objective: Student will discuss and brainstorm issues relating to country loyalty.

Subject: Social Studies	**Readiness Factor:** [2] Daily Living
Mode: Discussion	**Readiness Factor Category:** [h] Transportation/Travel/Worldliness
Training Zone: [Z] Socialization	

Ss 99: **Showing family loyalty**

Supplies: None

Point out to students that, unless one family member is harming another, it is good for a family to keep its problems to itself. Explain that this statement means that, outside of your closest friend, it is best not to tell others how much you hate your sister or the mean things your dad said when he was angry. Discuss that talking about such things prolongs and enhances problems rather than focusing on the good within the family. Make sure students understand that, if they are being abused in any way, they should seek help because family loyalty does not supercede personal health and safety.

Objective: Student will discuss the meaning and importance of family loyalty.

Subject: Social Studies **Mode:** Discussion **Training Zone:** [Z] Socialization	**Readiness Factor:** [2] Daily Living **Readiness Factor Category:** [i] Relationships

Ss 100: **Showing good sportsmanship**

Supplies: None

Discuss that no one who plays a game likes to lose, but that someone has to lose each competition. Point out that feeling anger or depression over losing brings unnecessary stress to a person's life. Explain that one of the easiest ways to handle a loss is to congratulate the winner(s) and strike up a friendly conversation.

Ask students to role play being gracious winners and losers by playing the parts of winners and losers in the following situations: basketball game, board game, informal race, bowling game, singing competition, test score comparison, straw drawing to choose which show to watch.

Objective: Student will role play examples of good sportsmanship.

Subject: Social Studies **Mode:** Role Play **Training Zone:** [F] Flexibility	**Readiness Factor:** [3] Personal/Social **Readiness Factor Category:** [i] Relationships

Ss 101: **Showing public courtesy**

Supplies: None

Ask students to draw pictures showing examples of public courtesy or abuses of public courtesy.

Answer (some possible topics):

• Playing a radio on a crowded bus or train

• Letting (or not letting) a driver into your lane in front of you

• Waiting in line at a store behind a shopper who has a problem

• Offering (or not offering) to help a person who has her hands full

• Watching TV in a waiting room with people who have different channel preferences than you have

Objective: Student will draw a picture showing a public courtesy.

Subject: Social Studies **Mode:** Drawing **Training Zone:** [Z] Socialization	**Readiness Factor:** [3] Personal/Social **Readiness Factor Category:** [k] Community Involvement and Responsibility

Ss 102: **Showing self control**

FUTR Tool: no
PACT: yes

Supplies: None

Discuss that "self control" is when a person holds natural feelings, words, or actions back (at least until later). Ask volunteers to give examples of and reasons for self control in each of the following situations:

a. Tess walks into her bedroom and finds her five-year-old brother coloring in her diary.

b. Pedro's mother says that, since he got home late last night, he cannot go out tonight.

c. Megan got her history test back and sees that she failed it, so she will be ineligible for the big match on Friday.

d. Nate and Alex checked the list of players chosen for the all-star game. Nate was chosen, but Alex was not.

Objective: Student will give examples and reasons for self control in given situations.

Subject: Social Studies **Mode:** Oral Response **Training Zone:** [S] Self-Awareness	**Readiness Factor:** [1] Career **Readiness Factor Category:** [b] Job Performance

Ss 103: **Showing two IDs**

FUTR Tool: no
PACT: no

Supplies: None

Discuss that some situations require two IDs. Ask students to identify what they would use if asked for two IDs. Encourage them to include ideas such as these:

• Driver's license

• Credit card

• School ID

• Debit card

• Social Security card

• Insurance card

• State non-driving ID

Objective: Student will identify what she will use if asked for two IDs.

Subject: Social Studies **Mode:** Oral Response **Training Zone:** [M] Manipulation	**Readiness Factor:** [2] Daily Living **Readiness Factor Category:** [e] Safety and Security

Ss 104: **Sorting bodies of water**

FUTR Tool: no
PACT: no

Supplies: None

Discuss the differences between ponds, lakes, rivers, and oceans. Name bodies of water in your local area as well as these bodies of water: Atlantic, Pacific, Mississippi, Nile, Thames, and Lake Michigan. Ask your students to identify each as a pond, lake, river, or ocean.

As a group, brainstorm names of additional ponds, lakes, rivers, and oceans and identify where each is located.

Objective: Student will name ponds, lakes, rivers, and oceans.

Subject: Social Studies **Mode:** Discussion **Training Zone:** [A] Analysis	**Readiness Factor:** [2] Daily Living **Readiness Factor Category:** [h] Transportation/Travel/Worldliness

Ss 105: Sorting land types

Supplies: None

Ask students to draw examples of the land types below. Next to each drawing, have them name an actual example of the land type from somewhere in the U.S.

- mountain
- meadow
- valley
- plateau
- river bed
- swamp
- forest

Objective: Student will draw examples of different land types and will identify a U.S. example of each.

Subject: Social Studies Mode: Discussion Training Zone: [A] Analysis	Readiness Factor: [2] Daily Living Readiness Factor Category: [h] Transportation/Travel/Worldliness

Ss 106: Sorting societal structures

Supplies: A typed list of cities or towns, countries, counties, states, and continents; scissors, magnets or tape

Discuss that the world is divided into societal structures including cities or towns, countries, and continents. Add that the U.S. also is divided into counties and states. Using about a 16 font, type up a whole page of cities or towns, countries, counties, states and continents. Print it out and cut it into slips of paper with one name on each slip. Put these headings on the board: cities or towns, countries, counties, states, and continents. Ask students to take turns drawing slips of paper and sticking them under the correct headings.

Objective: Student will sort cities or towns, countries, counties, states, and continents.

Subject: Social Studies Mode: Action Training Zone: [A] Analysis	Readiness Factor: [2] Daily Living Readiness Factor Category: [h] Transportation/Travel/Worldliness

Ss 107: Storing important papers safely

Supplies: None

Make a three-column chart on the board. Place the locations listed below in the left column. Label the other two columns "Pros" and "Cons" and, as a class, write reasons why each location would or would not be a good place to keep important papers.

Locations:

kitchen counter	family room couch	bedroom floor	filing cabinet
shoe box	back pack	car	safe
book shelf	dresser top	dining room table	shelf in garage
box in attic	phone book	can inside the freezer	

Objective: Student will write reasons why specific locations would or would not be good places to keep important papers.

Subject: Social Studies Mode: Graph or Chart Training Zone: [O] Organization	Readiness Factor: [3] Personal/Social Readiness Factor Category: [k] Community Involvement and Responsibility

Ss 108: Taking action when lost

Supplies: None

Discuss safe and wise choices when lost such as those below:

1. Stay in public areas with lots of people

2. If possible, call someone you know or 911

3. If someone is looking for you, stay in one place

4. Ask workers in public places, such as clerks and cashiers, for help

5. Do not go out of public areas with a stranger even if the stranger seems very nice.

Objective: Student will discuss safe and wise choices when lost.

Subject: Social Studies **Mode:** Discussion **Training Zone:** [U] Conclusion	**Readiness Factor:** [2] Daily Living **Readiness Factor Category:** [e] Safety and Security

Ss 109: Taking care of things you borrow

FUTR Tool: no
PACT: no

Supplies: None

Discuss that people do not have to lend you things, and if you do not take care of things you borrow, people might choose not to lend you things again. Ask students to identify things they have borrowed and make a list on the board. As a group, discuss examples of taking care of and not taking care of each of the borrowed items.

Objective: Student will help identify examples of taking care of and not taking care of borrowed items.

Subject: Social Studies **Mode:** Discussion **Training Zone:** [C] Conscientiousness	**Readiness Factor:** [3] Personal/Social **Readiness Factor Category:** [k] Community Involvement and Responsibility

Ss 110: Taking part in leisure activities

FUTR Tool: no
PACT: yes

Supplies: None

As a group, brainstorm some possible leisure activities and list them on the board. Then, ask students to think about leisure activities that they would enjoy. (Either those on the board or others) Have them each make a list of at least five leisure activities that sound like fun to them.

Objective: Student will make a list of leisure activities that sounds like fun to him.

Subject: Social Studies **Mode:** Brainstorming, Written **Training Zone:** [Z] Socialization	**Readiness Factor:** [3] Personal/Social **Readiness Factor Category:** [j] Leisure/Desires/Choices

Ss 111: Taking responsibility for one's own actions

FUTR Tool: no
PACT: no

Supplies: None

Discuss that "taking responsibility for one's own actions" means that you are willing to admit what you have done, and you are willing to accept the consequences. Explain that, when you have done something good or nice, such as putting the dishes away without being asked, it is easy to admit you did it and to take the consequences (such as a hug from your mother). On the other hand, point out that when you have done something bad or mean such as throwing someone's backpack in the trash can, it isn't easy to admit you did it, nor to accept the consequences (such as being told to dig in the trash can, get the bag, and apologize in public).

Divide the class into five teams. Ask each team to think of a situation where it would be hard to take responsibility for your actions and to role play someone taking responsibility in the given situation.

Objective: Student will discuss and role play taking responsibility for her own actions.

Subject: Social Studies **Mode:** Role Play **Training Zone:** [R] Responsibility	**Readiness Factor:** [3] Personal/Social **Readiness Factor Category:** [j] Leisure/Desires/Choices

Ss 112: Talking to bereaved friends and relatives

FUTR Tool: no
PACT: no

Supplies: None

Discuss that it is difficult to talk to people who have lost a friend or relative, but that people who are in mourning really need others to reach out to them. As a group, brainstorm a list of things that you could say to a person who has lost a friend or relative.

Some possible examples: I'm sorry for your loss, My sympathies, My prayers are with you, (Name) was a wonderful person and will be greatly missed, I'll call you next week and see if you feel like getting together, I remember when (Name)...., Please let me know if I can help in any way

Objective: Student will help brainstorm a list of things to say to a person who has lost a friend or relative.

Subject: Social Studies **Mode:** Brainstorming **Training Zone:** [Z] Socialization	**Readiness Factor:** [3] Personal/Social **Readiness Factor Category:** [k] Community Involvement and Responsibility

Ss 113: Talking to the boss

FUTR Tool: 50
PACT: yes

Supplies: None

Ask volunteers to play the parts of employees and bosses to role play the following situations:

a. Todd works for a large tire company. He wants to ask his boss if he can take Tuesday off so he can take his daughter to the doctor. What should Todd say?

b. Tonya made a mistake at work. She accidentally threw some papers away that she was supposed to file. What should she say when her boss asks her for the papers and she realizes she wasn't supposed to throw them away?

c. Beatrice saw a coworker take two handfuls of pens from the supply closet and then put them in her purse to take home. What should Beatrice do or say when the boss asks why the pen supply is going down so fast?

Objective: Student will role play a communication with the boss.

Subject: Social Studies **Mode:** Role Play **Training Zone:** [F] Flexibility	**Readiness Factor:** [1] Career **Readiness Factor Category:** [b] Job Performance

Ss 114: Understanding about candidates and voting

FUTR Tool: 69
PACT: yes

Supplies: None

Ask volunteers to answer the following questions:

a. Where do people in your neighborhood go to vote?

b. Can you register to vote at the voting place right before you vote? [no]

c. If you are going to be in a different town on Election Day, how can you vote?
   [Plan ahead to get an absentee ballot]

d. Can you vote if you are in prison? [no]

e. How old do you have to be to vote in the U.S.? [18]

f. What is a political candidate? [Person running for office]

Objective: Student will answer questions about candidates and voting.

Subject: Social Studies **Mode:** Oral Response **Training Zone:** [A] Analysis	**Readiness Factor:** [3] Personal/Social **Readiness Factor Category:** [k] Community Involvement and Responsibility

Ss 115: Understanding alcohol/drugs and driving

FUTR Tool: 47
PACT: yes

Supplies: Newspaper stories about accidents caused by drinking and driving (If available, use local stories)

Discuss that drinking and taking drugs never mixes well with driving. Point out that, even though not everyone who drives under the influence has an accident, the dangers of driving dangerously are so much higher that such drivers put themselves and everyone else on the road in terrible danger. Share newspaper stories about accidents caused by drinking and driving and discuss how impaired control took part in each accident.

Objective: Student will discuss results of driving under the influence.

Subject: Social Studies **Mode:** Discussion **Training Zone:** [C] Conscientiousness	**Readiness Factor:** [2] Daily Living **Readiness Factor Category:** [e] Safety and Security

Ss 116: Understanding and dealing with inappropriate words and touches from others

FUTR Tool: no
PACT: yes

Supplies: None

Explain that inappropriate words such as swear words, threats, and sexual comments are not OK and that, if you are ever in such a situation, you should talk to your parents or another adult you trust.

Explain that inappropriate touches are when someone touches your vagina, breasts, penis, or rear end. Point out that, no matter what the person says will happen to you if you tell, you should ask a trusted adult for help. Tell students that many young people are sexually abused for years and do not tell anyone because they are afraid. Explain that laws in the U.S. protect young people from such abuse, and you should ask for help no matter what threats or lies the abuser tells you.

Discuss that sometimes abuse is physical, but not sexual. Tell students that, if someone is hurting you, you should talk to a trusted adult for help.

Objective: Student will discuss abuse and where to turn for help.

Subject: Social Studies **Mode:** Discussion **Training Zone:** [U] Conclusion	**Readiness Factor:** [3] Personal/Social **Readiness Factor Category:** [l] Health, Diet, and Appearance

Ss 117: **Understanding general history timelines**

FUTR Tool: no
PACT: no

Supplies: None

Ask students to turn a piece of paper sideways. Have them draw an arrow like this ⬚ from one side of the paper to the other. At the left arrow, have them write 1800. At the right arrow, have them write 2000. Ask your student to place these activities in order on the timeline:

• First train tracks run from the East coast to the West coast in the U.S. [1st, 1860s]

• Man lands on the moon [4th, 1969]

• WWII ends [3rd–mid 1940s]

• Model Ts are popular car [2nd, early 1900s]

• Many people have home computers [5th–1980s or 90s]

Objective: Student will draw a timeline using some general historical happenings.

Subject: Social Studies **Mode:** Drawing **Training Zone:** [E] Exploration	**Readiness Factor:** [2] Daily Living **Readiness Factor Category:** [h] Transportation/Travel/Worldliness

Ss 118: **Understanding good customer service**

FUTR Tool: no
PACT: no

Supplies: None

Ask volunteers for ideas about what to expect in the way of customer service in each of the following situations.

1. You are in a store and you cannot find light bulbs. You ask an employee for help. What should you expect the employee to do—point you in the right direction, go with you and show you, or give you a landmark that you can see from where you are?

2. You are in a store and a young child is running without looking and knocks you down. You hit your head on a shelf and are feeling dizzy. An employee comes by and helps you up. What should you expect the employee to do?

3. You are returning something to a store, and you are in a hurry. There is a big line at the service counter. You tell an employee you are in a hurry and ask for help. What should you expect the employee to do?

Objective: Student will discuss customer-service expectations.

Subject: Social Studies **Mode:** Discussion **Training Zone:** [U] Conclusion	**Readiness Factor:** [1] Career **Readiness Factor Category:** [b] Job Performance

Ss 119: Understanding living location options

Supplies: None

Discuss different living location options such as these:

- with your parents
- in a group home
- in a supported living program
- in your own apartment with a roommate
- in your own apartment by yourself
- in a home you own

Objective: Student will discuss different after-high school living arrangements.

Subject: Social Studies **Mode:** Discussion **Training Zone:** [E] Exploration	**Readiness Factor:** [3] Personal/Social **Readiness Factor Category:** [k] Community Involvement and Responsibility

Ss 120: Understanding local, state, and national

FUTR Tool: 39
PACT: yes

Supplies: None

Ask students to tear a piece of paper in fourths. Have them write one of these words on each fourth: "local," "state," "national," and "international." Then, call out comments such as those below and ask students to raise the relevant piece of paper each time.

a. Would a news story about California by local, state, national or international news?

b. Is (name a local company) a local, state, national, or international company?

c. Is IBM a local, state, national, or international company?

d. Would a trip to England be local, state, national, or international?

e. Would a news story about (name your state governor) be local, state, national, or international?

f. Would a news story about (name your school) be local, state, national, or international?

Objective: Student will differentiate between local, state, national, and international.

Subject: Social Studies **Mode:** Action **Training Zone:** [O] Organization	**Readiness Factor:** [2] Daily Living **Readiness Factor Category:** [h] Transportation/Travel/Worldliness

Ss 121: Understanding parking options

FUTR Tool: no
PACT: no

Supplies: None

On the board, make a bar graph. Across the bottom, write these parking options: large parking lot, small parking lot, underground parking lot, street parking in front, street parking some distance away, parking ramp. Up the side, number by fives from 0 to 20. Up from each type of parking, create a "starter bar" that marks 0. Show students how to build a bar graph by adding to the starter bars. Ask students to name off a local place, identify which type of parking the place provides, and add to the bar for that type of parking. As some areas of the graph begin to fill up, ask students to try to think of other examples for the not-so-full areas. Ask a volunteer to summarize the graph in this way: "The types of parking that are commonly available in this area include.... and the types of parking that are not commonly available in this area include...."

Objective: Student will help create a bar graph showing types of local parking.

Subject: Social Studies **Mode:** Graph or Chart **Training Zone:** [A] Analysis	**Readiness Factor:** [2] Daily Living **Readiness Factor Category:** [h] Transportation/Travel/Worldliness

Ss 122: **Understanding registrations and licenses**

FUTR Tool: 45
PACT: yes

Supplies: None

Ask volunteers to answer the following questions:

a. How does a person get registration papers for a car? [From the car dealer or, in the case of a private purchase, from the State Department of Motor Vehicles.]

b. By law, do you have to have a fishing license or hunting license to fish or hunt on your own property? [depends on laws in the state where you own property]

c. Which of these careers require a license or certification: cutting hair, plumbing, farming, teaching, nursing, grocery clerking, real estate sales, singing, factory worker? [cutting hair, plumbing, teaching, nursing, real estate sales]

Objective: Student will indicate how to register a car and will identify other situations where licenses are needed.

Subject: Social Studies **Mode:** Oral Response **Training Zone:** [R] Responsibility	**Readiness Factor:** [3] Personal/Social **Readiness Factor Category:** [k] Community Involvement and Responsibility

Ss 123: **Understanding special needs assistance options**

FUTR Tool: no
PACT: no

Supplies: None

Discuss different special needs assistance and accommodation options such as these:

wheel chair	service animal	assisted living
reading assistance	sign language	textbook on tape
substitution of course	small-group or individual testing	job coach
tape recorder	practice tests prior to actual tests	personal attendant
special computer	special software	accessibility
computer testing	notetaker	

additional time to complete tests or work on activities

use of dictionary or other educational aids while taking tests

Objective: Student will discuss special needs assistance and accommodation options.

Subject: Social Studies **Mode:** Discussion **Training Zone:** [E] Exploration	**Readiness Factor:** [3] Personal/Social **Readiness Factor Category:** [k] Community Involvement and Responsibility

Ss 124: Understanding the 3-day right to rescind a contract
FUTR Tool: no
PACT: no

Supplies: A current calendar

Explain that, when you sign a contract, you have up to three business days to change your mind without having a legal problem. Make sure students can see a calendar. Ask volunteers to name the dates when you would be able to change your mind following the signing of contracts on these dates:

a. The 3rd of this month

b. The 8th of this month

c. The 12th of this month

d. The 15th of this month

e. The 17th of this month

f. The 20th of this month

Objective: Student will identify dates where the right to rescind can be used.

Subject: Social Studies	Readiness Factor: [2] Daily Living
Mode: Oral Response	Readiness Factor Category: [e] Safety and Security
Training Zone: [U] Conclusion	

Ss 125: Understanding the skills needed to perform a desired job
FUTR Tool: no
PACT: no

Supplies: None

Have students create job webs by drawing circles in the centers of their papers and drawing five radiating lines out. Ask students to each choose a job of interest and write the job title in the circle. At the end of each line, ask them to write a skill that is needed for the job. Encourage students to research as needed. Post the finished webs around the room so all students can learn about the different jobs.

Objective: Student will create a job web showing needed skills for a specific job.

Subject: Social Studies	Readiness Factor: [1] Career
Mode: Drawing	Readiness Factor Category: [a] Career Preparation
Training Zone: [E] Exploration	

Ss 126: Understanding U.S. road systems
FUTR Tool: 52
PACT: yes

Supplies: None

List these two columns of road descriptions on the board:

- U.S. highway
- Local road
- Interstate highway
- Bypass
- Toll road

- Gravel road
- Paved road
- Two-lane road
- Four-lane road
- Limited access road

Ask students to identify area roads and choose a matching description from each column for each road.

Objective: Student will describe local roads by road designations and types.

Subject: Social Studies	Readiness Factor: [2] Daily Living
Mode: Graph or Chart	Readiness Factor Category: [h] Transportation/Travel/Worldliness
Training Zone: [V] Observation	

Ss 127: Understanding wants versus needs

FUTR Tool: 41
PACT: yes

Supplies: None

As a group, brainstorm a list of things students have in their homes. Then, go back through the list and identify each item as a "want" or a "need." If you don't end up with very many "needs," ask students to do an add-on brainstorm to get more "needs."

Objective: Student will help create a list of items and will then help identify each item as a want or need.

Subject: Social Studies	**Readiness Factor:** [3] Personal/Social
Mode: Brainstorming	**Readiness Factor Category:** [j] Leisure/Desires/Choices
Training Zone: [L] Logic	

Ss 128: Understanding why the U.S. government needs taxes

FUTR Tool: no
PACT: no

Supplies: None

Discuss that taxes are used for running the government. Explain that "running the government" includes expenses for a wide range of services. Have students brainstorm a list of government expenses. Make sure they include ideas such as these: building buildings, paying government employees, funding the military, building roads, paying for transportation of government employees, and paying for public events at the White House.

Objective: Student will help make a list of tax-supported government expenses.

Subject: Social Studies	**Readiness Factor:** [2] Daily Living
Mode: Brainstorming	**Readiness Factor Category:** [c] Finances
Training Zone: [A] Analysis	

Ss 129: Understanding your values

FUTR Tool: 58
PACT: yes

Supplies: None

Ask students to write responses to the following questions:

a. Which matters most to you: fun or good grades? Explain why.

b. Which matters most to you: effort or being on time? Explain why.

c. Which matters most to you: family or friends? Explain why.

d. Which matters most to you: fairness or correctness? Explain why.

e. Which matters most to you: honesty or kindness? Explain why.

f. Which matters most to you: easy homework or interesting homework? Explain why.

Objective: Student will explore her values by taking stands between choices

Subject: Social Studies	**Readiness Factor:** [3] Personal/Social
Mode: Written	**Readiness Factor Category:** [l] Health, Diet, and Appearance
Training Zone: [S] Self-Awareness	

Ss 130: **Using a globe**

FUTR Tool: no
PACT: yes

Supplies: A globe

Discuss that a globe is like a map, only that a map is flattened out for ease of use and a globe is round like the Earth. Have students study a globe to answer these questions.

a. Which country on the other side of the Pacific ocean is closest to the U.S.? [Russia]

b. Find a U.S. city that is at about the same latitude as Paris, France [one possibility—Spokane, WA].

c. Find a U.S. city that is at about the same longitude as Cali, Columbia [one possibility—Allentown, PA]

d. Find a city in another country that is at about the same latitude as your local area.

e. Find a city in another country that is at about the same longitude as your local area.

Objective: Student will use a globe to find cities and countries at specified latitudes and longitudes.

Subject: Social Studies **Mode:** Hands-On **Training Zone:** [M] Manipulation	**Readiness Factor:** [2] Daily Living **Readiness Factor Category:** [h] Transportation/Travel/Worldliness

Ss 131: **Using a mall directory**

FUTR Tool: 53
PACT: yes

Supplies: Several copies of the directory from a local mall

Divide the class into groups so that each group can have a mall directory. Ask questions that are specific to the mall and can be answered by using the directory. For example, If you come into the mall's West Entrance, what shoe store will be closest?

Objective: Student will use a mall directory to answer questions about the mall.

Subject: Social Studies **Mode:** Hands-On **Training Zone:** [V] Observation	**Readiness Factor:** [2] Daily Living **Readiness Factor Category:** [h] Transportation/Travel/Worldliness

Ss 132: **Using a map legend**

FUTR Tool: no
PACT: yes

Supplies: Five different maps with legends, five pieces of posterboard, markers

Divide the class into five teams. Give each team a map, a piece of posterboard, and some markers and ask them to create a large version of the map legend. Then, have team members find an example of each legend marking on the map. Finally, have teams compare their map legends to see which markings they have in common and which are different.

Objective: Student will help make a large map legend, will use the legend, and will compare the legend with other teams' legends.

Subject: Social Studies **Mode:** Drawing **Training Zone:** [V] Observation	**Readiness Factor:** [2] Daily Living **Readiness Factor Category:** [h] Transportation/Travel/Worldliness

Ss 133: Using a road map or atlas

FUTR Tool: 64
PACT: yes

Supplies: At least five atlases or road maps of your state (alike if possible)

Divide the class into five groups (or more if you have more than five road maps or atlases). Give each group a road map or atlas. Ask each team to complete the following tasks:

a. Find the map coordinates for your city or town.

b. Find a river near where you live.

c. Find a city that is located near D-6 on the map.

d. Find the mark used to identify a city as being in the largest-city category.

e. Describe the method used to identify a four-lane road.

f. Find the mark used to identify an airport.

g. Find the mark used to identify a park.

Objective: Student will use and interpret a road map or atlas.

Subject: Social Studies **Mode:** Hands-On **Training Zone:** [M] Manipulation	**Readiness Factor:** [2] Daily Living **Readiness Factor Category:** [f] Shopping and Eating at Restaurants

Ss 134: Using community resources

FUTR Tool: 62
PACT: yes

Supplies: None

Either in pairs or individually, assign the following careers and places of business as role play identities: travel agent, banker, plumber, farmer, librarian, realtor, exercise gym, grocery store, hair salon, dry cleaner, restaurant, movie-rental store, flower shop, fabric shop, department store, home improvement store, gas station.

Ask questions such as the following and ask the relevant role players to stand and say "I can help you with that."

a. I want something inexpensive and fun to do this weekend.

b. I've got to do something about this weight I am gaining.

c. I'd like to take my daughter and her friends on a hayride.

d. I need some foam to fix a chair.

Objective: Student will role play being part of a community and offering a business service.

Subject: Social Studies **Mode:** Role Play **Training Zone:** [E] Exploration	**Readiness Factor:** [3] Personal/Social **Readiness Factor Category:** [k] Community Involvement and Responsibility

Ss 135: Using mailing and shipping services

FUTR Tool: 66
PACT: yes

Supplies: A breakable item, change-of-address forms

Choose a breakable item and ask students to make a list of issues to keep in mind when shipping the item. Make sure to include ideas such as using a sturdy box, using lots of packing or crating it (mail service facility can help), insuring it, having the complete destination address.

Pass out change-of-address forms. Have students practicing completing the form by using the school address as the new addresses. Explain that these forms are available at the local post office.

Discuss the cost of mailing with the U.S.Post Office vs. other mailing services and how the services compare. Also, discuss that C.O.D. (Cash on Delivery) is a shipping service that businesses sometimes use so that merchandise is paid for before it is in the purchaser's control.

Objective: Student will discuss mailing choices and services and will fill out a change of address form.

Subject: Social Studies **Mode:** Discussion, Written **Training Zone:** [M] Manipulation	**Readiness Factor:** [3] Personal/Social **Readiness Factor Category:** [k] Community Involvement and Responsibility

Ss 136: Using proper eating manners

FUTR Tool: no
PACT: yes

Supplies: None

Ask each students to take paper and pencil to the cafeteria at lunch time and make some notes so they can remember good and bad eating manners that they see. Back in the classroom, compile students' notes to make one large chart showing good eating manners and one showing bad eating manners.

Objective: Student will make note of good and bad eating manners and will help create charts showing good and bad eating manners.

Subject: Social Studies **Mode:** Graph or Chart **Training Zone:** [Z] Socialization	**Readiness Factor:** [2] Daily Living **Readiness Factor Category:** [f] Shopping and Eating at Restaurants

Ss 137: Using public transportation

FUTR Tool: 63
PACT: yes

Supplies: Local public transportation information

Discuss local public transportation options such as taxi, bus, plane, and train options. Ask students to assume they need to use public transportation and to discuss which option would be most logical for each of the following (or others that pertain directly to your local area):

a. Go to New York City

c. Go to the mall

e. Go to school

b. Go to the airport

d. Go to the grocery store

Objective: Student will discuss local transportation options.

Subject: Social Studies **Mode:** Discussion **Training Zone:** [E] Exploration	**Readiness Factor:** [2] Daily Living **Readiness Factor Category:** [h] Transportation/Travel/Worldliness

Ss 138: Volunteering in the community

FUTR Tool: no
PACT: no

Supplies: None

Point out examples of people volunteering in the community such as playing cards with people in nursing homes, helping newly-released hospitals patients get to their cars, and helping teachers assemble bulletin boards at schools. Discuss that volunteers work without pay to make the community a better place to live. Explain that when many people each help a little, a lot gets done.

Objective: Student will discuss community volunteering opportunities and how volunteering helps make a community a better place.

Subject: Social Studies **Mode:** Discussion **Training Zone:** [F] Flexibility	**Readiness Factor:** [3] Personal/Social **Readiness Factor Category:** [k] Community Involvement and Responsibility

Ss 139: Waiting in line calmly

FUTR Tool: no
PACT: no

Supplies: Drawing paper, markers or crayons

Discuss that there are many times in life when you will have to wait in line. Brainstorm a list of activities you can do to make waiting in line easier. Make sure to include ideas such as the following: Talk to other people in line, read a book, listen to music, make plans for later in the day, study, talk on a cell phone, eat lunch.

Ask students to each choose one of the brainstormed items to draw. Post the drawings around the room.

Objective: Student will help brainstorm a list of activities to do when waiting in line and will then draw one of the ideas.

Subject: Social Studies **Mode:** Drawing **Training Zone:** [Z] Socialization	**Readiness Factor:** [3] Personal/Social **Readiness Factor Category:** [k] Community Involvement and Responsibility

Ss 140: Walking and driving in parking lots

FUTR Tool: no
PACT: no

Supplies: None

Discuss that parking lots can be dangerous and that both drivers and pedestrians need to be careful. Discuss causes of parking lot dangers such as the following:

Most parking lots have few or no traffic-control signs.

The rows of cars in a parking lot make it hard to see moving vehicles.

Many drivers only pay attention to the parking spot they are trying to get or the road they are trying to leave on.

Parking lots are often tight areas.

Objective: Student will discuss the dangers of parking lots.

Subject: Social Studies **Mode:** Discussion **Training Zone:** [A] Analysis	**Readiness Factor:** [2] Daily Living **Readiness Factor Category:** [h] Transportation/Travel/Worldliness

Ss 141: **Working in a group**

FUTR Tool: no
PACT: yes

Supplies: Drawing paper, markers or crayons

Point out that, when working in a group, "minding your own business" is not the best tactic to take. Explain that group members need to pay attention to each other so they can be ready to help as needed.

Divide the class into five groups. Ask each group to divide the alphabet up amongst the group members and draw a picture for each letter. Tell them to all be very careful to help each other as needed so that all the work is done, all the work is done well, and no team members are standing around not working when there is still a lot of work to be completed.

Objective: Student will function as an involved group member.

Subject: Social Studies **Mode:** Action **Training Zone:** [F] Flexibility	**Readiness Factor:** [3] Personal/Social **Readiness Factor Category:** [i] Relationships

Science/
Health

Life Skill Lessons

Table of Contents: *Science/Health*

Sc 1: Adapting to workplace conditions

FUTR Tool: 86
PACT: yes

Supplies: None

Explain that every workplace has its own set-up and procedures. Point out that, since change is difficult for most people, adapting to a new workplace requires effort, attitude checks, and perseverance. Discuss that you are more likely to be successful in a new job if you start out planning to figure out how that specific workplace runs and try to go along with it. Also, address the issue that some workplaces are hot or cold, require uncomfortable dress, or have you standing for long periods of time—and that complaining about these kinds of issues rarely is in your best interest. Discuss that the best route to take is to do what you can to make yourself comfortable, and then work through it. Ask volunteers for ideas about how to make yourself comfortable if you have temperature, dress, or standing issues.

Objective: Student will discuss workplace conditions and how to deal with them.

Subject: Science/Health **Mode:** Discussion **Training Zone:** [F] Flexibility	**Readiness Factor:** [1] Career **Readiness Factor Category:** [b] Job Performance

Sc 2: Adjusting ring sizes

FUTR Tool: no
PACT: no

Supplies: None

Discuss that rings can be adjusted to fit a range of sizes. Point out that rings that are too large can be adjusted using a spacer that attaches to the inside of the ring or they can be cut down up to several sizes by a jeweler. Explain that rings that are too small can be stretched a size or two by a jeweler.

Objective: Student will discuss that rings can be enlarged and made smaller.

Subject: Science/Health **Mode:** Discussion **Training Zone:** [M] Manipulation	**Readiness Factor:** [2] Daily Living **Readiness Factor Category:** [f] Shopping and Eating at Restaurants

Sc 3: Asking for gardening advice

FUTR Tool: no
PACT: no

Supplies: Phone book yellow pages: enough to scatter around the class so all students can gather around one

Ask students to find some greenhouses and garden-supply businesses in the yellow pages. Have them choose two or three in your local area and write the company names, addresses, and phone numbers on the board. Point out that these businesses are great places to buy gardening supplies as well as get good gardening advice.

Objective: Student will find greenhouse and garden-supply businesses in the yellow pages and will discuss that these businesses can offer good gardening advice.

Subject: Science/Health **Mode:** Action **Training Zone:** [F] Flexibility	**Readiness Factor:** [3] Personal/Social **Readiness Factor Category:** [j] Leisure/Desires/Choices

Sc 4: Avoiding bug, bee, snake, mosquito, and spider bites

FUTR Tool: no
PACT: no

Supplies: None

Make a chart on the board and use tallies to indicate how many students have been bitten by each of the animals below. Ask volunteers for ideas about how to avoid being bitten. Make sure they include ideas such as those shown in the answers below.

1. bugs [bug repellent, screen rooms, fans, citronella candles, closed windows and doors]
2. bees [alertness, calmness]
3. snakes [alertness, use of paths]
4. mosquitoes [mosquito repellent, screen rooms, mosquito spraying or fogging]
5. spiders [house fog-bombing, baseboard spraying, pest control service]

Objective: Student will discuss ways to avoid being bitten by bugs, bees, snakes, mosquitoes, and spiders.

Subject: Science/Health **Mode:** Discussion **Training Zone:** [L] Logic	**Readiness Factor:** [3] Personal/Social **Readiness Factor Category:** [I] Health, Diet, and Appearance

Sc 5: Avoiding unplanned pregnancies

FUTR Tool: no
PACT: yes

Supplies: None

Ask students to write an answer to this question: What can you do so that you don't have children you aren't planning to have?

Answer: Accept abstinence or a trustworthy type of birth control.

Objective: Student will identify a method of preventing unplanned pregnancies.

Subject: Science/Health **Mode:** Written **Training Zone:** [R] Responsibility	**Readiness Factor:** [2] Daily Living **Readiness Factor Category:** [e] Safety and Security

Sc 6: Being a responsible driver/car owner

FUTR Tool: 81
PACT: yes

Supplies: None

Write this list on the board:

- oil
- oil change
- driver's license
- license plates
- insurance
- tires
- repairs
- tune-ups
- cleaning
- parking
- bad weather

Ask volunteers to describe how each item on the list relates to being a responsible driver or car owner.

Objective: Student will describe aspects of being a responsible driver/car owner.

Subject: Science/Health **Mode:** Oral Response **Training Zone:** [R] Responsibility	**Readiness Factor:** [2] Daily Living **Readiness Factor Category:** [e] Safety and Security

Sc 7: **Being patient with expectations of self and others**

FUTR Tool: 87
PACT: yes

Supplies: None

Ask students how many of them have ever wanted to run faster, have more friends, look better in clothes, or say funnier things. Point out that most people have thoughts like that at times, but you are really better off if you can relax and be happy with those things you do well and quit worrying about those things you do not do as well. Discuss that, if you are more patient with your expectations of yourself and others, you will have much less stress. Explain that being patient is not the same as no longer trying to improve, it is simply a way of taking the stress out of the efforts to improve.

Objective: Student will discuss being patient with expectations of self and others.

Subject: Science/Health **Mode:** Discussion **Training Zone:** [F] Flexibility	**Readiness Factor:** [3] Personal/Social **Readiness Factor Category:** [i] Relationships

Sc 8: **Being socially aware**

FUTR Tool: no
PACT: yes

Supplies: None

Ask students to number from a–g on a piece of paper using every other line. Then have them answer these questions:

a. Would the clothes you have on be OK to wear to a football game?

b. Name one of your close friends.

c. Give one reason why it will be important for you to get along with your parents when you are out of high school.

d. Why is it important to be nice to people you do not even know?

e. Why are good friends important?

f. Name a group activity that you enjoy, or could enjoy, taking part in.

g. Why is it important to brush your hair and teeth before you come to school?

Objective: Student will write answers to social awareness questions.

Subject: Science/Health **Mode:** Written **Training Zone:** [Z] Socialization	**Readiness Factor:** [3] Personal/Social **Readiness Factor Category:** [i] Relationships

Sc 9: **Believing in yourself (work and personal)**

FUTR Tool: 95
PACT: yes

Supplies: None

Ask students to get out a piece of paper and number from 1–10. Then, ask them to list ten things they do well. Discuss that identifying your strong points is definitely not an ego problem. Tell them it is a healthy and essential part of promoting yourself in the work setting. Explain that, on the other hand, if you constantly tell your friends and family about your strong points, they might see it as an ego problem. Point out that, in your personal life, helping others, being respectful, and putting out effort are all ways to show that you believe in yourself. Explain that these behaviors will also cause others to believe in you.

Objective: Student will make a list of ten things she does well and will discuss how to present that information in work and personal settings.

Subject: Science/Health **Mode:** Written **Training Zone:** [S] Self-Awareness	**Readiness Factor:** [3] Personal/Social **Readiness Factor Category:** [I] Health, Diet, and Appearance

Sc 10: **Breathing as a way to deal with pain or anger**

FUTR Tool: no
PACT: no

Supplies: None

Discuss that controlled breathing is a technique that can help people deal with pain. Ask students to do some controlled breathing together by following these steps as you call them out (repeat 1−4 four or five times):

1. Take a deep breath, 1−2−3−4 (Read the numbers slowly and calmly)

2. Hold it, 1−2−3−4

3. Blow it out slowly 1−2−3−4

4. Take four regular breaths, 1−2−3−4

Discuss that the mental focus on the breathing along with the slowed breathing rate helps to calm a person down and makes it easier to deal with pain or anger.

Objective: Student will do some controlled breathing and will discuss how it helps a person deal with pain or anger.

Subject: Science/Health **Mode:** Action **Training Zone:** [S] Self-Awareness	**Readiness Factor:** [3] Personal/Social **Readiness Factor Category:** [l] Health, Diet, and Appearance

Sc 11: **Caring for children**

FUTR Tool: no
PACT: no

Supplies: None

Discuss that caring for children means staying with them and paying attention to them. Explain that, due to their exploring natures, children can get into trouble easily if not given enough attention. Ask students to brainstorm problem situations children they know have gotten into and discuss how each problem might have been avoided. Discuss that not all problems can be foreseen, but by paying attention to children, you can prevent some problems.

Objective: Student will discuss how to care for children to avoid as many problems as possible.

Subject: Science/Health **Mode:** Discussion **Training Zone:** [R] Responsibility	**Readiness Factor:** [2] Daily Living **Readiness Factor Category:** [e] Safety and Security

Sc 12: **Caring for hair and teeth**

FUTR Tool: no
PACT: yes

Supplies: None

As a group, brainstorm two lists: One of actions people can take to care for their hair and one of actions people can take to take care of their teeth. [For hair, include ideas such as these: wash it every day or at least two or three times a week, comb it, brush it, use a blow dryer, use a curling iron, use gels or sprays, use shampoo and conditioner, get it trimmed every couple of months, eat a healthy diet. For teeth, include ideas such as these: brush teeth, floss teeth, use mouthwash, have regular checkups, eat apples, keep sweets at an acceptable level, eat a healthy diet.]

After the brainstorming is completed, ask volunteers to circle the actions that need to be part of everyone's basic hair and teeth care.

Objective: Student will help identify general and basic hair- and teeth-care actions.

Subject: Science/Health **Mode:** Brainstorming **Training Zone:** [C] Conscientiousness	**Readiness Factor:** [3] Personal/Social **Readiness Factor Category:** [l] Health, Diet, and Appearance

Sc 13: **Caring for pets**

FUTR Tool: no
PACT: no

Supplies: None

Discuss that people who decide to have pets need to accept the responsibility of taking care of a pet. Divide the class into six teams. Ask each team to choose one of these pets (or another as long as there are no duplicates): dog, cat, parrot, hamster, duck, horse. Ask each team to give a presentation about caring for its pet, making sure to include information on food, exercise, lodging, medical care, and affection.

Objective: Student will help put together a presentation on caring for a specific type of pet.

Subject: Science/Health **Mode:** Oral Response **Training Zone:** [R] Responsibility	**Readiness Factor:** [3] Personal/Social **Readiness Factor Category:** [j] Leisure/Desires/Choices

Sc 14: **Caring for self when sick**

FUTR Tool: 79
PACT: yes

Supplies: None

Brainstorm a list of actions a person can take to feel better when sick. Include ideas such as these:

1. Rest a lot.
2. Eat foods that are gentle on the digestive system.
3. Depending on how sick—either push yourself to do at least a partial version of your regular exercise or skip your exercise until you start feeling better.
4. Drink plenty of water.
5. Plan to stay home and take it easy.
6. Take over-the-counter medication as needed.
7. Depending on how sick—ask a friend or relative for help, call your doctor's office for advice, make an appointment with your doctor, or go to the emergency room.

Discuss examples of situations that call for taking care of yourself (alone or with the help of friends and relatives) versus those that call for getting professional medical help.

Objective: Student will help brainstorm actions to take when sick.

Subject: Science/Health **Mode:** Brainstorming **Training Zone:** [R] Responsibility	**Readiness Factor:** [3] Personal/Social **Readiness Factor Category:** [l] Health, Diet, and Appearance

Sc 15: **Checking fuses and breakers**

FUTR Tool: no
PACT: yes

Supplies: A tiny fuse (can be a blown one), a blow dryer or other appliance with a breaker

Show students the fuse and the breaker on the blow dryer (or other appliance). Discuss that many items, such as a string of Christmas lights, have fuses that have to be replaced when they blow. Point out that other items, such as a blow dryer, have a breaker switch that might pop and shut the item off and then have to be reset before the item can be used again. Also, point out that houses have a breaker box with switches that might pop and have to be reset. Explain that both fuses that blow out and breakers that pop off are designed to protect items or wiring from damage caused by electrical surges or overuse.

Objective: Student will discuss how fuses and breakers work.

Subject: Science/Health **Mode:** Discussion **Training Zone:** [E] Exploration	**Readiness Factor:** [2] Daily Living **Readiness Factor Category:** [e] Safety and Security

Science/Health 113

Sc 16: **Chewing food adequately**

FUTR Tool: no
PACT: yes

Supplies: None

Discuss that not chewing food enough can cause problems such as choking, stomach problems, and eating too much. Ask volunteers to share examples of times when they wished they had chewed their food a little more.

Objective: Student will discuss problems caused by not chewing food enough.

Subject: Science/Health **Mode:** Discussion **Training Zone:** [A] Analysis	**Readiness Factor:** [3] Personal/Social **Readiness Factor Category:** [l] Health, Diet, and Appearance

Sc 17: **Choosing a car**

FUTR Tool: no
PACT: no

Supplies: Newspaper sales ads with pictures of cars

Pass out the newspaper ads and discuss the different types of cars. Ask students which cars they like best and make a chart on the board to keep track of how many students like each of the different kinds of cars. Ask volunteers to share why they like the cars they chose. Discuss issues that are most important when choosing a car [some examples: price, size, gas mileage, age, condition].

Objective: Student will discuss which kinds of car he likes best and why.

Subject: Science/Health **Mode:** Graph or Chart **Training Zone:** [U] Conclusion	**Readiness Factor:** [2] Daily Living **Readiness Factor Category:** [f] Shopping and Eating at Restaurants

Sc 18: **Choosing appropriate clothing for the occasion**

FUTR Tool: 108
PACT: yes

Supplies: 15 or 20 magazines that includes pictures of people in clothing for different occasions; 5 sheets of posterboard

Divide the class into five teams and give each team some magazines and a poster board. Have them draw center lines down the posterboards and then draw two crosswise lines to divide the posterboard into six sections. Ask them to label the six sections with the words in the list below. Ask each team to look through the magazines to find pictures of appropriate clothing for men and women for each of these situations:

• wedding
• funeral
• picnic
• exercise
• office job
• factory job

Objective: Student will help create a chart showing clothing for different occasions.

Subject: Science/Health **Mode:** Graph or Chart **Training Zone:** [U] Conclusion	**Readiness Factor:** [3] Personal/Social **Readiness Factor Category:** [l] Health, Diet, and Appearance

Sc 19: **Choosing a protective place during a storm**

FUTR Tool: no
PACT: no

Supplies: None

Discuss that, during storms, the safest places are basements or lowest levels, areas away from windows, fortified areas such as closets under stairwells, other closets, and bathrooms. Point out that closets and bathrooms are good choices because closer walls helps provide more support to the roof. Also, explain that the center of the house is a good choice since every wall between you and the outside provides additional protection. Ask students to explain where they will go in their homes if there are tornado warnings.

Objective: Student will discuss the safest kinds of places to go during a storm, and will tell where he would go in his own house.

Subject: Science/Health **Mode:** Discussion **Training Zone:** [U] Conclusion	**Readiness Factor:** [2] Daily Living **Readiness Factor Category:** [e] Safety and Security

Sc 20: **Choosing comfortable clothes**

FUTR Tool: no
PACT: yes

Supplies: None

Have students each write a paragraph describing comfortable clothes. Ask volunteers to share their paragraphs. Discuss features that make clothes comfortable.

Objective: Student will write a paragraph describing comfortable clothes and will orally discuss features that make clothes comfortable.

Subject: Science/Health **Mode:** Written **Training Zone:** [S] Self-Awareness	**Readiness Factor:** [3] Personal/Social **Readiness Factor Category:** [l] Health, Diet, and Appearance

Sc 21: **Choosing cooking methods**

FUTR Tool: no
PACT: yes

Supplies: None

Ask each student to draw a line down the center of a piece of paper from top to bottom and again from left to right to divide the paper into four sections. Have them label the sections Oven, Stove, Microwave, Grill and then draw or list things that they think are best when cooked using the different methods.

Objective: Student will make a chart showing foods that are best when cooked in an oven, on a stove, in a microwave, and on a grill.

Subject: Science/Health **Mode:** Graph or Chart **Training Zone:** [O] Organization	**Readiness Factor:** [2] Daily Living **Readiness Factor Category:** [d] Household Care and/or Chores

Sc 22: **Choosing correct battery sizes**

FUTR Tool: no
PACT: no

Supplies: C battery, D battery, AA battery, AAA battery, 9-volt battery

Show students the different batteries and tell them the size of each. Discuss that batteries are available in different sizes including those you are showing. Explain that you can tell which size battery to use in one of two ways:

1. The package or product (or both) indicate the needed battery size in writing and/or with a picture.

2. Battery compartments are sized to only fit the size and number of batteries needed.

Objective: Student will see different battery sizes and will discuss how to know which size to use.

Subject: Science/Health **Mode:** Hands-On **Training Zone:** [V] Observation	**Readiness Factor:** [2] Daily Living **Readiness Factor Category:** [f] Shopping and Eating at Restaurants

Sc 23: **Choosing microwave containers**

FUTR Tool: 75
PACT: yes

Supplies: None

Ask students to draw a picture of a container and a lid that are safe for use in the microwave. Tell them to indicate if the pieces are made of glass, plastic, etc. Have volunteers share their pictures and discuss the variety of containers and lids that are safe for microwaves, making sure to include these containers: glass containers, plastic containers, and paper plates and these lids: glass lids, plastic lids, paper plates, plastic wrap, paper towels.

Discuss that foods that melt, such as cheese, can get too hot for some softer-plastic containers. Explain that melting foods work better in hard plastic or glass containers.

Objective: Student will draw a microwave-safe container and lid and will discuss containers that work best for melting foods.

Subject: Science/Health **Mode:** Drawing **Training Zone:** [O] Organization	**Readiness Factor:** [2] Daily Living **Readiness Factor Category:** [d] Household Care and/or Chores

Sc 24: **Choosing not to be taken advantage of**

FUTR Tool: no
PACT: no

Supplies: None

Discuss that sometimes friends or family members might take advantage of you by doing things like using your stuff without asking, assuming you will be available without asking, and making choices for you without getting your opinion. Explain that, when you think you are being taken advantage of, you should discuss the problem right away so that it neither gets out of hand nor becomes a regular pattern.

Objective: Student will discuss what it means to be taken advantage of and how to deal with such a situation.

Subject: Science/Health **Mode:** Discussion **Training Zone:** [U] Conclusion	**Readiness Factor:** [3] Personal/Social **Readiness Factor Category:** [i] Relationships

Sc 25: Choosing not to pollute

FUTR Tool: no
PACT: no

Supplies: Picture of a beautiful landscape, candy wrappers, wadded up paper

Show students a picture of a beautiful landscape. Then, stick some candy wrappers and wadded up paper on the landscape. Discuss that litter really does ruin the landscape. Ask volunteers to describe times when they have seen litter that they found upsetting. Discuss that we can all make the choice not to pollute and that these tips can help:

1. Put a garbage can or bag in your car.
2. Keep an eye out for garbage cans when you are eating and walking.
3. Remember that all stores and restaurants have garbage cans, and you can either use them yourself or ask an employee to throw something away for you.
4. Encourage your friends not to litter. Once disposing of garbage properly is a habit for all of you, you will all be less likely to ever consider littering.

Objective: Student will discuss issues about littering.

Subject: Science/Health **Mode:** Discussion **Training Zone:** [U] Conclusion	**Readiness Factor:** [3] Personal/Social **Readiness Factor Category:** [k] Community Involvement and Responsibility

Sc 26: Choosing workplace options

FUTR Tool: 96
PACT: yes

Supplies: None

Discuss that workplaces vary in many ways including temperature, dress code, cleanliness, indoor or outdoor, number of people, and formal or relaxed. Ask each student to identify five places that would seem fun to work. Have volunteers share their lists and tell what they think they would like about each of the workplaces.

Objective: Student will discuss how workplaces vary and identify some workplaces that she might like.

Subject: Science/Health **Mode:** Written **Training Zone:** [S] Self-Awareness	**Readiness Factor:** [1] Career **Readiness Factor Category:** [a] Career Preparation

Sc 27: Clearing ears in pressurized situations

FUTR Tool: no
PACT: no

Supplies: None

Show students how to close their mouths, plug their noses, and gently blow out of their ears to equalize the pressure in their ears. Explain that this technique is helpful on airplanes and in other situations where their ears plug up from pressure. Explain that another technique that helps equalize ear pressure is to suck on hard candy or chew food or small pieces of ice.

Objective: Student will practice clearing his ears and and will discuss optional ways of ear-clearing.

Subject: Science/Health **Mode:** Action **Training Zone:** [M] Manipulation	**Readiness Factor:** [3] Personal/Social **Readiness Factor Category:** [l] Health, Diet, and Appearance

Sc 28: **Comparing snacks**

FUTR Tool: no
PACT: yes

Supplies: None

As a group, brainstorm a list of snack foods. Then, mark each snack on the list as H (healthy), OK (not real healthy, but not real bad), or U (unhealthy). Discuss that, although people do not always have to choose healthy snacks, choosing healthy snacks most of the time is a good idea.

Objective: Student will help make a list of snack foods and then will help identify each as healthy, OK , or unhealthy.

Subject: Science/Health **Mode:** Brainstorming **Training Zone:** [A] Analysis	**Readiness Factor:** [3] Personal/Social **Readiness Factor Category:** [l] Health, Diet, and Appearance

Sc 29: **Conserving electricity**

FUTR Tool: no
PACT: no

Supplies: None

Point out that conserving electricity means to use only the electricity that is absolutely needed. Together, brainstorm ways to conserve electricity at home and at school. Make sure to include ideas such as these:

1. shutting off lights when you leave a room

2. heating to the high 60s instead of the low 70s

3. setting the heat lower at night

4. air conditioning to the low 80s instead of in the 70s

5. keeping doors and windows closed when heat or air conditioning is on

6. making sure to turn burners and ovens off when finished

Objective: Student will help list ways to conserve electricity.

Subject: Science/Health **Mode:** Brainstorming **Training Zone:** [R] Responsibility	**Readiness Factor:** [3] Personal/Social **Readiness Factor Category:** [k] Community Involvement and Responsibility

Sc 30: **Considering weather when packing**

FUTR Tool: 73
PACT: yes

Supplies: None

Divide the class into four teams. Assign each team one of these destinations:

• New York City, NY

• Minneapolis, MN

• Seattle, WA

• Dallas, TX

• Orlando, FL

Ask teams to assume they are traveling to their destinations next week and to plan what clothes they will take to stay for four days and be ready for the weather.

Objective: Student will help plan clothes to pack to be ready for the weather in a specific location.

Subject: Science/Health **Mode:** Role Play **Training Zone:** [O] Organization	**Readiness Factor:** [2] Daily Living **Readiness Factor Category:** [h] Transportation/Travel/Worldliness

Sc 31: **Counting calories**

FUTR Tool: no
PACT: no

Supplies: Calorie counting book or a calorie-counting chart from an Internet site

Have students list the foods they have eaten over the last 24 hours. Then, have them determine how many calories they have eaten. Discuss the role calories play in maintaining weight. Also, have students identify foods they like that are high and low in calories. Discuss that low-calories foods they like make good snacks between meals.

Objective: Student will count the number of calories she eats in a 24-hour period.

Subject: Science/Health **Mode:** Calculation **Training Zone:** [V] Observation	**Readiness Factor:** [3] Personal/Social **Readiness Factor Category:** [l] Health, Diet, and Appearance

Sc 32: **Dealing with ants, etc. in a home**

FUTR Tool: no
PACT: yes

Supplies: Five phone book yellow pages

Divide the class into five teams and give each team a phone book yellow pages book. Ask teams to find a local company that deals with residential pest control. Either through an ad or a phone call, find out what types of pests the companies typically deal with. (Typical pest control ads target animals such as scorpions, termites, roaches, ants, rats, mice, rodents, bees, fleas, ticks.) Discuss that minor pest problems such as a few ants, mice, roaches, or bees can be handled at home by using over-the-counter sprays and traps.

Objective: Student will find a local pest control company and will discuss commercial vs. personal handling of pest control.

Subject: Science/Health **Mode:** Action **Training Zone:** [C] Conscientiousness	**Readiness Factor:** [2] Daily Living **Readiness Factor Category:** [d] Household Care and/or Chores

Sc 33: **Dealing with death**

FUTR Tool: no
PACT: yes

Supplies: None

Discuss that death is a part of life, but that doesn't make it any easier to lose a loved one. Explain that it is normal to feel sad when someone dies, and it is even common to have a loss of energy for a while. Discuss the following tips for dealing with a loss:

1. Talk with friends and relatives about how you feel.
2. Try not to spend too much time alone.
3. Take a little time off from responsibilities, if needed.
4. Plan something nice to do for yourself.
5. Be patient, healing takes a while.

Objective: Student will discuss how to deal with losing a friend or relative.

Subject: Science/Health **Mode:** Discussion **Training Zone:** [Z] Socialization	**Readiness Factor:** [3] Personal/Social **Readiness Factor Category:** [l] Health, Diet, and Appearance

Sc 34: **Dealing with garbage and recycling**

FUTR Tool: no
PACT: yes

Supplies: None

Make a seven-column chart on the board and label it with the days of the week. Take a poll in the classroom to see how many garbage pickups are held on each day.

Discuss that not so long ago—in the 1980s—garbage and recycling items were all thrown together as garbage in most U.S. households. Explain that since the 1980s, most U.S. households have begun to recycle items such as newspaper, plastic, aluminum, and glass. Ask volunteers to share examples of preparing items for the recycling bin.

Objective: Student will discuss issues relating to garbage and recycling.

Subject: Science/Health **Mode:** Graph or Chart **Training Zone:** [R] Responsibility	**Readiness Factor:** [3] Personal/Social **Readiness Factor Category:** [k] Community Involvement and Responsibility

Sc 35: **Dealing with leftover food**

FUTR Tool: no
PACT: yes

Supplies: None

Ask students to name foods that they often have as leftovers. Discuss how to store and prepare each of the different leftovers.

Objective: Student will discuss how to store and prepare leftovers.

Subject: Science/Health **Mode:** Discussion **Training Zone:** [U] Conclusion	**Readiness Factor:** [2] Daily Living **Readiness Factor Category:** [e] Safety and Security

Sc 36: **Dealing with stress**

FUTR Tool: 91
PACT: yes

Supplies: None

Discuss that stress is the result of people getting upset, and that too much stress is unhealthy so you should look for ways to relieve your stress. Ask volunteers for examples of ways to be less upset and have less stress such as the following:

1. Talk to the person who upset you. Often, the situation is really not as bad as you think, and talking can clear it up.
2. Exercise to relieve stress—Take a walk, go for a swim, or do some other activity.
3. Relax to relieve stress—Read a book, watch TV, or take a nap.
4. Talk to friends. Sharing problems with friends often makes you feel better.
5. Give yourself some time—Some time without big expectations is often the most helpful.

Objective: Student will discuss ways to alleviate stress.

Subject: Science/Health **Mode:** Discussion **Training Zone:** [Z] Socialization	**Readiness Factor:** [3] Personal/Social **Readiness Factor Category:** [l] Health, Diet, and Appearance

Sc 37: **Dealing with teasing**

Supplies: None

Create a Pros and Cons chart on the board. As a group, fill the chart in with pros and cons that have to do with teasing. Include ideas such as the following:

• Pros: can be fun, is often an easy way to communicate, can lighten a heavy time, can be nice to receive the attention

• Cons: can hurt feelings, can get out of control, can give unwanted attention

Objective: Student will help make a pros and cons chart about teasing.

Subject: Science/Health **Mode:** Graph or Chart **Training Zone:** [F] Flexibility	**Readiness Factor:** [3] Personal/Social **Readiness Factor Category:** [i] Relationships

Sc 38: **Dealing with unusual or dangerous odors**

FUTR Tool: no
PACT: no

Supplies: None

Discuss that odors can send a lot of messages such as something good is cooking, something is burning, someone just took a shower, someone is sick, there is a dog around, someone is smoking. Explain that, when you smell an unusual or dangerous odor such as fire, gas, chemical, something burning, or a dead animal, you should search it out. Point out that you should try to find the source so that you can be sure all is OK. Ask volunteers to share examples of times when they smelled unusual or dangerous odors.

Objective: Student will discuss noticing and searching out unusual or dangerous odors.

Subject: Science/Health **Mode:** Discussion **Training Zone:** [V] Observation	**Readiness Factor:** [2] Daily Living **Readiness Factor Category:** [e] Safety and Security

Sc 39: **Deciding when to open eyes in water**

FUTR Tool: no
PACT: no

Supplies: None

Discuss that some people always swim with their eyes closed, but that others like to open their eyes when they are in clear water. Discuss that most swimmers can safely open their eyes in a pool with a well-balanced chemistry. Point out that some swimmers' eyes react to chlorine, so they are best off swimming with their eyes closed. Also point out that swimmers should keep their eyes closed in lakes and oceans because of all the critters, sand, and debris.

Objective: Student will discuss when to swim with eyes open and closed.

Subject: Science/Health **Mode:** Discussion **Training Zone:** [C] Conscientiousness	**Readiness Factor:** [3] Personal/Social **Readiness Factor Category:** [l] Health, Diet, and Appearance

Sc 40: Describing a person

FUTR Tool: no
PACT: no

Supplies: None

Explain to students that, when describing a person, they should use features that make the person stand out as different from others. Point out the following levels of descriptions and their usefulness:

1. Saying a person has hair is not useful unless the person is in a room with mostly bald people.

2. Saying a person has dark hair might be a little more helpful, depending on other hair colors.

3. Saying a person has long dark hair will be even a little more helpful as long as some people in the room have short hair.

4. Saying a person has waist-length dark curly hair would almost always be helpful since it tells how long, what color, and what style—and since waist-length hair is not common.

Ask students to each choose one classmate and write a description. Have students put both their names and the names of the people they are describing on their papers. Collect the papers and choose some to read aloud to see if students can guess who is being described. Discuss additions that might help each description.

Objective: Student will describe another student.

Subject: Science/Health Mode: Written Training Zone: [V] Observation	Readiness Factor: [3] Personal/Social Readiness Factor Category: [k] Community Involvement and Responsibility

Sc 41: Describing yourself

FUTR Tool: no
PACT: no

Supplies: None

Explain to students that, when describing yourself, you should use features that make you stand out as different from other people. Point out the following levels of descriptions and their usefulness:

1. Saying you are a teenager helps if comparing yourself to all people, but not if comparing yourself to students in a high school.

2. Saying you are pretty doesn't help since "pretty" to one person might not be "pretty" to all.

3. Saying you are female helps since it rules out many people (unless the group is all female).

4. Saying you are about 5′4″ helps as long as all others in the room are not the same height.

Ask students to write descriptions of themselves. Have students put their names on their papers. Collect the papers and choose some to read aloud to see if students can guess who is being described. Discuss additions that might help each description.

Objective: Student will write a description of herself.

Subject: Science/Health Mode: Written Training Zone: [S] Self-Awareness	Readiness Factor: [3] Personal/Social Readiness Factor Category: [l] Health, Diet, and Appearance

Sc 42: Detecting the source (direction) of noises and voices

FUTR Tool: no
PACT: no

Supplies: None

Ask students to close their eyes. Tell them that you are going to move around the room and call student names and that the student you call is to point in the direction of your voice. Randomly move around the room calling student names until every student has had a chance to participate.

Objective: Student will identify the direction of a voice.

Subject: Science/Health	Readiness Factor: [2] Daily Living
Mode: Action	Readiness Factor Category: [e] Safety and Security
Training Zone: [V] Observation	

Sc 43: Dieting sensibly

FUTR Tool: no
PACT: no

Supplies: None

Discuss that being overweight is unhealthy, so dieting has a place. But, point out that improper dieting is also unhealthy. Tell your student that the best way to diet is to eat smaller portions than usual and to exercise more than usual.

As a group, brainstorm different diet plans and discuss whether each is healthy or unhealthy.

Objective: Student will help make a list of diet plans and will discuss whether each is healthy or unhealthy.

Subject: Science/Health	Readiness Factor: [3] Personal/Social
Mode: Brainstorming	Readiness Factor Category: [l] Health, Diet, and Appearance
Training Zone: [R] Responsibility	

Sc 44: Differentiating between water and permanent markers

FUTR Tool: no
PACT: yes

Supplies: Water marker, permanent marker, small piece of fabric, empty plastic milk jug, piece of paper, wet paper towel, sink or bowl of water

Discuss that water markers and permanent markers function in different ways. Demonstrate the following uses of markers:

1. Make a line on the paper with each marker. Show how the permanent marker shows more easily on the back side of the paper. Take a wet paper towel and swipe across the two lines to show that the water marker will smear even after it has "dried."

2. Make a line on the fabric with each marker. Rub the lines under water to show that the water marker washes out and the permanent marker does not.

3. Make a line on the milk jug with each marker and give the lines a moment to dry.
   Then, try to rub the two lines off.

4. If desired, use the two markers to do a "wash-off" test on your hand.

Objective: Student will discuss the differences between water and permanent markers and watch a demonstration showing some of the differences.

Subject: Science/Health	Readiness Factor: [3] Personal/Social
Mode: Demonstration	Readiness Factor Category: [j] Leisure/Desires/Choices
Training Zone: [V] Observation	

Sc 45: Differentiating between wild and tame animals

FUTR Tool: no
PACT: no

Supplies: None

Make a two-column chart on the board. Label one column "wild" and one column "tame." As a group, brainstorm a list of animals to put in each column. Some possibilities: Wild—tigers, elephants, lions, bears, owls, deer, crickets, worms; Tame—dogs, cats, horses, domesticated rabbits, dairy cows.

Objective: Student will help make a list of wild animals and a list of tame animals.

Subject: Science/Health **Mode:** Graph or Chart **Training Zone:** [V] Observation	**Readiness Factor:** [2] Daily Living **Readiness Factor Category:** [e] Safety and Security

Sc 46: Doing laundry

FUTR Tool: 83
PACT: yes

Supplies: None
Ask volunteers to answer the following questions:

1. Why is it important not to wash clothes that say "dry clean only"? [Might ruin them]
2. Why do some people hang their jeans to dry instead of putting them in the dryer? [Won't shrink]
3. What color clothing causes the most problems when washed with other things? [Red]
4. How much does it cost to wash clothes at a laundromat? [Current wash and dry prices]
5. How many days should you wear each item below before you wash it?

t-shirt	exercise shorts	pair of jeans	pair of socks
coat	underwear	dressy shirt	pajamas

Objective: Student will answer questions about doing laundry.

Subject: Science/Health **Mode:** Oral Response **Training Zone:** [C] Conscientiousness	**Readiness Factor:** [2] Daily Living **Readiness Factor Category:** [d] Household Care and/or Chores

Sc 47: Dressing appropriately for the weather

FUTR Tool: no
PACT: yes

Supplies: None

Divide students into five-person teams. Ask each team to create the following five pictures:

1. Clothes to wear on a rainy day
2. Clothes to wear on a cold winter day
3. Clothes to wear on a warm summer day
4. Clothes to wear on a cool and sunny fall day
5. Clothes colors that help you be cool in hot weather [white and light colors] and clothes colors that help you be warmer in cool weather [black and dark colors]

Objective: Student will draw a picture of weather-appropriate clothing.

Subject: Science/Health **Mode:** Drawing **Training Zone:** [L] Logic	**Readiness Factor:** [3] Personal/Social **Readiness Factor Category:** [l] Health, Diet, and Appearance

Sc 48: Drinking enough water

FUTR Tool: 104
PACT: yes

Supplies: None

Explain that water is one of the basic needs of the human body and that drinking liquids such as soda and tea cannot replace the need for water.

Discuss that some people believe in drinking at least eight glasses of water per day, while others say eight glasses is more than necessary. Point out that, at a minimum, a person should drink a large glass of water with each meal. Add that a having a large glass between meals is also a good plan.

Ask students to keep track of the amount of water they drink and then discuss whether they need to try to drink more or not.

Objective: Student will discuss the amount of water people need and will then keep track of the water he drinks and decide if it is enough or not.

Subject: Science/Health **Mode:** Discussion, Action **Training Zone:** [A] Analysis	**Readiness Factor:** [3] Personal/Social **Readiness Factor Category:** [I] Health, Diet, and Appearance

Sc 49: Eating a balanced diet

FUTR Tool: 85
PACT: yes

Supplies: None

Divide students into teams of three students. Ask each team to create a balanced meal plan for one day. Collect all the meal plans and have the class choose the healthiest, most balanced plan(s) [up to five "best" plans depending on number of teams]. Discuss why some plans are healthier than others. Discuss which foods add no value to a meal plan [junk food such as chips, donuts, and candy].

Objective: Student will help create a balanced meal plan for one day.

Subject: Science/Health **Mode:** Written **Training Zone:** [F] Flexibility	**Readiness Factor:** [3] Personal/Social **Readiness Factor Category:** [I] Health, Diet, and Appearance

Sc 50: Exercising

FUTR Tool: no
PACT: yes

Supplies: None

Discuss that exercise is as important to good health as are eating and sleeping. Brainstorm a list of exercise choices. Make sure to include some that are fun-based as well as some that are straight exercise.

Objective: Student will help make a list of exercise choices.

Subject: Science/Health **Mode:** Brainstorming **Training Zone:** [R] Responsibility	**Readiness Factor:** [3] Personal/Social **Readiness Factor Category:** [I] Health, Diet, and Appearance

Sc 51: Feeling differences in temperatures

FUTR Tool: no
PACT: yes

Supplies: Four water bottles: one warmed in a microwave, one room temperature, one that has been in a refrigerator, and one that is frozen; a blindfold

Blindfold a volunteer and ask him to identify the four bottles of water as warm, room temperature, refrigerator-cold, or frozen. Repeat with other volunteers.

Objective: Student will identify differences in temperature, including warm, room temperature, refrigerator-cold, and frozen

Subject: Science/Health **Mode:** Action **Training Zone:** [M] Manipulation	**Readiness Factor:** [1] Career **Readiness Factor Category:** [b] Job Performance

Sc 52: Feeling differences in thicknesses

FUTR Tool: no
PACT: yes

Supplies: None

Divide the class into teams of two or three students. Ask each team to find three sets of items that meet the following descriptions:

1. Two items that are about the same thickness

2. Two items that are different, but close in thickness

3. Two items that are very different in thickness

Objective: Student will find items that meet varying thickness-comparison qualifications.

Subject: Science/Health **Mode:** Action **Training Zone:** [M] Manipulation	**Readiness Factor:** [1] Career **Readiness Factor Category:** [b] Job Performance

Sc 53: Freezing foods properly and safely

FUTR Tool: no
PACT: no

Supplies: None

Explain that you can take steps to make frozen foods taste better and have less freezer burn. Discuss the following tips for freezing foods:

1. When using containers, make sure to choose containers that have lids that seal.

2. Freezer bags are thicker than other zipper bags and the word "freeze" or "freezer" is on the box. Look carefully when choosing.

3. Eat frozen leftovers within three months.

4. Check labels on packaged frozen foods for length-of-freezing-time recommendations.

5. Set containers with liquids level so they do not leak.

6. Place waxed paper between soft food items, such as pieces of cheesecake, so they do not freeze together.

Objective: Student will discuss tips for freezing foods.

Subject: Science/Health **Mode:** Discussion **Training Zone:** [C] Conscientiousness	**Readiness Factor:** [2] Daily Living **Readiness Factor Category:** [e] Safety and Security

Sc 54: Getting enough sleep

Supplies: None

Discuss with your students that it is important that they get at least eight hours of sleep each night to keep up with their growth and development as well as their busy schedules. Also, explain that, if possible, it is best to have a set schedule for going to bed and getting up. For two weeks, have them keep a chart showing when they go to bed and when they get up each day. Discuss whether their schedules are healthy or not as well as these sleep concepts:

1. If you eat right and take vitamins, can you be healthy without much sleep? [No, there are no substitutes for proper rest]
2. What is likely to happen to a person who goes night after night without enough sleep? [Will become run down, possibly become ill]

Objective: Student will discuss healthy amounts of sleep, will keep a chart showing his sleep habits for two weeks, and will discuss whether or not his sleep habits are healthy.

Subject: Science/Health **Mode:** Graph or Chart **Training Zone:** [S] Self-Awareness	**Readiness Factor:** [3] Personal/Social **Readiness Factor Category:** [l] Health, Diet, and Appearance

Sc 55: Getting stains out

Supplies: Hair spray, bar of soap and cup of water, bottle of club soda, purchased stain remover for clothing, purchased stain remover for carpet (product containers can be empty)

Place the following items where students can see them: hair spray, bar of soap and cup of water, bottle of club soda, commercial stain remover for clothing, commercial stain remover for carpet.

Discuss how each item gets stains out.

Answer:
• Hair spray—use without water for stains such as ink
• Soap and water—apply and scrub
• Club soda—apply and scrub
• Purchased stain remover for clothing—apply and wash in washing machine
• Purchased stain remover for carpet—apply, let dry, rub

Objective: Student will discuss different methods of getting stains out.

Subject: Science/Health **Mode:** Hands-On **Training Zone:** [C] Conscientiousness	**Readiness Factor:** [2] Daily Living **Readiness Factor Category:** [d] Household Care and/or Chores

Sc 56: Getting the roots when pulling weeds

FUTR Tool: no
PACT: no

Supplies: None

Draw an actual-sized weed on the board. Choose a weed that spreads both up and out. Include the roots, and draw a line marking the top of the soil. With your fingers, show students how to put your fingers touching the soil so you can grasp the stem as far down as possible. Also, demonstrate how to gather all the leaves together so you are pulling on the whole core of the weed.

Objective: Student will see how to pull a weed so that the whole root is most likely to come out.

Subject: Science/Health **Mode:** Demonstration **Training Zone:** [A] Analysis	**Readiness Factor:** [2] Daily Living **Readiness Factor Category:** [d] Household Care and/or Chores

Sc 57: Giving medical histories

FUTR Tool: 80
PACT: yes

Supplies: Copies of a medical history form from either a doctor and/or dentist office

Give each student a medical history form to fill out. Discuss why doctors and dentists require the different pieces of information.

If needed, have students take the forms home to get help filling out parts they do not know.

Objective: Student will fill out a medical history form.

Subject: Science/Health **Mode:** Action **Training Zone:** [R] Responsibility	**Readiness Factor:** [3] Personal/Social **Readiness Factor Category:** [l] Health, Diet, and Appearance

Sc 58: Guessing people's ages

FUTR Tool: no
PACT: no

Supplies: People pictures (from magazines) showing an assortment of ages and/or video tapes showing people

Discuss that telling ages is always just a guess—but most of the time, a guess can be within ten years. One at a time, hold up the people pictures and ask students to guess their ages. For each, discuss clues they can use to guess. OR Show the video collection of people, pausing on each person to give students a chance to guess. (The video tape can be of people in your daily life or taped off the television.)

Objective: Student will guess ages of people in pictures or on video.

Subject: Science/Health **Mode:** Oral Response **Training Zone:** [V] Observation	**Readiness Factor:** [3] Personal/Social **Readiness Factor Category:** [i] Relationships

Sc 59: Handling electricity safely

FUTR Tool: no
PACT: no

Supplies: Something that plugs in, a not-plugged-in surge protector

Discuss that outlets have one hole a little larger than the other, plugs have one prong a little wider than the other, and the wider prong must go into the wider hole. Also, discuss that when unplugging from an outlet, you should take hold of the plug itself and pull—as opposed to grabbing the cord and pulling.
Have students practice plugging in and unplugging an electrical cord.

Discuss that plugs that get very hot, are frayed, or have exposed wires are not safe to use. Also, discuss that electrical items should be kept away from water because water and electricity are an unsafe mix.

Objective: Student will properly plug and unplug an electrical cord.

Subject: Science/Health **Mode:** Action **Training Zone:** [M] Manipulation	**Readiness Factor:** [2] Daily Living **Readiness Factor Category:** [e] Safety and Security

Sc 60: Having well check-ups

FUTR Tool: no
PACT: no

Supplies: None

Ask volunteers to answer the following questions about well check-ups with doctors and dentists.

1. What is a well check-up? [A doctor or dentist appointment that is not for the purpose of a known problem. The point of the appointment is to prevent problems.]
2. How often should a person have a well check-up with a doctor? [Preferably, once a year]
3. How often should a person have a well check-up with a dentist? [Preferably, once a year]
4. What is the danger of never having well check-ups? [You might have a small problem that unnecessarily becomes a large problem.]
5. Will insurance pay for well check-ups? [Some insurance plans do, some do not]

Objective: Student will discuss issues about well check-ups with doctors and dentists.

Subject: Science/Health **Mode:** Oral Response **Training Zone:** [R] Responsibility	**Readiness Factor:** [3] Personal/Social **Readiness Factor Category:** [l] Health, Diet, and Appearance

Sc 61: Identifying and using serrated- and smooth-bladed knives

FUTR Tool: no
PACT: no

Supplies: None

Draw two knives on the board—a serrated one and a smooth one. Discuss that a serrated knife is best for cutting meat and bread, and a smooth knife is best for cutting cheese. Point out that either type of knife works well for cutting fruits and vegetables.

Objective: Student will discuss the different uses for serrated and smooth knives.

Subject: Science/Health **Mode:** Discussion **Training Zone:** [A] Analysis	**Readiness Factor:** [2] Daily Living **Readiness Factor Category:** [d] Household Care and/or Chores

Sc 62: **Identifying smells**

FUTR Tool: 88
PACT: yes

Supplies: About five brown bags with items that can be identified by smell (See some possibilities below.)

As a group, brainstorm smells that you can identify without seeing where it is coming from. Include ideas such as the following: fire, glue, new tires, gasoline, pizza, bacon, bleach, soap, rubber bands, cinnamon, pepper, a rose, nail polish, coffee, bubble gum, chocolate.

For each brown bag, ask five volunteers to smell (without seeing) and write (without saying aloud) what they think is in the bag. Then, take the item out and see who was right. Give each student at least one turn to identify a smell.

Objective: Student will identify an item by its smell.

Subject: Science/Health **Mode:** Action **Training Zone:** [V] Observation	**Readiness Factor:** [2] Daily Living **Readiness Factor Category:** [e] Safety and Security

Sc 63: **Identifying things by touch**

FUTR Tool: no
PACT: no

Supplies: About five brown bags with items that can be identified by feel (See some possibilities below.)

As a group, brainstorm items that you can identify by touching (without seeing). Include ideas such as the following: stapler, remote control, cell phone, pen with a cap, pencil, book, lid, hair clip, wallet, ruler, spoon, plastic cup or glass, tube of chapstick.

For each brown bag, ask five volunteers to feel (without seeing) and write (without saying aloud) what they think is in the bag. Then, take the item out and see who was right. Give each student at least one turn to identify a touch.

Objective: Student will identify an item by touching it.

Subject: Science/Health **Mode:** Action **Training Zone:** [M] Manipulation	**Readiness Factor:** [1] Career **Readiness Factor Category:** [b] Job Performance

Sc 64: **Identifying things you shouldn't touch**

FUTR Tool: 103
PACT: yes

Supplies: None

As a group, brainstorm a list of things that you should not touch with your hands. Make sure to include things that could make you dirty, things that could cut you, and things that could chemically hurt you.

Objective: Student will help make a list of things that he should not touch with his hands.

Subject: Science/Health **Mode:** Brainstorming **Training Zone:** [A] Analysis	**Readiness Factor:** [3] Personal/Social **Readiness Factor Category:** [l] Health, Diet, and Appearance

Sc 65: Identifying your hair as oily or dry

Supplies: None

Discuss that some people have oily hair that begins to look somewhat wet when it hasn't been washed for a while, other people have dry hair that doesn't get the wet look, and still others have "normal" hair which is in between oily and dry. Point out that normal hair doesn't get oily after one or two days, but it probably would get oily if not washed for a week. Ask volunteers to share whether they have oily, normal, or dry hair and how they know. Explain that knowing your hair type is helpful when buying shampoo since many shampoos advertise that they are for either oily, normal, or dry hair.

Objective: Student will determine whether her hair is oily, normal, or dry.

Subject: Science/Health **Mode:** Discussion **Training Zone:** [S] Self-Awareness	**Readiness Factor:** [3] Personal/Social **Readiness Factor Category:** [l] Health, Diet, and Appearance

Sc 66: Interpreting weather reports

Supplies: Newspaper weather report on an overhead or copied for individual students , video of a TV weather report

Have students study the newspaper and TV weather reports. Discuss the meaning and certainty of the weather reports.

Discuss the meanings of these weather terms:

drought	flood	tornado	hurricane
thunderstorm	frostbite	fire threat	humidity
pollen count	chapped skin	sleet	hail
cloudy	severe weather	unseasonal weather	rain
snow	precipitation	chance of rain	skin exposure

Objective: Student will interpret weather reports and discuss weather terms.

Subject: Science/Health **Mode:** Hands-On **Training Zone:** [U] Conclusion	**Readiness Factor:** [2] Daily Living **Readiness Factor Category:** [e] Safety and Security

Sc 67: **Judging the safety of a surface when walking, running, or driving**

FUTR Tool: no
PACT: no

Supplies: None

Divide the class into three teams. Assign one team to answer questions from the point of view of a person who is walking, one to answer questions from the point of view of a person who is running, and one to answer questions from the point of view of a person who is driving. Then, ask these questions:

What should you do if you come to a place in the sidewalk or street that

1. is wet?
2. is icy?
3. is covered with broken glass?
4. has a tree branch across it?
5. has a dog standing in it?
6. has a sort of scary looking man standing in it?
7. is covered with a deep snow drift?
8. is uneven from broken concrete?

Objective: Student will offer solutions to sidewalk and street problems for walkers, runners, and drivers.

Subject: Science/Health **Mode:** Oral Response **Training Zone:** [A] Analysis	**Readiness Factor:** [2] Daily Living **Readiness Factor Category:** [e] Safety and Security

Sc 68: **Keeping a car clean and tuned**

FUTR Tool: no
PACT: yes

Supplies: None

Discuss that cars can only be clean if they are washed every week or two. Explain that some people like to keep their cars clean while others are not as concerned and therefore do not wash their cars as often. Point out that cars that are kept clean tend to be in better overall condition. Discuss different choices for cleaning a car such as the following: wash it in your driveway, go to a car wash, hire a teenage neighbor, hire a professional car detailer.

Discuss that manufacturers suggest a mileage point where cars should be tuned-up (often about every 50,000 miles). Explain that cars that are not kept tuned on schedule tend to develop problems. Point out that both dealerships and automotive shops perform tune-ups.

Objective: Student will discuss keeping a car clean and tuned.

Subject: Science/Health **Mode:** Discussion **Training Zone:** [C] Conscientiousness	**Readiness Factor:** [2] Daily Living **Readiness Factor Category:** [h] Transportation/Travel/Worldliness

Sc 69: **Keeping a home tidy**

FUTR Tool: 82
PACT: yes

Supplies: None

Make a four-column chart on the board. Label the columns with these headings: Once a day, Once a week, Once a month, Once a year. Make three rows below the columns to create three "boxes" below each heading. Ask volunteers to fill the chart with 12 household-cleaning tasks that need to be completed once a day, once a week, once a month, and once a year (three in each category).

Ask volunteers to explain how to complete each task in the chart.

Objective: Student will help create a chart showing cleaning tasks that need to be completed once a day, once a week, once a month, and once a year

Subject: Science/Health **Mode:** Graph or Chart **Training Zone:** [C] Conscientiousness	**Readiness Factor:** [2] Daily Living **Readiness Factor Category:** [d] Household Care and/or Chores

Sc 70: **Keeping a yard in good shape**

FUTR Tool: no
PACT: yes

Supplies: None

Discuss that yards require ongoing care including tasks such as the following:

- grass mowing
- leaf raking
- bush and tree trimming
- flower planting
- garden-area weeding
- unwanted lawn grass and weed removal
- lawn fertilizing
- grass watering
- ground aerating
- soil refurbishing
- border edging

Objective: Student will discuss specific tasks involved in keeping a yard in good shape.

Subject: Science/Health **Mode:** Discussion **Training Zone:** [C] Conscientiousness	**Readiness Factor:** [2] Daily Living **Readiness Factor Category:** [d] Household Care and/or Chores

Sc 71: **Keeping clothes from shrinking**

FUTR Tool: no
PACT: no

Supplies: None

Foe each statement below, ask students to choose the option that is least likely to cause clothing to shrink:

1. Washing in [**cold,** hot] water
2. Using the [dryer, **clothesline**] to dry clothes
3. Drying until [**somewhat dry,** completely dry]
4. Cleaning by [**dry cleaning,** machine washing]

Objective: Student will choose laundry options that are least likely to cause shrinkage.

Subject: Science/Health **Mode:** Oral Response **Training Zone:** [C] Conscientiousness	**Readiness Factor:** [2] Daily Living **Readiness Factor Category:** [d] Household Care and/or Chores

Sc 72: Keeping the bathroom mirror from fogging up

FUTR Tool: no
PACT: no

Supplies: None

Ask students how many of them have had the bathroom mirror fog up on them when they were showering or bathing. Discuss that the high water content in the air settles on the mirror to create the fog. Ask volunteers for ways to keep a bathroom mirror from fogging. Make sure the answers include the following ideas: turn on the exhaust fan, leave the door open, spray a purchased anti-fogger (might or might not be effective).

Objective: Student will discuss ways to keep a bathroom mirror from fogging up.

Subject: Science/Health **Mode:** Oral Response **Training Zone:** [A] Analysis	**Readiness Factor:** [2] Daily Living **Readiness Factor Category:** [d] Household Care and/or Chores

Sc 73: Keeping your fingernails clean and trimmed

FUTR Tool: no
PACT: yes

Supplies: None

Ask students to brainstorm choices that will help to keep their fingernails clean. Make sure the answers include ideas such as wash your hands often, wear gloves when doing messy work, use a fingernail brush and soap, keep an eye on your nails, and remove visible dirt right away.

Make a chart on the board with these headings: Straight across, Rounded, Rounded sides with straight tips, Cropped close to the fingers, Other. Survey students to see how they wear their fingernails. Use tallies to mark their responses.

Objective: Student will discuss ways to keep his fingernail clean and will become familiar with a variety of ways to shape fingernails.

Subject: Science/Health **Mode:** Brainstorming, Graph or Chart **Training Zone:** [S] Self-Awareness	**Readiness Factor:** [3] Personal/Social **Readiness Factor Category:** [l] Health, Diet, and Appearance

Sc 74: Keeping yourself clean

FUTR Tool: 84
PACT: yes

Supplies: None

Discuss that overall cleanliness depends on more than just taking showers and baths. As a group, brainstorm different steps a person can take to be clean. Make sure to include ideas such as the following:

- Take shower and baths regularly
- Wear clean clothes
- Wash your hands often
- Shampoo your hair often
- Ride in clean vehicles
- Brush and floss your teeth
- Wear deodorant
- Sleep in sheets that are washed regularly

Objective: Student will help make a list of steps a person can take to be clean.

Subject: Science/Health **Mode:** Brainstorming **Training Zone:** [C] Conscientiousness	**Readiness Factor:** [3] Personal/Social **Readiness Factor Category:** [l] Health, Diet, and Appearance

Sc 75: Knowing and following safety rules at work

FUTR Tool: no
PACT: no

Supplies: None

As a group, brainstorm a list of local businesses. Next to each business name, write one safety rule that might logically be in place at that business. Discuss that employees must take the effort to learn their companies' safety rules both for their own protection and for the protection of the company.

Objective: Student will help make a list of local businesses and safety rules that might logically be associated with them.

Subject: Science/Health **Mode:** Brainstorming **Training Zone:** [C] Conscientiousness	**Readiness Factor:** [1] Career **Readiness Factor Category:** [b] Job Performance

Sc 76: Knowing foods that are high in proteins, fats, carbs, or calories

FUTR Tool: no
PACT: yes

Supplies: None

Discuss that carbs (carbohydrates), fats, and proteins are three main components of foods. Make a chart on the board with these side labels: carbs, fats, proteins. Make five columns with food headers as follows: (Ask students to name) one dairy food, one vegetable, one meat, one grain, and one dessert. Have students use nutrition charts (from books or the Internet) to decide whether each food has a low (L), medium (M), or high (H) content of carbs, fats, and proteins. Discuss that many nutrition experts believe that people are more likely to be overweight when eating diets high in fats, and that people who have diabetic tendencies need to eat diets that are low in carbohydrates.

Objective: Student will help make a chart comparing the carbs, fats, and proteins in five different foods.

Subject: Science/Health **Mode:** Graph or Chart **Training Zone:** [U] Conclusion	**Readiness Factor:** [3] Personal/Social **Readiness Factor Category:** [l] Health, Diet, and Appearance

Sc 77: Knowing how to cook foods so they are safe to eat

FUTR Tool: no
PACT: yes

Supplies: None

Discuss that some foods must be cooked to a certain level to be safe. Ask volunteers to name some of these foods. Make sure they include chicken, eggs, pork, hamburger, some fish, turkey, and dough or batter that includes eggs. Discuss how to safely cook each of the foods.

Point out that many foods do not have such safety issues. Ask volunteers to name some foods that are safe to eat raw, cooked a little, or cooked a lot. [Some possibilities: carrots, broccoli, mushrooms, apples, cured ham, some fish, cheese]

Objective: Student will discuss the safety-related cooking needs of different foods.

Subject: Science/Health **Mode:** Discussion **Training Zone:** [C] Conscientiousness	**Readiness Factor:** [3] Personal/Social **Readiness Factor Category:** [l] Health, Diet, and Appearance

Sc 78: Knowing kinds of dairy foods

FUTR Tool: no
PACT: no

Supplies: None

Point out that dairy foods are an important part of a daily diet. Ask students to number a piece of paper from 1–10 and write ten dairy foods. Start a master list on the board by having one student read his ten things. Then, have other students add foods they have that are not already on the list.

Objective: Student will make a list of dairy foods.

Subject: Science/Health **Mode:** Written **Training Zone:** [V] Observation	**Readiness Factor:** [2] Daily Living **Readiness Factor Category:** [f] Shopping and Eating at Restaurants

Sc 79: Knowing kinds of grain foods

FUTR Tool: no
PACT: no

Supplies: None

Make a "grain foods" web on the board by starting with a small circle. Write "grain foods" inside of the circle. Then, have volunteers name different grain foods. As each food is named, draw a line out from the circle and write the named food at the end of the line.

Objective: Student will help identify a variety of grain foods.

Subject: Science/Health **Mode:** Graph or Chart **Training Zone:** [V] Observation	**Readiness Factor:** [2] Daily Living **Readiness Factor Category:** [f] Shopping and Eating at Restaurants

Sc 80: Knowing kinds of meat and fish

FUTR Tool: no
PACT: no

Supplies: Four pieces of posterboard, markers

Divide the class into four teams. Assign each team one of these meat and fish sources: cows, pigs, chicken and other fowl, fish. Ask each team to create a poster showing the source as well as meat or fish items that come from the source.

Objective: Student will help make a poster showing food items from cows, pigs, chicken and other fowl, or fish.

Subject: Science/Health **Mode:** Drawing **Training Zone:** [V] Observation	**Readiness Factor:** [2] Daily Living **Readiness Factor Category:** [f] Shopping and Eating at Restaurants

Sc 81: Knowing main car parts

FUTR Tool: no
PACT: yes

Supplies: A car—either in the school automotive shop or parking lot

Take students to the automotive shop in the school or out to the school parking lot. Ask volunteers to point out car parts such as the following: Inside the car—steering wheel, horn, clutch (if there is one), gas pedal, brake, cruise control, air conditioner switch, heat switch, defroster, speedometer, odometer, gas gauge, temperature gauge, voltage gauge; Under the hood—radiator, battery, oil dipstick, automatic transmission dipstick, windshield washing solution, fan belt, alternator, air cleaner, brake cylinder reservoir, water pump, air conditioner pump; Under the car—muffler, shocks, brake lines, tire treads

Objective: Student will point out car parts on a car.

Subject: Science/Health **Mode:** Action **Training Zone:** [V] Observation	**Readiness Factor:** [2] Daily Living **Readiness Factor Category:** [h] Transportation/Travel/Worldliness

Sc 82: Knowing parent and baby animal names

FUTR Tool: no
PACT: yes

Supplies: None

Ask volunteers to act out each of the animals listed below. Have other students guess the animal, and then give the father, mother, and offspring names. (Example: Volunteer acts out a cow, students guess cow and then say "Bull, cow, calf")

- horse [stud or stallion, mare, colt]
- chicken [rooster, chicken, chick]
- pig [boar, sow, piglet]
- cat [tom cat, cat, kitten]
- deer [buck, doe, fawn]
- human [man, woman, child]
- duck [drake, duck, duckling]
- goose [gander, goose, gosling]
- goat [billy, nanny, kid)]
- rabbit [buck, doe, bunny]

Objective: Student will identify various animal family member names.

Subject: Science/Health **Mode:** Action **Training Zone:** [O] Organization	**Readiness Factor:** [3] Personal/Social **Readiness Factor Category:** [i] Relationships

Sc 83: Knowing parts of a routine physical

FUTR Tool: 74
PACT: yes

Supplies: None

Write the list below on the board. Assign students to teams of two or three and assign one procedure from the list to each team. Ask each team to explain what its procedure is and if it is part of a routine physical.

- Take your temperature [yes]
- Take your blood pressure [yes]
- Do a chest X-ray [no]
- Check your weight [yes]
- Check your heart rate [yes]
- Realign your spine [no]
- Check for illegal drug use [no]
- Take a urine test [yes]
- Do a blood test [yes]
- Do simple surgery [no]
- Check inside ear [yes]
- Look inside your throat [yes]
- Do a reflex test [yes]
- Give a cancer treatment [no]
- Remove warts [no]

Objective: Student will identify and explain parts of a routine physical.

Subject: Science/Health **Mode:** Action **Training Zone:** [O] Organization	**Readiness Factor:** [3] Personal/Social **Readiness Factor Category:** [l] Health, Diet, and Appearance

Sc 84: Knowing the difference between over-the-counter and prescription medications

FUTR Tool: no
PACT: no

Supplies: Several empty prescription medication containers and several empty over-the-counter medication containers

Place several empty prescription medication containers and several empty over-the-counter medication containers where students can see them. Ask volunteers to select either a prescription or an over-the-counter medication container and then tell whether it is prescription or over-the-counter. Repeat with other volunteers until all containers have been chosen.

Objective: By looking at the container, student will determine whether a medication is over-the-counter or prescription.

Subject: Science/Health Mode: Hands-On Training Zone: [A] Analysis	Readiness Factor: [3] Personal/Social Readiness Factor Category: [l] Health, Diet, and Appearance

Sc 85: Knowing the names of fruits and vegetables

FUTR Tool: no
PACT: no

Supplies: None

Divide the class into three teams and play a picture-identification game. Ask each team to send one representative to the front of the room. Show the representative one of the words on the list below. Ask the representative to draw the item on the board while team members guess what it is. The first team to guess gets a point. Continue with different representatives and foods.

apple	pear	banana	orange	rhubarb	blueberries	plum
watermelon	cantaloupe	honeydew	strawberries	raspberries	blackberries	peach
carrot	celery	peas	beans	potatoes	pumpkin	squash
asparagus	cauliflower	mushrooms	broccoli	tomato	lettuce	radish

Objective: Student will draw vegetables and fruits for other students to guess and will guess names of fruits and vegetables when others draw them.

Subject: Science/Health Mode: Drawing Training Zone: [V] Observation	Readiness Factor: [2] Daily Living Readiness Factor Category: [f] Shopping and Eating at Restaurants

Sc 86: Knowing when to get a tetanus shot

FUTR Tool: no
PACT: no

Supplies: None

Discuss that tetanus shots keep you from getting serious infections as a result of receiving a deep puncture or cut. Explain that, if you get a puncture or deep cut, and do not know if you have had a tetanus shot recently, you should call your doctor and ask to have your records checked.

Objective: Student will discuss purpose and timing for a tetanus shot.

Subject: Science/Health Mode: Discussion Training Zone: [U] Conclusion	Readiness Factor: [3] Personal/Social Readiness Factor Category: [l] Health, Diet, and Appearance

Sc 87: Knowing when you need medical help

Supplies: None

Ask volunteers to match each of the problems below with one of these options: Take care of it yourself, Make a doctor's appointment, Go to the emergency room.

1. You have something in your eye and can't open it. [emergency room]
2. You have a sore that isn't healing. [doctor appointment]
3. You cut yourself and can't make it stop bleeding. [emergency room]
4. You have a large pimple. [yourself]
5. One of your eyes has been red and itchy for a couple of days. [doctor appointment]
6. Your eyes are tired. [yourself]

Objective: Student will match health problems with medical help choices.

Subject: Science/Health **Mode:** Oral Response **Training Zone:** [S] Self-Awareness	**Readiness Factor:** [3] Personal/Social **Readiness Factor Category:** [I] Health, Diet, and Appearance

Sc 88: Knowing where magnets will stick

FUTR Tool: no
PACT: no

Supplies: A bunch of decorative magnets

Divide the class into groups of two or three. Give each team a magnet and ask members to make a list of things in the room to which the magnets will stick. Ask teams to present their lists. Then, discuss that magnets stick to metal (not aluminum).

Objective: Student will find items to which magnets will stick.

Subject: Science/Health **Mode:** Action **Training Zone:** [A] Analysis	**Readiness Factor:** [2] Daily Living **Readiness Factor Category:** [h] Transportation/Travel/Worldliness

Sc 89: Knowing your body parts

FUTR Tool: no
PACT: yes

Supplies: None

Randomly call out the following body parts and ask students to point to them as you say the names.

ankle	nose	elbow	thumb	neck	ear
hand	thigh	heel	mouth	eye	wrist
knee	jaw	forearm	calf	hip	ribs
throat	toe	finger	shoulder	knuckle	instep

Objective: Student will point to her body parts as the names are called.

Subject: Science/Health **Mode:** Action **Training Zone:** [S] Self-Awareness	**Readiness Factor:** [3] Personal/Social **Readiness Factor Category:** [I] Health, Diet, and Appearance

Sc 90: Leaving things you see in public places

FUTR Tool: no
PACT: no

Supplies: None

Discuss that when you see things that are in public places (for example: on the ground, a road, a floor, a table, or a chair), you should leave them there and not touch them. Explain that since you do not know where the things have been nor what might be on them, you put yourself in danger by touching them. Ask volunteers to share situations where they have seen things they would like to have picked up, but knew they should not touch.

Objective: Student will discuss that things found in public places should not be touched.

Subject: Science/Health **Mode:** Discussion **Training Zone:** [U] Conclusion	**Readiness Factor:** [2] Daily Living **Readiness Factor Category:** [e] Safety and Security

Sc 91: Letting scabs heal

FUTR Tool: 105
PACT: yes

Supplies: None

Discuss that scabs are one of the body's natural healing procedures, and that, as a rule, they should be left in place to do their healing work until they are ready to fall off on their own. Explain that picking scabs off can slow the healing process and sometimes result in bigger scars. Point out that, in some situations, a doctor will advise a patient to remove a scab and, if that happens to you, you should do as the doctor says.

Ask volunteers to share experiences they have had with scabs.

Objective: Student will discuss the purpose of scabs and how to handle them.

Subject: Science/Health **Mode:** Discussion **Training Zone:** [A] Analysis	**Readiness Factor:** [3] Personal/Social **Readiness Factor Category:** [l] Health, Diet, and Appearance

Sc 92: Loading electrical outlets properly

FUTR Tool: no
PACT: yes

Supplies: An electrical strip, four conversion plugs that each allow multiple plugs to plug into one outlet

Show students how the strip and the conversion plugs can all be plugged into one outlet thus allowing 15 or 20 (count your total possible) items to plug into one two-plug outlet. Explain that using power strips is usually acceptable, but using multiple converters along with a power strip is definitely an overload. Also, using multiple converters without a power strip would also most likely cause an overload situation. In addition, point that, when several items with high electrical demand are plugged into a power strip, even a single power strip is sometimes an overload. Explain that, one way to know for sure that a plug is overloaded is if it feels warm, or if it trips the breaker.

Objective: Student will watch an example of an overloaded outlet.

Subject: Science/Health **Mode:** Demonstration **Training Zone:** [L] Logic	**Readiness Factor:** [2] Daily Living **Readiness Factor Category:** [e] Safety and Security

Sc 93: **Making a regular exercise plan**

FUTR Tool: no
PACT: yes

Supplies: None

As a group, brainstorm ways to build exercise into a busy life. Make sure to include ideas such as choose some recreational activities that double as exercise, join a gym and go on a regular schedule, get up one hour earlier and exercise before work or school, exercise during at least one TV show at night.

Objective: Student will help brainstorm ways to build exercise into a busy life.

Subject: Science/Health **Mode:** Brainstorming **Training Zone:** [O] Organization	**Readiness Factor:** [3] Personal/Social **Readiness Factor Category:** [I] Health, Diet, and Appearance

Sc 94: **Making choices when pregnant**

FUTR Tool: no
PACT: no

Supplies: None

Discuss that pregnant women have to take care of both themselves and their babies. As a group, brainstorm a list of activities that people might normally do, but that would not be a good idea for a pregnant person to do.

[Some possible responses: ride wild fair rides, run marathons, drink alcohol, smoke cigarettes, wear tight clothes, take over-the-counter medications without a doctor's advice]

Objective: Student will discuss activities that are not a good idea for pregnant people.

Subject: Science/Health **Mode:** Discussion **Training Zone:** [R] Responsibility	**Readiness Factor:** [3] Personal/Social **Readiness Factor Category:** [I] Health, Diet, and Appearance

Sc 95: **Making health decisions**

FUTR Tool: 107
PACT: yes

Supplies: None

Ask students to say "stay home" or "go to school" for each of the following students to tell which of the kids should stay home and which should go to school.

- Matt has a temperature of 98.6° [go]
- Antoine has a headache [go]
- Maisy has a temperature of 102.5° [stay]
- Jason's nose will not stop bleeding [stay]
- Liza is tired. [go]
- Anna is in a wheel chair. [go]
- Beth is upset with a friend [go]
- Dino has five stitches. [go]
- Garth is too dizzy to walk. [stay]
- Richard has the hiccups [go]
- Lynette woke up with blood from her ear all over her pillow [stay]

Objective: Student will decide whether different conditions warrant staying home from school.

Subject: Science/Health **Mode:** Oral Response **Training Zone:** [U] Conclusion	**Readiness Factor:** [3] Personal/Social **Readiness Factor Category:** [I] Health, Diet, and Appearance

Sc 96: Making non-driving weather-related decisions

FUTR Tool: no
PACT: yes

Supplies: None

Ask students to answer the following questions:

1. What can a person who sunburns easily do to keep from getting sunburned? [Use sun screen, stay out of the sun, wear protective clothing]
2. When, if ever, is it too hot to take a long walk? [Anything over 80° or 90°]
3. Children sometimes enjoy playing in the rain. During what kind of rainstorm should they not be allowed to play outside? [Heavy, flooding rain OR Rain with lightning]
4. When should you take an umbrella with you even if it isn't raining? [Looks like rain, cloudy, weather report calls for rain]

Objective: Student will answer weather-related questions.

Subject: Science/Health **Mode:** Oral Response **Training Zone:** [U] Conclusion	**Readiness Factor:** [2] Daily Living **Readiness Factor Category:** [e] Safety and Security

Sc 97: Noticing changing moles

FUTR Tool: no
PACT: yes

Supplies: None

Draw a human arm on the board. Draw a mole on the arm. Discuss that many people have moles that are not a problem, but if you have a mole that changes, you should have a doctor check it out, because it could be a sign of a problem. Draw three more arms on the board. On one of them, and in the same spot as on the first arm, draw a mole that is a little bigger than the first mole. On another of the arms, draw a mole that is darker. On the third arm, draw a mole that is a different shape. Discuss that moles can change in size, color, and shape.

Objective: Student will see how moles can change and will discuss the need to see a doctor.

Subject: Science/Health **Mode:** Demonstration **Training Zone:** [V] Observation	**Readiness Factor:** [3] Personal/Social **Readiness Factor Category:** [l] Health, Diet, and Appearance

Sc 98: Performing basic first aid

FUTR Tool: 102
PACT: yes

Supplies: None

Divide the class into small teams. Ask each team to role play one of the following basic first aid situations.

1. Taking care of an irritating mosquito bite [Anti-itch medication, bandaid]
2. Taking care of a sliver [tweezers, needle]
3. Taking care of a sunburn [sunburn spray, vinegar, lotion]
4. Taking care of a skinned knee [soap and water, disinfectant cream, bandaid]
5. Taking care of a small cut [soap and water, disinfectant cream, bandaid]
6. Taking care of a simple burn [ice]
7. Taking care of a slightly turned ankle [sit, leg up, ice]

Objective: Student will role play basic first aid treatments.

Subject: Science/Health **Mode:** Role Play **Training Zone:** [M] Manipulation	**Readiness Factor:** [3] Personal/Social **Readiness Factor Category:** [l] Health, Diet, and Appearance

Sc 99: **Planning yard and garden work**

FUTR Tool: no
PACT: yes

Supplies: None

Divide the class into twelve teams. Assign each team one of the months and ask teams to draw pictures showing typical yard or garden work during their months.

[Depending on climate, students might show these activities in logical months: mowing grass, raking leaves, pruning bushes and trees, shoveling snow, planting flowers, tilling a garden, planting a garden, weeding a garden, harvesting a garden, pulling dead plants out of a garden, edging a lawn, watering a lawn or garden or landscaping, picking up sticks, fertilizing, aerating, gutter cleaning, cleaning up piles or litter or clutter]

Objective: Student will draw a picture of seasonal yard work.

Subject: Science/Health	**Readiness Factor:** [3] Personal/Social
Mode: Drawing	**Readiness Factor Category:** [j] Leisure/Desires/Choices
Training Zone: [O] Organization	

Sc 100: **Predicting whether an item will float**

FUTR Tool: no
PACT: no

Supplies: A small tub full of water, small "do they float?" items made of materials such as wood, plastic, rock or brick, paper, metal, concrete, glass, fabric, rubber, styrofoam

Place the tub of water and the "do they float" items where students can work with them. Have a student choose one of the items, say what it is made of, predict if it will float or not, and then try it. Repeat with each item and different students.

Objective: Student will experiment with different items to see if they will float.

Subject: Science/Health	**Readiness Factor:** [2] Daily Living
Mode: Action	**Readiness Factor Category:** [d] Household Care and/or Chores
Training Zone: [L] Logic	

Sc 101: **Preparing food**

FUTR Tool: 100
PACT: yes

Supplies: None

Ask volunteers to explain the steps involved in making food items they know how to make. Ask them to list the needed ingredients before they explain how to make the dish. For each volunteer, ask for a second volunteer to write the steps as they are given. Discuss that writing ingredients and food-preparation steps is the same as writing a recipe and that it is a good way to be sure you can make the dish yourself later.

Objective: Student will share steps to make a specific food item and/or write a recipe as another student explains it.

Subject: Science/Health	**Readiness Factor:** [2] Daily Living
Mode: Action	**Readiness Factor Category:** [d] Household Care and/or Chores
Training Zone: [M] Manipulation	

Sc 102: **Preparing for season changes**

FUTR Tool: no
PACT: yes

Supplies: None

Discuss typical tasks that people in your area perform as they move from one season to the next. Make sure to include ideas such as those listed below.

1. Winter turns to Spring: Rake leaves, sticks, and debris; plant spring flowers
2. Spring turns to Summer: Plant garden, get lawn mower ready, get patio furniture out, fill pool
3. Summer turns to Fall: Clean out finished garden plants, drain pool
4. Fall turns to Winter: Put patio furniture away, rake leaves, make sure snow blower is ready

Objective: Student will discuss typical tasks that people perform to get ready for the next season.

Subject: Science/Health **Mode:** Discussion **Training Zone:** [F] Flexibility	**Readiness Factor:** [2] Daily Living **Readiness Factor Category:** [d] Household Care and/or Chores

Sc 103: **Preventing athlete's foot**

FUTR Tool: no
PACT: no

Supplies: None

Discuss that athlete's foot is a painful foot condition that is easily spread in damp areas where lots of people are barefoot, such as a locker room. Tell students they should wear shoes, such as flip flops, at all times while in a locker room—even in the shower. Invite volunteers to share athlete-foot experiences.

Objective: Student will discuss athlete's foot and how to prevent it.

Subject: Science/Health **Mode:** Discussion **Training Zone:** [C] Conscientiousness	**Readiness Factor:** [3] Personal/Social **Readiness Factor Category:** [l] Health, Diet, and Appearance

Sc 104: **Preventing household problems**

FUTR Tool: 78
PACT: yes

Supplies: None

Divide the class into four teams. Ask each team to role play one of the following problems as well as explain how to avoid the problem.

1. You are cooking soup. You run to the store, and the soup boils over while you are gone. [Do not leave the house while food is cooking on the stove.]
2. You come downstairs to get a drink of water during the night and slip on your tennis shoes. [Do not leave items such as shoes and toys on steps or in walking paths.]
3. Your niece spills the bleach in her lap. It burns her leg, ruins her clothes, and ruins the carpet. [Keep cleaners and other potentially dangerous products out of the reach of children.]
4. You are too full to eat your whole sandwich, so you leave it on the table. Later, ants are crawling on it. [Keep food in the refrigerator or in containers and keep the kitchen clean.]

Objective: Student will role play a household hold problem and a possible solution.

Subject: Science/Health **Mode:** Role Play **Training Zone:** [L] Logic	**Readiness Factor:** [2] Daily Living **Readiness Factor Category:** [d] Household Care and/or Chores

Sc 105: Protecting a kitchen counter

FUTR Tool: no
PACT: yes

Supplies: None

Ask volunteers to describe kitchen counter problems they have seen such as s burns, scratches, chips, and stains. Discuss that some kitchen counter materials are stronger and more chip-resistant than others. Discuss steps to take to make sure you do not harm a kitchen counter. Include ideas such as these:

- Use hotpads or boards to protect the counter against hot pans.
- Be careful not to drop heavy things on the counter.
- Always use a cutting board when using a knife.
- Wipe up spilled foods immediately.

Objective: Student will discuss steps to take to protect a kitchen counter.

Subject: Science/Health **Mode:** Discussion **Training Zone:** [L] Logic	**Readiness Factor:** [2] Daily Living **Readiness Factor Category:** [d] Household Care and/or Chores

Sc 106: Protecting against frost bite

FUTR Tool: no
PACT: no

Supplies: None

Ask students to touch these body parts as you call them out: nose, cheeks, chin, all 10 fingers, all 10 toes, soles of feet, heels. Point out that body extremities, such as those they have just touched, are particularly susceptible to frost bite when you are outside in very cold temperatures. Make sure students understand that frostbite is when a body part partially freezes or completely freezes. Explain that you can protect these body parts in extreme cold temperatures by keeping them covered, keeping them dry, moving those that can move, staying outdoors for only short periods of time.

Objective: Student will identify body parts that are susceptible to frost bite and will discuss how to protect body parts from frost bite.

Subject: Science/Health **Mode:** Action **Training Zone:** [L] Logic	**Readiness Factor:** [3] Personal/Social **Readiness Factor Category:** [l] Health, Diet, and Appearance

Sc 107: Protecting your ears from loud noises

FUTR Tool: no
PACT: no

Supplies: None

As a group, brainstorm ways to deal with noise overload. Include ideas such as the following:

- Limit your exposure.
- Wear ear plugs or stuff pieces of cotton or tissue in your ears.
- Keep your distance.
- Cover your ears with your hands.
- Hold pillows over your ears.
- Take frequent breaks from the noisy area.
- If you have control when listening to music, turn the volume down and keep it down most of the time. Listening to loud music for a short time (like during one song) is usually not harmful.

Objective: Student will help identify ways to protect her ears from loud noises.

Subject: Science/Health **Mode:** Brainstorming **Training Zone:** [L] Logic	**Readiness Factor:** [3] Personal/Social **Readiness Factor Category:** [l] Health, Diet, and Appearance

Sc 108: Protecting your skin

FUTR Tool: no
PACT: yes

Supplies: None

Divide the class into nine teams. Ask each team to role play of these skin-protection ideas:

1. Use sunscreen or clothing to prevent sun burn.
2. Use lotion after bathing and to help chapped skin.
3. Use gloves to protect hands when using harsh products.
4. Wear gloves when doing garden and yard work.
5. Wear gloves when lifting heavy or sharp-edged things.
6. Wear gloves or mittens in cold weather.
7. Keep your hands clean and dry.
8. Avoid foods, lotions, or creams that make you break out.
9. Wear shirts under sweaters that itch.

Objective: Student will role play a skin-protection idea.

Subject: Science/Health **Mode:** Role Play **Training Zone:** [R] Responsibility	**Readiness Factor:** [3] Personal/Social **Readiness Factor Category:** [l] Health, Diet, and Appearance

Sc 109: Putting batteries in correctly

FUTR Tool: no
PACT: no

Supplies: None

Draw a typical battery case and battery on the board. Point out the "+" and "−" ends. Also, point out the little projection at the "+" end of the battery and how it matches the shape on the battery case. Discuss that most battery cases have either the "+" and "−" or the battery shape as clues and that some have both. Explain that, if neither clue is given, you should put the flat end of the battery next to the spring or springy bent piece of metal and put the projection end next to the metal contact point.

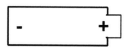 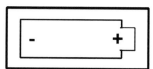

Objective: Student will discuss how to put batteries in correctly.

Subject: Science/Health **Mode:** Demonstration **Training Zone:** [V] Observation	**Readiness Factor:** [2] Daily Living **Readiness Factor Category:** [d] Household Care and/or Chores

Sc 110: Reacting when something breaks or spills

FUTR Tool: no
PACT: yes

Supplies: None

Ask volunteers to describe times when something broke or spilled. In each case, discuss how to clean it up and why it is important to clean it up in a timely fashion.

Answer: Some possible reasons why it is important to clean breaks or spills in a timely fashion:

- So no one gets hurt
- So nothing is stained
- So the house is not a mess
- So it doesn't draw ants or other animals

Objective: Student will discuss how to clean breaks or spills and why the cleaning should be done in a timely fashion.

Subject: Science/Health **Mode:** Oral Response **Training Zone:** [U] Conclusion	**Readiness Factor:** [2] Daily Living **Readiness Factor Category:** [e] Safety and Security

Sc 111: **Reading a thermometer**

FUTR Tool: no
PACT: yes

Supplies: None

Draw samples of a traditional thermometer and a digital thermometer (ear or mouth version) on the board. Ask a volunteer to read the digital thermometer. Make sure volunteer reads "one hundred point two degrees fahrenheit." Then, ask another volunteer to fill in the mercury column so that the traditional thermometer also reads 100.2°F. Discuss that, today, most people use digital thermometers.

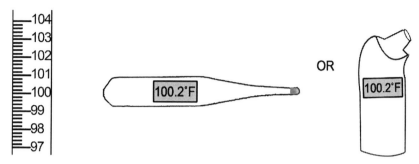

Objective: Student will read traditional and digital thermometers.

Subject: Science/Health **Mode:** Action **Training Zone:** [V] Observation	**Readiness Factor:** [3] Personal/Social **Readiness Factor Category:** [l] Health, Diet, and Appearance

---

Sc 112: **Recognizing a safe tire tread**

FUTR Tool: no
PACT: no

Supplies: None

Discuss that a tire's tread is the surface of the tire that touches the road and that safe tires have treads that are distinctly notched. Explain that worn-down treads allow tires to slip and slide too easily. Draw the four treads shown below and ask volunteers to identify each as safe or not safe.

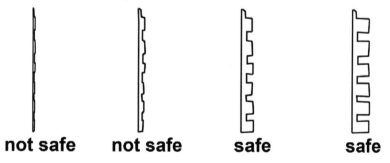

not safe   **not safe**   **safe**   **safe**

Objective: Student will identify tire treads as safe or not safe.

Subject: Science/Health **Mode:** Oral Response **Training Zone:** [U] Conclusion	**Readiness Factor:** [2] Daily Living **Readiness Factor Category:** [e] Safety and Security

Sc 113: **Recognizing common baking ingredients**

FUTR Tool: no
PACT: yes

Supplies: Collection of common baking ingredients (can be empty containers or packages)

Ask volunteers to identify a collection of common baking ingredients. Include items such as those below:

sugar	flour	eggs	milk	cinnamon
salt	pepper	soda	cocoa	yeast
vanilla	ginger	cloves	baking powder	brown sugar

Objective: Student will identify common baking ingredients.

Subject: Science/Health **Mode:** Hands-On **Training Zone:** [V] Observation	**Readiness Factor:** [2] Daily Living **Readiness Factor Category:** [d] Household Care and/or Chores

---

Sc 114: **Recognizing durable materials**

FUTR Tool: no
PACT: no

Supplies: Collect the list of items in numbers 1-5 below.

Place the following sets of items together and ask a volunteer to rank each set in order from most to least durable.

1. cloth purse, fake-leather purse, leather purse
2. flip-flop, non-leather dress shoe, tennis shoe
3. manila folder, non-glossy two-pocket folder, glossy two-pocket folder
4. thin-fabric pants, medium-thick-fabric pants, denim pants
5. knee high nylons, dress socks, gym socks

Objective: Student will rank items in order from most to least durable.

Subject: Science/Health **Mode:** Hands-On **Training Zone:** [V] Observation	**Readiness Factor:** [2] Daily Living **Readiness Factor Category:** [f] Shopping and Eating at Restaurants

---

Sc 115: **Recognizing noise overload**

FUTR Tool: no
PACT: yes

Supplies: None

As a group, brainstorm sounds that are so loud that they could harm a person's hearing. Make sure to include sounds such as very loud music, jet engines, large trucks, some factory equipment, and some construction equipment.

Objective: Student will help identify noise overload situations.

Subject: Science/Health **Mode:** Brainstorming **Training Zone:** [S] Self-Awareness	**Readiness Factor:** [3] Personal/Social **Readiness Factor Category:** [l] Health, Diet, and Appearance

Sc 116: **Recognizing proper posture**

FUTR Tool: no
PACT: yes

Supplies: None

Ask students to freeze—hold all muscles still—in their current positions. Ask them to, without moving, think about whether or not they are using proper posture. Tell them they can move, and then demonstrate while you discuss that proper standing posture incorporates features such as these: standing squarely on both feet, head level, back straight, eyes forward, shoulders back, stomach in. Demonstrate and discuss that sitting posture incorporates features such as these: both hips on a level seat, feet flat on floor, shoulders back, and back straight. Ask students to move and then freeze again and again think about whether or not they are using proper posture.

Objective: Student will evaluate his own posture and will discuss proper posture.

Subject: Science/Health **Mode:** Action, Discussion **Training Zone:** [S] Self-Awareness	**Readiness Factor:** [3] Personal/Social **Readiness Factor Category:** [I] Health, Diet, and Appearance

Sc 117: **Respecting nature**

FUTR Tool: no
PACT: no

Supplies: None

Discuss that Earth will only be a nice place to live if people work to keep it that way. Point out these steps students can take to do their part: use trash cans, recycle, car pool or take public transportation, obey hunting rules, conserve on all products—don't be wasteful. Ask students to draw pictures showing ways they can respect nature.

Objective: Student will draw a picture showing a way she can respect nature.

Subject: Science/Health **Mode:** Drawing **Training Zone:** [C] Conscientiousness	**Readiness Factor:** [3] Personal/Social **Readiness Factor Category:** [k] Community Involvement and Responsibility

Sc 118: **Responding to emergencies**

FUTR Tool: no
PACT: no

Supplies: None

From the news, select a variety of emergencies over a period of a few days. For each, discuss how the emergency came about, and looking at the situation before the emergency happened, discuss best choices for the different people involved.

Objective: Student will discuss how to respond to different emergencies.

Subject: Science/Health **Mode:** Discussion **Training Zone:** [M] Manipulation	**Readiness Factor:** [2] Daily Living **Readiness Factor Category:** [e] Safety and Security

Sc 119: Ridding hair and clothes of static electricity

FUTR Tool: no
PACT: no

Supplies: None

Discuss that static electricity causes hair and clothing to stick together and to stick to other things. Point out that it can also cause you to give or receive shocks when touching other people. Ask volunteers to share experiences involving static electricity. Explain that static electricity can be controlled using actions such as the following: using fabric softener, using a humidifier, rubbing damp hands on clinging clothes, using a purchased anti-cling spray, using hair conditioner.

Objective: Student will discuss causes of, and solutions for, static cling.

Subject: Science/Health **Mode:** Discussion **Training Zone:** [M] Manipulation	**Readiness Factor:** [3] Personal/Social **Readiness Factor Category:** [l] Health, Diet, and Appearance

Sc 120: Searching for a reason a flashlight will not work

FUTR Tool: no
PACT: no

Supplies: Working flashlight

Out of the sight of students, shut the flashlight off and remove the batteries and bulb. Place the batteries and bulb where they are hidden from sight but can easily be gotten by you as needed. Tell students that you do not think the flashlight works. Ask if anyone has an idea how to make it work. Try each idea as it is suggested. Continue asking for suggestions until the flashlight has the bulb and batteries in place, is turned on, and is working.

Objective: Student will help think of steps to take to make a flashlight work.

Subject: Science/Health **Mode:** Demonstration **Training Zone:** [E] Exploration	**Readiness Factor:** [2] Daily Living **Readiness Factor Category:** [d] Household Care and/or Chores

Sc 121: Setting and following a routine

FUTR Tool: no
PACT: no

Supplies: None

Explain that a routine is a regular order in which you do things. Discuss that having a routine is one way to stay organized. Ask students to either describe (in writing) routines they have for part of their school days or to describe hypothetical routines that would help their days be more organized.

Objective: Student will give a written description of a routine that does (or could) help his day be more organized.

Subject: Science/Health **Mode:** Written **Training Zone:** [O] Organization	**Readiness Factor:** [2] Daily Living **Readiness Factor Category:** [g] Time and Order

Sc 122: **Starting to eat after having been sick**

Supplies: None

Ask volunteers to say which of the following pairs of food items would work best when starting to eat after having been sick—and why.

1. burrito or meatloaf [probably meatloaf since it is must less spicy]
2. chicken noodle soup or chili [probably chicken noodle soup since both the noodles and the broth are quite gentle and non-spicy]
3. ice cream or cherry pie [probably ice cream since the cherry pie is more complex and the cherries will be somewhat acidic]
4. toast or waffles [probably toast since waffles usually involve a sweet topping]
5. potato or broccoli [probably potato since it is easier to digest than a green vegetable]

Objective: Student will choose foods that would work best when starting to eat after having been sick.

Subject: Science/Health **Mode:** Oral Response **Training Zone:** [L] Logic	**Readiness Factor:** [3] Personal/Social **Readiness Factor Category:** [l] Health, Diet, and Appearance

Sc 123: **Storing food**

Supplies: None

Divide the class into three teams. Ask each team to make a list of foods that should be stored in each of the following locations: Cupboard (or pantry), freezer, refrigerator. Have teams share some of the items on their lists.

Objective: Student will help make lists of foods that should be stored in a cupboard, freezer, and refrigerator.

Subject: Science/Health **Mode:** Written **Training Zone:** [L] Logic	**Readiness Factor:** [2] Daily Living **Readiness Factor Category:** [e] Safety and Security

Sc 124: **Taking a child for proper medical care**

Supplies: None

Discuss that babies and small children often cry for lots of reasons since, given the lack of capability to use words, crying is a main form of communication for them. Point out that the frequent crying makes it difficult to know when they are just uncomfortable and when they need medical care. Explain that the following symptoms are definite signs of a need for medical care:

- An obvious increase in usual amount of crying
- A fever over 99°
- Unwillingness to eat
- Not sleeping as usual
- Unusual bowels or lack of bowel movements
- Constant tugging at an ear
- Unusual lack of activity

Objective: Student will discuss signs that a baby or child needs medical care.

Subject: Science/Health **Mode:** Discussion **Training Zone:** [R] Responsibility	**Readiness Factor:** [3] Personal/Social **Readiness Factor Category:** [l] Health, Diet, and Appearance

Sc 125: Taking action in response to TV and radio weather warnings

FUTR Tool: no
PACT: no

Supplies: None

Ask students to discuss the best options in the following situations:

1. You are getting ready to drive across town to the mall to do a little "shopping for fun" when you hear that there is a thunderstorm warning for your area. What should you do?

2. The weather report says that ten inches of snow will blanket the area during the night. You normally get up at 6:15 and leave for work at 7:00. What should you do differently tomorrow and why?

3. You have friends coming to visit for the weekend. You are planning to go to a movie Saturday afternoon, go out to eat Saturday night, and go on a picnic on Sunday. You hear that it is supposed to rain on Sunday. How might you change your plans?

Objective: Student will discuss changing plans based on weather reports.

Subject: Science/Health **Mode:** Discussion **Training Zone:** [U] Conclusion	**Readiness Factor:** [2] Daily Living **Readiness Factor Category:** [e] Safety and Security

Sc 126: Taking care of indoor plants

FUTR Tool: no
PACT: yes

Supplies: None

Discuss that you must water indoor plants on a regular schedule to keep them alive. Point out that a logical plan for most plants is to choose a day (such as Monday) and water the plant(s) every week on that day.

Also, discuss that plants need enough water, but not too much water. Tell them that, if the dirt is still wet a week later, the plant has too much water. Explain that you should let a wet-dirt plant dry out before watering it. Then, explain that you should give it less water from then on so the plant can use the water in a week.

Objective: Student will discuss how to care for indoor plants.

Subject: Science/Health **Mode:** Discussion **Training Zone:** [M] Manipulation	**Readiness Factor:** [2] Daily Living **Readiness Factor Category:** [d] Household Care and/or Chores

Sc 127: Taking medication on time

FUTR Tool: no
PACT: no

Supplies: None

Discuss that medications often must be taken on a set schedule, and that remembering to follow the schedule is sometimes difficult. As a group, brainstorm ways to remember to take medications on time. Include ideas such as the following: set a timer, take medication with a meal and keep the medication where you will see it at each meal such as in front of your chair at the table, write yourself a note, ask a friend or family member to help remind you.

Objective: Student will help make a list of ways to remember to take medications on time.

Subject: Science/Health **Mode:** Brainstorming **Training Zone:** [M] Manipulation	**Readiness Factor:** [3] Personal/Social **Readiness Factor Category:** [l] Health, Diet, and Appearance

Sc 128: Taking medication safely

Supplies: None

Discuss that medication can be unsafe in the following situations:

1. When taken along with alcohol or other drugs
2. When taken in incorrect amounts
3. When symptoms do not match the drug's capabilities
4. When you are driving and the warnings indicate that driving is not safe
5. When a prescription drug is taken by someone other than the intended person
6. When a drug that is to be taken with food or liquid is taken without food or liquid

Objective: Student will discuss situations that cause medications to be unsafe.

Subject: Science/Health **Mode:** Discussion **Training Zone:** [C] Conscientiousness	**Readiness Factor:** [3] Personal/Social **Readiness Factor Category:** [l] Health, Diet, and Appearance

Sc 129: Thawing frozen foods safely

Supplies: None

Explain that the safest way to thaw food is by putting it into the refrigerator for a day or two. Discuss that when you want to thaw food more quickly, you can immerse it in water or microwave it a little. Tell students that it is usually not safe to thaw foods by just leaving them on the counter for a day.

Objective: Student will discuss safe ways to thaw frozen foods.

Subject: Science/Health **Mode:** Discussion **Training Zone:** [M] Manipulation	**Readiness Factor:** [2] Daily Living **Readiness Factor Category:** [e] Safety and Security

Sc 130: Treating insect bites

Supplies: Box of bandaids

Discuss that stores sell creams and pills that help stop insect bites from itching. Also, explain that covering insect bites with bandaids can help since the bandaids will stop the bites from being tickled by breezes or touched by clothing.

Give each student a bandaid. Have them each choose a spot on an arm. Ask them to blow on the spots and then to rub clothing over the spots. Then, have them put the bandaids on the spots and repeat the blowing and rubbing. Discuss how much less they can feel the blowing and rubbing when the bandaid is in place. Explain that this protection from breezes and clothing is how a bandaid helps to keep an insect bite from itching by lessening the irritation.

Objective: Student will experiment to see how a bandaid can protect an insect bite from irritation.

Subject: Science/Health **Mode:** Action **Training Zone:** [M] Manipulation	**Readiness Factor:** [3] Personal/Social **Readiness Factor Category:** [l] Health, Diet, and Appearance

Sc 131: Trying not to spread an illness

FUTR Tool: 76
PACT: yes

Supplies: None

Ask students to brainstorm ways that illnesses are spread and how they can avoid spreading illnesses through each of the "spreading methods." Encourage responses such as the following:

1. Spread by mouth: Do not kiss others when you are ill
2. Spread by touch: Keep your hands away from your face, wash your hands often, do not touch other people, do not touch other people's things
3. Spread through the air: Cover your mouth when you talk or cough, look away from people when you cough, moving away from others who are coughing
4. Spread by being around others: Stay home

Objective: Student will help list ways that illnesses are spread and ways to avoid spreading illnesses.

Subject: Science/Health **Mode:** Brainstorming **Training Zone:** [L] Logic	**Readiness Factor:** [3] Personal/Social **Readiness Factor Category:** [l] Health, Diet, and Appearance

Sc 132: Turning car off at gas pump or inside garage

FUTR Tool: no
PACT: no

Supplies: None

Discuss that you should always turn a car off at a gas pump or when inside a closed garage, even if that means you will get too hot or too cold. Explain that a running engine could cause a car to blow up at a gas pump and a car in a closed garage could be deadly because of trapped carbon monoxide.

Objective: Student will discuss the need to turn a car off at a gas pump and inside a closed garage.

Subject: Science/Health **Mode:** Discussion **Training Zone:** [C] Conscientiousness	**Readiness Factor:** [2] Daily Living **Readiness Factor Category:** [h] Transportation/Travel/Worldliness

Sc 133: Understanding causes of stress

FUTR Tool: no
PACT: no

Supplies: None

Discuss that stress can be caused by many different situations. As a group, brainstorm sources of stress. Make sure to include sources in each of the following categories:

1. Loss through death or divorce
2. Hurt feelings
3. Work or school problems
4. Guilt from something you have done
5. Health issues

Objective: Student will help identify some causes of stress.

Subject: Science/Health **Mode:** Brainstorming **Training Zone:** [A] Analysis	**Readiness Factor:** [3] Personal/Social **Readiness Factor Category:** [l] Health, Diet, and Appearance

Sc 134: **Understanding common illnesses and diseases**

FUTR Tool: 98
PACT: yes

Supplies: None

As a group, make a chart of illnesses and diseases on the board. Include common and uncommon ones such as flu, cold, leg cramps, broken neck, fever, pneumonia, cancer, AIDS, strep throat, scarlet fever, ear infection, diabetes, heart attack, kidney failure, glaucoma, and alzheimer's. Next to each illness or disease, use tallies to mark the number of students who have had the illness or disease. Discuss that common illnesses and diseases are those that most people get and that uncommon ones are those that most people do not get. Circle each common illness or disease.

Objective: Student will help make a chart of illnesses and diseases and decide which are common and which are not.

Subject: Science/Health	**Readiness Factor:** [3] Personal/Social
Mode: Graph or Chart	**Readiness Factor Category:** [l] Health, Diet, and Appearance
Training Zone: [E] Exploration	

Sc 135: **Understanding heredity**

FUTR Tool: no
PACT: no

Supplies: None

Discuss it is common to inherit colorings and shapes of different body parts from your parents. Ask students to each make a chart on a piece of paper with these headings: hair color, eye color, hand-shape (short wide fingers, long thin fingers, etc.), skin tone, nose shape (long and pointed, short and flat, etc). Down the side, have them put ME, Mom, Dad. Ask them to fill in as much of the chart as they can and then to take it home and finish it. Then, under the Mom and Dad columns, ask them to circle each trait that they think they inherited.

Objective: Student will create a chart to focus on traits inherited from his parents.

Subject: Science/Health	**Readiness Factor:** [3] Personal/Social
Mode: Graph or Chart	**Readiness Factor Category:** [i] Relationships
Training Zone: [A] Analysis	

Sc 136: **Understanding hospital conditions**

FUTR Tool: no
PACT: yes

Supplies: None

Write these hospital health conditions on the board: good, fair, stable, serious, guarded, touch and go, intensive care, critical, life-threatening, non-responsive. Ask volunteers to describe accident victims that fit into each category.

Objective: Student will describe accident victims that fit specific hospital health conditions.

Subject: Science/Health	**Readiness Factor:** [3] Personal/Social
Mode: Discussion	**Readiness Factor Category:** [l] Health, Diet, and Appearance
Training Zone: [O] Organization	

Sc 137: Understanding how to practice safe sex

FUTR Tool: no
PACT: no

Supplies: None

Discuss that safe sex means one of the following:

1. You do not have sex until after you and your partner have both been tested so you know you are disease-free. Then you only have sex with each other. These choices and actions would theoretically allow you to practice safe sex for life. However, one of you could get AIDS through a channel such as a blood transfusion.

2. Use a condom when you have sex.

Objective: Student will discuss safe-sex choices.

Subject: Science/Health **Mode:** Discussion **Training Zone:** [S] Self-Awareness	**Readiness Factor:** [3] Personal/Social **Readiness Factor Category:** [l] Health, Diet, and Appearance

Sc 138: Understanding light bulbs

FUTR Tool: no
PACT: no

Supplies: Several types of lightbulbs and their packages

Show students the different lightbulbs. From the packages, read how the lightbulbs vary and the intended uses for each. Make sure to discuss the watts for each bulb. Explain that many lamps call for a 60 watt bulb, and some are rated for up to 100 watts. Explain that using a higher wattage bulb than a lamp is approved for might result in the lamp getting too hot and being damaged or unsafe.

Objective: Student will study different lightbulbs and discuss their differences and uses.

Subject: Science/Health **Mode:** Hands-On **Training Zone:** [V] Observation	**Readiness Factor:** [2] Daily Living **Readiness Factor Category:** [f] Shopping and Eating at Restaurants

Sc 139: Understanding optical illusions

FUTR Tool: no
PACT: yes

Supplies: None

Discuss that your eyes can play tricks on you, or rather, that some things are not as they seem. On the board, draw the four items below. Make sure to make all four lines the same length and place them randomly so it is not easy to compare their lengths. Ask students to number the items from longest line to shortest line. Then explain that the lines are all the same length—Discuss that the circle, arrows, and upright lines create optical illusions.

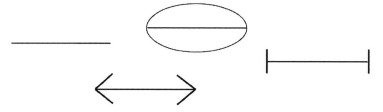

Objective: Student will experience and discuss an optical illusion.

Subject: Science/Health **Mode:** Oral Response **Training Zone:** [L] Logic	**Readiness Factor:** [2] Daily Living **Readiness Factor Category:** [h] Transportation/Travel/Worldliness

Sc 140: Understanding puberty and aging

FUTR Tool: 89
PACT: yes

Supplies: None

Discuss that the human body undergoes a series of changes as it progresses from birth to old age. Ask volunteers to name changes and typical ages for the changes. Make sure they include ideas and average age ranges such as the following:

- Strength to walk—age 1
- Hair grows longer and thicker—ages 2–6
- Head becomes proportionally smaller—ages 2–5
- Toddler voice disappears—ages 4–7

- Physical strength allows for sports—ages 5–10
- Childhood voice disappears—ages 14–22
- Voice lowers (most obvious in boys)—ages 14–21
- Breasts grow (girls)—ages 10–18

Objective: Student will identify human-body changes and typical related ages.

Subject: Science/Health **Mode:** Oral Response **Training Zone:** [V] Observation	**Readiness Factor:** [3] Personal/Social **Readiness Factor Category:** [l] Health, Diet, and Appearance

Sc 141: Understanding talking and traveling

FUTR Tool: 97
PACT: yes

Supplies: None

As a group, brainstorm topics that are too personal to discuss with strangers you meet when traveling.

As a group, brainstorm topics that are OK to discuss with strangers you meet when traveling.

Ask volunteers to role play some of the discussion topics.

Objective: Student will brainstorm some topics that are too personal and some that are OK to discuss with strangers when traveling.

Subject: Science/Health **Mode:** Brainstorming **Training Zone:** [E] Exploration	**Readiness Factor:** [2] Daily Living **Readiness Factor Category:** [h] Transportation/Travel/Worldliness

Sc 142: Understanding the diet implications of eating at home versus at restaurants

FUTR Tool: no
PACT: yes

Supplies: None

Have each student get out a piece of paper. On one half of their papers, ask students to draw what they usually eat for evening meals at their favorite restaurants. On the other half of their papers, ask them to draw what they ate at their last evening meals at home. Discuss that meals made at home are usually lower in quantity, calories, and fat—and therefore are healthier and less likely to make you gain weight. Explain that eating at restaurants once or twice a week usually works out, but that more frequent eating out often begins to create a diet problem.

Objective: Student will draw home and restaurant meals and compare the quantity, calories, and fat in the two meals.

Subject: Science/Health **Mode:** Drawing **Training Zone:** [L] Logic	**Readiness Factor:** [3] Personal/Social **Readiness Factor Category:** [l] Health, Diet, and Appearance

Sc 143: Understanding the four seasons

FUTR Tool: no
PACT: no

Supplies: Four pieces of posterboard; markers

Discuss the weather associated with the four seasons in your area. Discuss areas where the seasons are different from your area. Divide the class into four teams. Ask each team to create a poster depicting one of the four seasons in your local area.

Objective: Student will help create a poster depicting one of the four seasons.

Subject: Science/Health Mode: Drawing Training Zone: [V] Observation	Readiness Factor: [2] Daily Living Readiness Factor Category: [g] Time and Order

Sc 144: Understanding the importance of washing your hands

FUTR Tool: 92
PACT: yes

Supplies: None

Discuss that one way to help fight off illnesses is to wash your hands often, particularly before and after every meal and whenever you touch something that could have an unusual amount of germs on it. As a group, brainstorm a list of things that you might typically touch and that it would be wise to follow with a handwashing. Include ideas such as the following: tennis shoes, remote control, door knobs away from home, chairs at a gathering, seats in a school bus.

As a group, brainstorm a list of problems that can result from failing to wash your hands often enough. Include ideas such as the following: spread illnesses to others, catch illnesses from others, make dirty marks on walls and other things, find that some foods taste bad, get dirt in your mouth.

Objective: Student will help list things that, when touched, should be followed by a handwashing. Also, student will help make a list of problems that can result from failing to wash her hands often enough.

Subject: Science/Health Mode: Brainstorming Training Zone: [Z] Socialization	Readiness Factor: [3] Personal/Social Readiness Factor Category: [l] Health, Diet, and Appearance

Sc 145: Understanding the nature of illnesses

FUTR Tool: 93
PACT: yes

Supplies: None

As a group, brainstorm a list of illnesses along with descriptions of the symptoms of each. Discuss which illnesses on the list people can handle themselves and which require ongoing doctor care.

Objective: Student will help make a list of illnesses along with descriptions of the symptoms of each and whether or not each requires ongoing doctor care.

Subject: Science/Health Mode: Brainstorming Training Zone: [Z] Socialization	Readiness Factor: [3] Personal/Social Readiness Factor Category: [l] Health, Diet, and Appearance

Sc 146: **Understanding the pregnancy process and related issues**

FUTR Tool: no
PACT: no

Supplies: Pictures depicting the stages of pregnancy

Show students pictures depicting the stages of pregnancy. Discuss the overall process and that pregnancy usually begins to show between the 3rd and 5th months. Discuss that pregnant women should have regular check-ups and should follow the doctors' orders along the way. Explain that, in most cases, a pregnant woman can keep working, exercising, and being generally active right up until delivery day. However, point out that, even pregnant women who are very healthy might need to sleep more than they did before their pregnancies.

Objective: Student will discuss the pregnancy process and related issues.

Subject: Science/Health **Mode:** Discussion **Training Zone:** [R] Responsibility	**Readiness Factor:** [3] Personal/Social **Readiness Factor Category:** [l] Health, Diet, and Appearance

Sc 147: **Understanding types of doctors**

FUTR Tool: no
PACT: yes

Supplies: None

Ask students to create simple crossword puzzles using types of doctors (about five across and five down). Make sure they include clues. Then, have them exchange with a partner and solve each other's puzzles. Some types of doctors they might include are pediatrician (babies and children), obstetrician (pregnant women and childbirth), anesthesiologist (anesthesia for surgery), dentist (teeth), bariatrics doctor (weight control), dermatologist (skin), family practitioner (general), hematologist (blood), nephrologist (kidneys), neurologist (nerves), oncologist (cancer), orthopedic (bones and joints), neonatologist (premature babies), ophthalmologist (eyes), psychiatrist (mind), radiologist (x-rays).

Objective: Student will make a crossword puzzle using names of different types of doctors and will then exchange puzzles with a partner and solve the partner's puzzle.

Subject: Science/Health **Mode:** Drawing **Training Zone:** [E] Exploration	**Readiness Factor:** [3] Personal/Social **Readiness Factor Category:** [l] Health, Diet, and Appearance

Sc 148: **Using a lawn mower**

FUTR Tool: no
PACT: no

Supplies: None

Divide the class into two teams. Ask one team to role play using a push lawn mower and the other to role play using a riding lawn mower. Ask the teams to each include dealing with the lawn mowing issues listed below. Have each team include a moderator who explains how the person mowing is handling each obstacle.

Obstacles:

- sticks and rocks
- buildings
- trees
- open grassy areas
- sidewalk
- neighbor's dog
- corners

Objective: Student will help role play a lawn mowing situation.

Subject: Science/Health **Mode:** Role Play **Training Zone:** [M] Manipulation	**Readiness Factor:** [2] Daily Living **Readiness Factor Category:** [d] Household Care and/or Chores

Sc 149: **Using a seat belt**

FUTR Tool: no
PACT: no

Supplies: None

Discuss that safe drivers make it a habit or routine to latch their seatbelts before staring the car. Also, suggest that, before taking off, drivers should wait for passengers to get their seatbelts on.

At their desks, ask students to simultaneously role play putting on a seat belt and then turning the key to start the car.

Objective: Student will both discuss and role play putting a seat belt on before starting a car.

Subject: Science/Health **Mode:** Discussion, Role Play **Training Zone:** [C] Conscientiousness	**Readiness Factor:** [2] Daily Living **Readiness Factor Category:** [h] Transportation/Travel/Worldliness

Sc 150: **Using a vacuum cleaner**

FUTR Tool: no
PACT: no

Supplies: None

Discuss that modern-day vacuum cleaners require simple pushing and pulling as long as the operator pays attention to these issues:

1. Chunks rarely vacuum up well. Pick them up ahead of time.

2. Loud noises are usually a sign that something that should not be there has been sucked into the vacuum cleaner. Shut the vacuum cleaner off right away and look for the problem.

3. If the vacuum cleaner is sluggish or makes the air smell like dirt, the collection compartment is probably full. Turn off the vacuum cleaner and empty the compartment (or insert a new bag).

4. Vacuum cleaners usually have settings for no carpet, low carpet, and high carpet. Choose a setting that matches your floor.

Objective: Student will discuss how to use a vacuum cleaner.

Subject: Science/Health **Mode:** Discussion **Training Zone:** [M] Manipulation	**Readiness Factor:** [2] Daily Living **Readiness Factor Category:** [d] Household Care and/or Chores

Sc 151: **Using an iron**

FUTR Tool: no
PACT: no

Supplies: Iron, ironing board, old wrinkled clothing

Discuss that some fabrics do not wrinkle and therefore do not require ironing, but that other fabrics must be ironed to look nice. Point out that clothing tags often indicate an iron heat level. Also, point out that some fabric can go without being ironed if dried in a dryer and removed before hard-dried. Explain that the air in a dryer often fluffs the wrinkles out and the clothes look quite nice as long as they are removed and folded or hung up right away.

Bring an iron and some old wrinkled clothes to school and let students practice ironing. Make sure they read the tags before starting.

Objective: Student will discuss issues about ironing and will iron some clothing.

Subject: Science/Health **Mode:** Discussion, Action **Training Zone:** [M] Manipulation	**Readiness Factor:** [2] Daily Living **Readiness Factor Category:** [d] Household Care and/or Chores

Sc 152: **Using appropriate cleaning solutions**

FUTR Tool: 99
PACT: yes

Supplies: An assortment of cleaning solutions—see ideas below

Display a collection of cleaning solutions (empty containers are fine) such as a glass cleaner, dusting spray, toilet bowl cleaner, scrubbing cleanser, laundry detergent, dishwashing liquid (for hand washing), dishwashing detergent (for dishwashers), bar soap, and shampoo. Number the items and ask students to number their papers to match. Then, ask them to identify a use for each cleanser.

Objective: Student will identify uses for different cleansers.

Subject: Science/Health **Mode:** Written **Training Zone:** [E] Exploration	**Readiness Factor:** [2] Daily Living **Readiness Factor Category:** [d] Household Care and/or Chores

Sc 153: **Using basic appliances and tools**

FUTR Tool: 101
PACT: yes

Supplies: Straight screwdriver, phillips screwdriver, board with screws (straight and phillips), pliers, pencil, hammer, nail, board, pencil sharpener

Ask students each to do each of the following tasks:

1. Use a screwdriver to remove a screw and then put it back in.
2. Use a pliers to hold a pencil.
3. Use a hammer to hammer a nail part way into a board, and then use the hammer to pull it back out.
4. Use a pencil sharpener to sharpen a pencil.

Objective: Student will use some basic appliances and tools.

Subject: Science/Health **Mode:** Action **Training Zone:** [M] Manipulation	**Readiness Factor:** [2] Daily Living **Readiness Factor Category:** [d] Household Care and/or Chores

Sc 154: **Using bleach safely**

FUTR Tool: no
PACT: no

Supplies: None

Discuss that bleach (and some other powerful cleansers) will remove color instantly. Point out that you want to take great care to avoid dribbling bleach on fabric or carpet unintentionally. Ask volunteers to share examples of times when bleach (or another powerful cleanser) caused unplanned color removal. Explain that bleach works best when used to whiten cotton whites. Tell students they should always carefully read the instructions on a bleach container.

Objective: Student will discuss how to use bleach safely.

Subject: Science/Health **Mode:** Discussion **Training Zone:** [V] Observation	**Readiness Factor:** [2] Daily Living **Readiness Factor Category:** [d] Household Care and/or Chores

Sc 155: Using coasters to protect furniture

FUTR Tool: no
PACT: no

Supplies: An 8-1/2 x 11 piece of cardboard for each student, paints or markers, scissors, round items for tracing

Discuss that furniture, particularly wooden furniture, can easily be damaged by wet circles left from the bottom of a drink. Explain that you should use coasters to protect your own nice furniture, and when at others' houses, you should always ask your host if he or she would like you to use a coaster. Discuss that coasters are made of different materials such as cardboard, plastic, cork, wood, and ceramic. Ask students to decorate and cut out a set of six coasters. Have them trace round items to make circles or use their rulers to measure out squares.

Objective: Student will discuss the purpose of coasters and will then create a set of coasters.

Subject: Science/Health **Mode:** Discussion, Action **Training Zone:** [C] Conscientiousness	**Readiness Factor:** [2] Daily Living **Readiness Factor Category:** [d] Household Care and/or Chores

Sc 156: Using dew levels to predict rain

FUTR Tool: no
PACT: no

Supplies: None

Explain to students that, one way to predict a no-rain day is to check to see if the grass has a heavy dew. Tell them that, when grass has a heavy dew, there is very little chance of rain that day.

Objective: Student will discuss the relationship between dew and rain.

Subject: Science/Health **Mode:** Discussion **Training Zone:** [V] Observation	**Readiness Factor:** [3] Personal/Social **Readiness Factor Category:** [h] Transportation/Travel/Worldliness

Sc 157: Using good posture

FUTR Tool: no
PACT: no

Supplies: None

Have your students practice standing, walking, and sitting with good posture. Ask all students to stand next to their desks and to make sure they are standing squarely on both feet with their heads level, their backs straight, their eyes forward, their shoulders back, and their stomachs in. Then, ask all students to walk forward ten steps and focus on keeping their heads up, their shoulders back, their stomachs in, and their backs straight while they swing their hands in unison with their legs. Finally, ask all students to sit down and keep their hips level, feet flat on the floor, shoulders back, and backs straight.

Ask them to pay special attention to their standing, walking, and sitting posture for one week.

Objective: Student will practice good standing, walking, and sitting posture.

Subject: Science/Health **Mode:** Action **Training Zone:** [S] Self-Awareness	**Readiness Factor:** [3] Personal/Social **Readiness Factor Category:** [l] Health, Diet, and Appearance

Sc 158: **Using kitchen appliances**

FUTR Tool: no
PACT: yes

Supplies: None

As a group, brainstorm a list of kitchen appliances such as blenders, can openers, slow cookers, mixers, electric knives, electric frying pans, electric griddles, and bread makers. Ask volunteers to describe a use for each appliance, and then role play actually using it.

Objective: Student will help make a list of kitchen appliances, describe how to use them, and role play using them.

Subject: Science/Health **Mode:** Brainstorming, Role Play **Training Zone:** [M] Manipulation	**Readiness Factor:** [2] Daily Living **Readiness Factor Category:** [d] Household Care and/or Chores

Sc 159: **Using taste words**

FUTR Tool: no
PACT: no

Supplies: Enough of these foods for each student to have a tiny taste: lemon, honey, coffer grounds, white bread or plain potato, fish, spice cake, jalapenos, fresh lemonade

Make sure students understand common taste words by using descriptive words as they taste each of these foods (or logical substitutions): lemon (sour), honey (sweet), coffee grounds (bitter), plain white sliced bread or potatoes with nothing added (drab), fish (salty), spice cake (spicy/flavorful), jalapenos (spicy/hot), fresh-squeezed lemonade that is sweetened (tangy).

If using real foods is problematic, ask students questions such as the following:

1. Which is often sour, lemonade or 7-up?
2. Which tastes sweet, milk or apple pie?
3. Which tastes bitter, potatoes or coffee grounds?

Objective: Student will taste different foods to help understand taste words.

Subject: Science/Health **Mode:** Action **Training Zone:** [U] Conclusion	**Readiness Factor:** [3] Personal/Social **Readiness Factor Category:** [l] Health, Diet, and Appearance

Sc 160: **Using the freezer to keep non-freezer foods fresh**

FUTR Tool: no
PACT: no

Supplies: None

Discuss that a freezer can help to keep some non-freezer foods fresh, such as nuts, cheese, and sunflower seeds. Tell students that, if you have a food that gets stale or old faster than you can eat it, you should experiment with keeping it in the freezer.

Objective: Student will discuss how to use the freezer to keep some non-freezer foods fresh.

Subject: Science/Health **Mode:** Discussion **Training Zone:** [F] Flexibility	**Readiness Factor:** [2] Daily Living **Readiness Factor Category:** [d] Household Care and/or Chores

Sc 161: Using vending machines

FUTR Tool: no
PACT: yes

Supplies: None

As a group, brainstorm foods and drinks that are available in vending machines. Include choices such as soda, coffee, lemonade, juices, water, milk, candy bars, bag candies, chips, sandwiches, gum, fruit, crackers, pastries, nuts, and granola bars. Discuss how different vending machines work and how much different items cost.

Objective: Student will help list foods and drinks that are available in vending machines and will discuss vending machine procedures and prices.

Subject: Science/Health **Mode:** Brainstorming **Training Zone:** [E] Exploration	**Readiness Factor:** [2] Daily Living **Readiness Factor Category:** [g] Time and Order

Sc 162: Using your teeth properly

FUTR Tool: no
PACT: no

Supplies: None

Discuss that teeth are for chewing food and can be harmed when used in other ways such as in the following types of activities:

Holding things (Example: pen or screwdriver)

Breaking things (Example: a string or a plastic shopping tag holder)

Opening things (Example: a bag of chips, a can of soda, or a walnut)

Objective: Student will discuss what teeth should and should not be used for.

Subject: Science/Health **Mode:** Discussion **Training Zone:** [C] Conscientiousness	**Readiness Factor:** [2] Daily Living **Readiness Factor Category:** [e] Safety and Security

Sc 163: Visiting a hospital patient

FUTR Tool: no
PACT: no

Supplies: None

Put a small circle on the board and write "visiting a hospital patient" inside it. Draw lines out from the circle and, as a group, add ideas such as the following:

1. Before going to visit a patient at a hospital, you should call to make sure that the privacy laws will allow you to get in.
2. When you are able to visit a patient, you need to make sure that you keep the patient's best interests upper most in your mind.
3. Keep in mind that a patient might get too tired for visitors.
4. Be ready to help since a patient might need assistance to do something.
5. Make sure to stay out of the way of the medical staff.
6. Be considerate so you do not infringe on a patient's roommate.

Objective: Student will help make a web showing issues related to visiting a hospital patient.

Subject: Science/Health **Mode:** Graph or Chart **Training Zone:** [V] Observation	**Readiness Factor:** [2] Daily Living **Readiness Factor Category:** [e] Safety and Security

Sc 164: **Washing dishes**

FUTR Tool: no
PACT: yes

Supplies: None

Divide the class into two teams. Ask one team to role play washing dishes by hand and the other to role play washing dishes in a dish washer. Tell them to begin and end with an empty sink or an empty dishwasher. Have each team provide a moderator to explain the actions that are being role played.

Objective: Student will role play washing dishes.

Subject: Science/Health **Mode:** Role Play **Training Zone:** [M] Manipulation	**Readiness Factor:** [2] Daily Living **Readiness Factor Category:** [d] Household Care and/or Chores

Sc 165: **Washing fresh produce**

FUTR Tool: no
PACT: no

Supplies: None

Discuss that you should wash all fresh produce before eating it. Explain that, for example, even if an apple looks shiny and great, you should wash it, because you do not know what has touched it or where it has been—so you do not know if it is safe to eat or not. Make sure students understand to wash produce thoroughly under strong running water.

Objective: Student will discuss how and why to wash fresh produce.

Subject: Science/Health **Mode:** Discussion **Training Zone:** [M] Manipulation	**Readiness Factor:** [2] Daily Living **Readiness Factor Category:** [e] Safety and Security

Sc 166: **Washing hands before eating**

FUTR Tool: no
PACT: no

Supplies: None

Ask volunteers to explain how you can wash your hands before eating in each of the situations below. Look for answers such as use the kitchen sink, go to the rest room, use a wet wipe, use waterless handcleaner, and use a water fountain.

1. at home
2. in the school cafeteria
3. in a restaurant
4. at a street vendor
5. in a mall

Objective: Student will help identify ways of washing hands when eating in different locations

Subject: Science/Health **Mode:** Discussion **Training Zone:** [C] Conscientiousness	**Readiness Factor:** [3] Personal/Social **Readiness Factor Category:** [l] Health, Diet, and Appearance

Sc 167: **Watching car oil and temperature gauges**

FUTR Tool: 90
PACT: yes

Supplies: A car either in the school automotive shop or parking lot OR pictures of car oil and temperature gauges.

Discuss that car oil and temperature gauges are one way to know if a car has a serious problem and that keeping an eye on them is one way to keep a car from having a problem. Go to the automotive shop or parking lot and show students what some gauges look like and what to watch for.

If going out to the shop or parking lot is a problem, take a picture of the dials along with some of the surrounding car parts. Use the picture as an overhead and show students what some gauges look like and what to watch for.

Objective: Student will see car oil and temperature gauges and will learn what they mean and how to watch them.

Subject: Science/Health **Mode:** Demonstration **Training Zone:** [V] Observation	**Readiness Factor:** [2] Daily Living **Readiness Factor Category:** [h] Transportation/Travel/Worldliness

Sc 168: **Watching for drug side effects**

FUTR Tool: no
PACT: no

Supplies: None

Discuss that, when taking prescription or over-the-counter drugs, you could have a negative reaction. Explain that a negative reaction is a side effect that makes you do things such as swell up, get a rash, have trouble breathing, be unable to sleep, vomit, be dizzy, and lose your appetite. Point out that, when you have an unexpected or bad reaction to medication, you should call your doctor. Make sure students understand that drugs that are not working correctly in your body can be very dangerous, possibly even deadly.

Objective: Student will discuss how to recognize and handle drug side effects.

Subject: Science/Health **Mode:** Discussion **Training Zone:** [S] Self-Awareness	**Readiness Factor:** [3] Personal/Social **Readiness Factor Category:** [l] Health, Diet, and Appearance

Sc 169: **Watching for use-by dates when grocery shopping**

FUTR Tool: no
PACT: no

Supplies: Several empty food boxes or bags with use-by dates; numbers on pieces of paper (see below)

Tape a number onto each food box and bag. Have students each get out a piece of paper and number to match the number of food boxes and bags. Pass the boxes and bags around the room and ask students to find the use-by dates and write them on their papers next to the correct numbers.

Objective: Student will locate use-by dates on a group of food products.

Subject: Science/Health **Mode:** Action **Training Zone:** [V] Observation	**Readiness Factor:** [2] Daily Living **Readiness Factor Category:** [d] Household Care and/or Chores

Expressive Literacy

Life Skill Lessons

Table of Contents: *Expressive Literacy*

EI 1: Addressing a problem with a purchase

FUTR Tool: 124
PACT: yes

Supplies: None

Divide the class into four teams. Ask each team to role play a conversation at a store service counter about one of the problems below.

1. You bought a DVD player three weeks ago, and now it is not working right.
2. You receive a cooler for a gift. About four months later you go to use it for the first time and discover that it leaks. It still has a tag on it, so you know it came from a certain local store.
3. You buy a bag of candy. When you get to the car, you realize the bag has a hole in the side.
4. You buy some things at a department store. When you get home, you realize you are missing several things that are on your sales slip. You go back to the store, but the check-out person is not the same one, and the person who is there knows nothing about your things, and you do not see your things anywhere

Objective: Student will role play talking to an employee at a service counter about a problem with a purchase.

Subject: Expressive Literacy **Mode:** Role Play **Training Zone:** [V] Observation	**Readiness Factor:** [2] Daily Living **Readiness Factor Category:** [f] Shopping and Eating at Restaurants

EI 2: Addressing an envelope

FUTR Tool: no
PACT: yes

Supplies: A box of blank envelopes

Pass out the envelopes and ask each student to address it to his parents at his home address. Have them use their own names and addresses as return addresses. If possible, use the envelopes when you have some correspondence to send to the parents.

Objective: Student will address an envelope.

Subject: Expressive Literacy **Mode:** Action **Training Zone:** [C] Conscientiousness	**Readiness Factor:** [1] Career **Readiness Factor Category:** [b] Job Performance

EI 3: Anticipating consequences

FUTR Tool: no
PACT: yes

Supplies: None

Discuss that part of making wise choices is anticipating the consequences. Point out that most choices involve both positive and negative consequences, and you have to decide if the positives outweigh the negatives. As a group, list some possible consequences for the choices below. Make sure to look at both the positive and negative possibilities.

1. Bob chose to go to sleep instead of doing his homework.
2. Anika chose to have three helpings of meatloaf.
3. Melissa chose to play a game with her little sister.
4. Guillermo's mother asked him to clean his room on Saturday. He chose to get up early and do it before breakfast.

Objective: Student will help list possible consequences for some choices.

Subject: Expressive Literacy **Mode:** Oral Response **Training Zone:** [L] Logic	**Readiness Factor:** [3] Personal/Social **Readiness Factor Category:** [i] Relationships

EI 4: **Apologizing gracefully**

FUTR Tool: no
PACT: no

Supplies: None

Explain that you are going to read two apologies and you want the students to tell you which one they think is best. Read these two apologies:

1. Even though you are way oversensitive, I'm sorry you didn't like what I said.

2. I'm sorry what I said offended you. I was just trying to make a joke.

Discuss that you are often better off to apologize when you offend others, even if you thought what you said was OK. Explain that the apology can be gracefully directed at apologizing for having offended rather than actually apologizing for what you said.

Objective: Student will choose the best apology out of two options and will discuss issues about apologizing.

Subject: Expressive Literacy Mode: Oral Response Training Zone: [Z] Socialization	Readiness Factor: [3] Personal/Social Readiness Factor Category: [k] Community Involvement and Responsibility

EI 5: **Applying for registrations and licenses**

FUTR Tool: 116
PACT: yes

Supplies: Copies of application forms for a registration or license, such as a fishing license, driver's license, or adult ed class registration

Pass out the application forms and ask each student to fill one in. Discuss what they would have to do with the form if they were actually applying for the registration or license. As a group, brainstorm situations that involve registrations and licenses such as driving, fishing, attending class, going to a conference, hunting, and diving.

Objective: Student will fill out an application form for a registration or license and will discuss related procedures.

Subject: Expressive Literacy Mode: Written Training Zone: [R] Responsibility	Readiness Factor: [3] Personal/Social Readiness Factor Category: [k] Community Involvement and Responsibility

EI 6: **Arranging babysitters**

FUTR Tool: no
PACT: yes

Supplies: Computer (optional) OR overhead projector (optional)

Discuss that, when preparing for babysitters, one good idea is to have a babysitter information sheet so that you do not have to remember everything you want the sitter to know and so the babysitter doesn't have to remember everything you say. Point out that a babysitter information sheet can have general information that doesn't change, such as your cell phone number, where snacks are and which TV channels are allowable as well as blanks for information that changes such as where you are going, when you will be back, and what time the kids are to go to bed. As a group, decide what pieces of information you want to include and then create a babysitter information sheet on the board, in a computer, or on an overhead.

Objective: Student will discuss babysitter information sheets and will help create one.

Subject: Expressive Literacy Mode: Discussion, Action Training Zone: [R] Responsibility	Readiness Factor: [2] Daily Living Readiness Factor Category: [e] Safety and Security

EI 7: Asking a pharmacist for advice

FUTR Tool: no
PACT: no

Supplies: None

Discuss that stores that offer prescription-filling services employ pharmacists. Explain that pharmacists know a lot about drugs and are good people to ask if you want to know information about prescription or over-the-counter drugs. As a group, brainstorm a list of local stores that have pharmacies, and therefore employ pharmacists. Point out that pharmacists usually know about drug side effects, which drugs work best for which symptoms, and facts about how, how often, and when to take specific drugs.

Objective: Student will discuss asking pharmacists for advice and will help make a list of local pharmacies.

Subject: Expressive Literacy **Mode:** Brainstorming **Training Zone:** [Z] Socialization	**Readiness Factor:** [2] Daily Living **Readiness Factor Category:** [f] Shopping and Eating at Restaurants

EI 8: Asking for help when needed

FUTR Tool: 112
PACT: yes

Supplies: None

Discuss that everyone needs help sometimes, and you need to figure out when you should ask for help and when you should put out the effort to do a little more work on your own. Discuss whether you should ask for help in each of these situations:

1. You are to clean up because you are having a party, but you want to talk with friends online right now. You know, if you wait, your mother will help you clean up later. Should you wait for her help?
2. You are in a wheelchair and you need a dish that is on a high shelf. You think you might be able to pull yourself up and maybe reach it. Your sister is in the next room. Should you ask for help?

Objective: Student will discuss when to ask for help.

Subject: Expressive Literacy **Mode:** Discussion **Training Zone:** [L] Logic	**Readiness Factor:** [3] Personal/Social **Readiness Factor Category:** [i] Relationships

EI 9: Asking for help with activities

FUTR Tool: 134
PACT: yes

Supplies: None

Discuss that you will need help doing things from time to time. Point out that, when you need help, you should ask for it and that, whether or not people will want to help you will often depend on how you ask. Draw a circle on the board and write "ask for help" in it. Then draw lines out from the circle and write related tips that the class generates as a group. Include ideas such as these: be polite, be specific so the person knows what you want, be considerate of the person's time, be aware of the person's abilities, only ask if you really need help, make sure you are doing as much or more than you ask the other person to do.

Objective: Student will help generate tips for asking others for help.

Subject: Expressive Literacy **Mode:** Brainstorming **Training Zone:** [E] Exploration	**Readiness Factor:** [3] Personal/Social **Readiness Factor Category:** [i] Relationships

EI 10: Asking questions for clarification

FUTR Tool: no
PACT: yes

Supplies: None

Discuss that when you do not understand what someone says, you should ask questions to clarify. Tell students that you are going to make some comments and you want them to ask clarifying questions until it is clear to them what you are saying.

1. (In your mind, choose a location, time, and reason.) Do you want to come with me?
2. (In your mind, picture a knight from the neck up.) How would you start if you were drawing a picture of a knight?
3. (In your mind, choose a subject and page number.) Remember to do 1–10- for homework.
4. (In your mind, picture one of your pens.) Has anyone seen my pen?
5. (In your mind, think of a current uncertain local happening.) Do you think it is really true?

Objective: Student will ask questions to clarify what she has heard.

Subject: Expressive Literacy	**Readiness Factor:** [1] Career
Mode: Discussion	**Readiness Factor Category:** [b] Job Performance
Training Zone: [E] Exploration	

EI 11: Being persistent with important issues

FUTR Tool: no
PACT: no

Supplies: None

Discuss that the saying "Pick your battles" means that you should let the little things go and be persistent with the important issues. Create a two-column chart on the board with these headers:

• Little things you should let go

• Important issues you should be persistent about

As a group, brainstorm at least five ideas for each list.

Objective: Student will help identify little things he should let go and important issues about which he should be persistent.

Subject: Expressive Literacy	**Readiness Factor:** [3] Personal/Social
Mode: Brainstorming	**Readiness Factor Category:** [k] Community Involvement and
Training Zone: [C] Conscientiousness	Responsibility

EI 12: Being positive

FUTR Tool: 121
PACT: yes

Supplies: None

Discuss that most everything can be presented in either a positive or a negative way. Write these ideas on the board:

• The shirt is orange.   • Paul let my dog out.   • We had peas for lunch.

Ask volunteers to restate each statement twice—once in a positive way and once in a negative way. Discuss that, when you say things positively, you set a positive tone around you and positive tones tend to bring out positive comments from others. Point out that positive comments create a positive atmosphere and that positive atmospheres are less stressful for everyone.

Objective: Student will present ideas in positive and negative tones and will discuss the benefits of creating positive atmospheres.

Subject: Expressive Literacy	**Readiness Factor:** [3] Personal/Social
Mode: Oral Response	**Readiness Factor Category:** [i] Relationships
Training Zone: [F] Flexibility	

EI 13: **Being Tactful**

Supplies: None

Explain that an example of tact is recognizing that a situation might be upsetting to another person and therefore taking care to avoid discussing the situation or discussing it in a way that won't be so upsetting.

Divide the class into four teams. Ask each team to come up with a tactful way to tell a friend that her jeans look bad on her. Ask teams to share their tactful comments. As a group, vote on the best tactful comment.

Objective: Student will word a difficult statement in a tactful way.

Subject: Expressive Literacy **Mode:** Oral Response **Training Zone:** [F] Flexibility	**Readiness Factor:** [3] Personal/Social **Readiness Factor Category:** [i] Relationships

EI 14: **Brainstorming with a group**

Supplies: None

Discuss that, in relaxed brainstorming, a group quickly generates a list of ideas. Explain that more formal brainstorming is quite similar, but actually includes a few rules. Point out that some of the most important rules include the following:

1. Encourage as many ideas as possible.
2. Accept all ideas without judgment—show no approval or disapproval.
3. Write all ideas down.
4. Build on each others' ideas.

Use the brainstorming rules to make a list of ten fun things to do on a weekend.

Objective: Student will use basic brainstorming rules to participate in a brainstorming session.

Subject: Expressive Literacy **Mode:** Brainstorming **Training Zone:** [E] Exploration	**Readiness Factor:** [1] Career **Readiness Factor Category:** [b] Job Performance

EI 15: **Calling about a job opening**

Supplies: Several want ad pages

Discuss that, when you initially call about a job opening, you should have a question in mind and it should be something you didn't learn in the ad.

Have students each choose a job from the want ads. Then, ask volunteers to role play calling about the job opening they chose.

Objective: Student will choose a job from the want ads and will role play a phone call about the job opening.

Subject: Expressive Literacy **Mode:** Hands-On **Training Zone:** [E] Exploration	**Readiness Factor:** [1] Career **Readiness Factor Category:** [a] Career Preparation

EI 16: Calling directory assistance

FUTR Tool: 135
PACT: yes

Supplies: None

Model a call to directory assistance by saying, "May I please have a listing for Clyde Smith." Point out that cities often have multiple listings for the same town, and that knowing the street the person lives on is helpful. Also explain that, if you do not know the street, you might have to try a couple of numbers before you find the house you want.

Have students pair up with partners and take turns being a caller and a directory assistance worker. Tell callers to call and request a phone number. So that the directory assistance role player knows the requested number, it works well to have callers request the home number of the person role playing the directory assistance position. Make sure the caller requests the phone of the person whose name the phone is listed in (probably a parent).

Objective: Student will role play a call to directory assistance.

Subject: Expressive Literacy **Mode:** Role Play **Training Zone:** [E] Exploration	**Readiness Factor:** [3] Personal/Social **Readiness Factor Category:** [k] Community Involvement and Responsibility

EI 17: Choosing appropriate discussion topics

FUTR Tool: no
PACT: no

Supplies: None

Explain that whether or not a discussion topic is appropriate depends on who will be part of the discussion and where the discussion will take place. Make a chart on the board with these top headings: During School, At Home, During Work, At a Party. Use these side labels: Friends, Siblings, Parents, Grandparents, Teachers, Boss. Use vertical lines to subdivide each column into four sections to make space for four different answers.

As a group, decide which combinations would be appropriate for a discussion about the four topics below. Use Xs to mark appropriate situations in the chart.

1. My grandmother is ill.
2. Who is Ashley dating?
3. I was arrested for shoplifting.
4. I can't decide what to wear to the school dance.

Objective: Student will help decide with whom and where specific discussion topics are appropriate.

Subject: Expressive Literacy **Mode:** Graph or Chart **Training Zone:** [F] Flexibility	**Readiness Factor:** [3] Personal/Social **Readiness Factor Category:** [j] Leisure/Desires/Choices

EI 18: Choosing Internet search words

FUTR Tool: no
PACT: no

Supplies: None

Divide students into four teams. Ask each team to make a list of search words to use for an Internet Search on one of the following topics.

1. Training programs for airline stewards and stewardesses [Some possibilities: airline steward or stewardess training, flight attendant training, airline training, airline employment, specific airlines]

2. Directions for making a kite [Some possibilities: kites, kite directions, kite instructions, kite construction, kite building]

3. Resorts in Kansas [Some possibilities: Kansas resorts, Kansas vacations, Kansas tourism, Kansas/specific resort hotels, Kansas visitors]

4. Tennis shoes for sale [Some possibilities: tennis shoes, shoes, specific brand shoes, running shoes, walking shoes]

Objective: Student will help make a list of search words for an Internet search.

Subject: Expressive Literacy **Mode:** Written **Training Zone:** [A] Analysis	**Readiness Factor:** [1] Career **Readiness Factor Category:** [b] Job Performance

EI 19: Communicating with fellow employees

FUTR Tool: no
PACT: no

Supplies: None

Discuss that getting along with the people you work with will be very important in determining if you like your job or not. Point out that, for this reason, it is always a good idea to stop and think before using angry words with a coworker. Also, point out that you should work to develop friendships with your coworkers since it is more fun to work with friends.

Objective: Student will discuss the importance of being friendly with coworkers.

Subject: Expressive Literacy **Mode:** Discussion **Training Zone:** [Z] Socialization	**Readiness Factor:** [1] Career **Readiness Factor Category:** [b] Job Performance

EI 20: Completing a college/trade school application

FUTR Tool: no
PACT: yes

Supplies: Copies of college and trade school applications

Discuss that many jobs require a college degree or a certification from a trade school. Explain that when planning on taking training, you should talk with a counselor at the school or center. Point out that the counselor will help you understand exactly what courses you need. As a group, brainstorm a list of jobs that require college degrees [Examples: teacher, federal law enforcement officer, librarian, accountant, bank officer, social worker, pilot, engineer, nurse] and a list that requires certification from a trade school [Examples: construction worker, electrician, plumber, mechanic, air conditioning/heating technician, welder, computer technician, truck driver, hair dresser].

Ask students to choose either a college application or a trade school application to complete.

Objective: Student will help list jobs that require college degrees and jobs that require trade school certification and will fill out an application for a college or trade school.

Subject: Expressive Literacy **Mode:** Brainstorming, Hands-On **Training Zone:** [S] Self-Awareness	**Readiness Factor:** [1] Career **Readiness Factor Category:** [a] Career Preparation

EI 21: Completing a job application

FUTR Tool: 131
PACT: yes

Supplies: A copy of a job application for each student

Discuss that a job application is often a person's main introduction to a workplace, so you want your application to look as professional as possible. Tell students that, when possible, you should take the application home to fill it out. Point out that, by taking it home, you can make a copy of it, fill out the copy as a rough draft, and then complete the real application. Make sure students understand that you will sometimes have to fill out an application without leaving the place of business.

Give each student a job application to fill out. Tell them to write neatly, to be sure about what they want to write before they start writing, and to try to complete all the blanks.

Objective: Student will fill out a job application.

Subject: Expressive Literacy **Mode:** Hands-On, Written **Training Zone:** [S] Self-Awareness	**Readiness Factor:** [1] Career **Readiness Factor Category:** [a] Career Preparation

EI 22: Compromising

FUTR Tool: 114
PACT: yes

Supplies: None

Explain that compromising is the process of arriving at an agreement by each person giving up a little. Give students this example of a compromise: Janine and Jessie are twins and they are having a birthday party. Janine wants to have the party from 6:00 p.m. until 9:00 p.m. so she can go to sleep early. Jessie wants to have the party from 9:00 p.m. until midnight so she can take a nap first. They agree to have the party from 7:30 p.m. until 10:30 p.m. so that Jessie can still take a nap first, and Janine can go to sleep well ahead of midnight.

Ask two volunteers to role play compromising. Tell them to begin with the stands below and to agree on a lunch plan.

1. Pizza, chips, and soda will taste great for lunch.

2. Turkey sandwiches, carrot sticks, and milk will make a healthy lunch.

Objective: Student will discuss and role play compromising.

Subject: Expressive Literacy **Mode:** Discussion, Role Play **Training Zone:** [L] Logic	**Readiness Factor:** [3] Personal/Social **Readiness Factor Category:** [i] Relationships

EI 23: Controlling emotional reactions

FUTR Tool: no
PACT: no

Supplies: None

Discuss that sometimes you should control your emotional reactions to give yourself time to think about the situation and to avoid sending a message you do not want to send. Point out that you sometimes need to control both angry and happy emotions such as in these situations:

1. You come home and find your little brother in your room, and you are so angry that you want to hit him. But, hitting your brother won't solve anything, so it is best to talk calmly and make an agreement from this point on.

2. You just got invited to a party and you are so excited that you want to talk about it, even though you know your friend who is listening was not invited. But, talking about it to your friend is like rubbing it in that he is being left out. Since you don't want to hurt your friend, it is best to talk about something else.

Objective: Student will discuss situations where controlling emotions can be helpful.

Subject: Expressive Literacy **Mode:** Discussion **Training Zone:** [Z] Socialization	**Readiness Factor:** [3] Personal/Social **Readiness Factor Category:** [k] Community Involvement and Responsibility

EI 24: Conversing on topics chosen by others

FUTR Tool: 123
PACT: yes

Supplies: None

Use this activity to give students a chance to practice conversing on topics chosen by others:

1. Divide the class into groups with three or four students each.

2. Give each group one of these topics to discuss:
   Should public schools operate year round?
   Should sports be eliminated from high schools?
   Should schools break for religious holidays such as Thanksgiving and Christmas?
   Should public schools require students to wear uniforms?
   Should public schools provide transportation?
   Should students be allowed to have cell phones in class?

3. Encourage students to give their opinions, listen to others, and ask questions as ways to start conversations and keep them going.

Objective: Student will converse on topics chosen by others.

Subject: Expressive Literacy **Mode:** Discussion **Training Zone:** [F] Flexibility	**Readiness Factor:** [3] Personal/Social **Readiness Factor Category:** [i] Relationships

EI 25: Creating a computer password you can remember

FUTR Tool: no
PACT: yes

Supplies: None

Discuss that you often need to provide a password when doing things online, and that it is frustrating when you forget your password. Suggest these tips for choosing and remembering passwords:

1. Choose a name or word with 8–10 letters to fall easily within typical requested ranges.
2. Choose a name or word that you know how to spell and that has only one spelling so you do not find yourself using different spellings.
3. Always use all lowercase letters so you do not have to remember if you used upper or lower.
4. Keep a password list near your computer so you do not have to remember what passwords you have used where. Make sure to add to the list each time you create a new password.

Objective: Student will discuss tips for choosing and remembering passwords.

Subject: Expressive Literacy **Mode:** Discussion **Training Zone:** [U] Conclusion	**Readiness Factor:** [2] Daily Living **Readiness Factor Category:** [e] Safety and Security

EI 26: Describing a problem to a lawyer

FUTR Tool: no
PACT: yes

Supplies: None

Discuss these two main features of conversations with your lawyer:

1. Time is money (your money).
2. Whatever you say will be kept confidential—even if it makes you look bad.

Discuss whether you should discuss the following issues with your lawyer while on a business call:

1. Your favorite kind of car [No, you don't want to pay for time to discuss it.])
2. Even though the police said the accident was the other guy's fault, you feel a little responsible [Yes, it is better to discuss it now than when others are around.]
3. Things you cannot do with your arm since the accident [Yes, the injury is relevant.]

Objective: Student will discuss things to say and not say when talking to a lawyer.

Subject: Expressive Literacy **Mode:** Discussion **Training Zone:** [V] Observation	**Readiness Factor:** [2] Daily Living **Readiness Factor Category:** [e] Safety and Security

EI 27: Describing symptoms to a doctor

FUTR Tool: 126
PACT: yes

Supplies: None

Ask volunteers to "go back in time" to times when they were sick and to role play telling a doctor how they feel. Make sure they include the following categories:

1. Whether or not they have a fever
2. location of pain or discomfort
3. length of time they have had the problem
4. all associated symptoms
5. presence or absence of bodily discharges, vomiting, or bleeding
6. desire (or not) to eat

Objective: Student will role play describing symptoms to a doctor.

Subject: Expressive Literacy **Mode:** Role Play **Training Zone:** [V] Observation	**Readiness Factor:** [2] Daily Living **Readiness Factor Category:** [e] Safety and Security

EI 28: Enunciating clearly

FUTR Tool: no
PACT: no

Supplies: Cassette recorder; blank cassette

Ask a volunteer to tell what he is doing after school tonight and record what he says. Point out that casual English is speckled with cut-off and slurred words. Explain that casual talking is fine for casual, in-person situations, but for school, work, and over-the-phone conversations, clear enunciation is a good choice, because it is easier to understand.

Ask the volunteer to repeat what he is doing after school tonight, being careful to use clear enunciation. Record what he says. Compare the two statements and discuss how they are alike and different.

Objective: Student will discuss the difference between casual and clear enunciation and where each is appropriate.

Subject: Expressive Literacy **Mode:** Discussion **Training Zone:** [S] Self-Awareness	**Readiness Factor:** [1] Career **Readiness Factor Category:** [b] Job Performance

EI 29: Exploring situation-appropriate speech/actions

FUTR Tool: no
PACT: yes

Supplies: None

Discuss that home is a personal, private place where you can say and do things that you would not say or do away from home. As a group, brainstorm things you can talk about or do at home, but not in other places. For each item on the list, discuss why it belongs on the list.

Objective: Student will help identify some things that should only be discussed or done at home and discuss why these things belong only at home.

Subject: Expressive Literacy **Mode:** Discussion **Training Zone:** [A] Analysis	**Readiness Factor:** [1] Career **Readiness Factor Category:** [b] Job Performance

EI 30: Expressing self with feeling words

Supplies: None

Point out that a good way to share your thoughts with other people is to use feeling words. Ask volunteers to express thoughts using these words:

angry	excited	pleased	lucky	sad
lonely	enraged	ashamed	depressed	shy
shocked	bored	surprised	suspicious	happy
guilty	cautious	confident	smug	overwhelmed
jealous	confused			

Objective: Student will use feeling words to express thoughts.

Subject: Expressive Literacy **Mode:** Oral Response **Training Zone:** [A] Analysis	**Readiness Factor:** [3] Personal/Social **Readiness Factor Category:** [i] Relationships

EI 31: Filling or refilling a prescription

Supplies: None

Ask volunteers to role play asking to have an allergy medication prescription refilled. Have one person play the part of the customer and one the part of the pharmacist employee. Encourage the pharmacist employee to ask questions and use procedures such as these:

1. Your name?

2. Phone number?

3. Address?

4. Doctor's name?

5. Do you have insurance?

After the customer answers the questions, have the pharmacist employee ask the customer to sign for the prescription. Charge a $24.95 fee, unless the customer indicated he had insurance, then charge a $15 co-pay.

Objective: Student will participate in a prescription refill role play.

Subject: Expressive Literacy **Mode:** Role Play **Training Zone:** [M] Manipulation	**Readiness Factor:** [2] Daily Living **Readiness Factor Category:** [e] Safety and Security

EI 32: **Filling out personal information forms**

FUTR Tool: 130
PACT: yes

Supplies: A personal information form—either find one to copy or create one

Pass out the personal-information forms and ask students to complete them in ink. Remind them to be both neat and accurate.

Make sure the form includes personal information such as the following:

first/middle/last name	address	phone #
e-mail address	next of kin	schools attended
place of employment	height	weight
hair color	eye color	parents' names
mother's maiden name	siblings names	place of birth

Objective: Student will complete a personal information form.

Subject: Expressive Literacy **Mode:** Hands-On, Written **Training Zone:** [S] Self-Awareness	**Readiness Factor:** [1] Career **Readiness Factor Category:** [a] Career Preparation

EI 33: **Following food preparation directions**

FUTR Tool: 133
PACT: yes

Supplies: Three empty boxes for easy-to-prepare food items such as macaroni and cheese, a cake, and a box meal to which hamburger is to be added.

Divide the class into three groups. Give each group one of the food boxes. Ask the group to choose a reader and a food-preparation role player. Ask each team to have the reader read the directions as the role player acts them out. Tell them to make sure the readers do not get ahead of the role players (or vice versa).

Objective: Student will be part of a food-preparation role play.

Subject: Expressive Literacy **Mode:** Role Play **Training Zone:** [E] Exploration	**Readiness Factor:** [2] Daily Living **Readiness Factor Category:** [d] Household Care and/or Chores

EI 34: **Giving "How to" directions**

FUTR Tool: 125
PACT: yes

Supplies: None

Ask students to each choose a simple activity, such as How to Sharpen a Pencil, and write explicit step-by-step directions for doing the activity. Choose a couple of the written directions and test them out by following them exactly.

Objective: Student will write step-by-step "how to" directions.

Subject: Expressive Literacy **Mode:** Written **Training Zone:** [V] Observation	**Readiness Factor:** [3] Personal/Social **Readiness Factor Category:** [j] Leisure/Desires/Choices

EI 35: Giving an opinion on a movie

FUTR Tool: no
PACT: yes

Supplies: None

Ask students to choose movies they have seen and tell what they liked and did not like about the movies and whether or not they would recommend that others see the movies. Have each student give an opinion on at least one movie.

Objective: Student will give an opinion on a movie.

Subject: Expressive Literacy **Mode:** Oral Response **Training Zone:** [U] Conclusion	**Readiness Factor:** [3] Personal/Social **Readiness Factor Category:** [j] Leisure/Desires/Choices

EI 36: Giving compliments

FUTR Tool: no
PACT: yes

Supplies: None

Pair each student with a partner. Ask students to think of compliments to give to their partners. Then, one at a time, have students give their compliments to their partners. Ask them to stand and give the compliments aloud so the whole class can hear them.

Objective: Student will give a compliment to a classmate.

Subject: Expressive Literacy **Mode:** Action **Training Zone:** [Z] Socialization	**Readiness Factor:** [3] Personal/Social **Readiness Factor Category:** [i] Relationships

EI 37: Giving people enough physical space

FUTR Tool: no
PACT: no

Supplies: None

Discuss that people are uncomfortable when others stand too close to them. Explain that anything closer than two feet is too close. Ask students to experiment with standing "too close" and standing at a "good distance."

Objective: Student will experiment with standing "too close" and standing at a "good distance."

Subject: Expressive Literacy **Mode:** Action **Training Zone:** [Z] Socialization	**Readiness Factor:** [3] Personal/Social **Readiness Factor Category:** [i] Relationships

EI 38: Giving verbal clarification

FUTR Tool: no
PACT: yes

Supplies: None

Discuss that, when speaking over the phone, some letters require clues because it is hard to hear the difference between like-sounding letters. Point out that when saying or spelling words or names with confusing letters, it is helpful to offer a clue such as "That's F as in Frank."

Make a three-column chart on the board. In the left column, write these often mis-heard letters:

f   s   m   n   p   g   t   v   b   d

In the other two columns across from the "f," write "Frank" and "fantastic." Point out that "Frank" and "fantastic" are both good clues for clarifying the letter "F." Add that, since "f" is often confused with "s," the word "sunny" would not be a good clue because it could be heard as "funny," unless you say "sunny" like in a "sunny day." As a group, fill in the rest of the two columns with one name and one word that could be clues for each letter.

Objective: Student will discuss using letter clues for clarification and will help make a list of letter clues.

Subject: Expressive Literacy **Mode:** Graph or Chart **Training Zone:** [F] Flexibility	**Readiness Factor:** [1] Career **Readiness Factor Category:** [a] Career Preparation

EI 39: Handling personal issues at work

FUTR Tool: no
PACT: yes

Supplies: None

Discuss that all employees have times when they deal with personal issues at work, but that, in fairness to employers, you should do as few personal things at work as possible. As a group, decide whether it is fair to handle each of the following issues at work:

1. You want to invite a fellow employee to go to a movie over the weekend. [Yes]

2. You wrote a 50-page story, and you want to read it to a fellow employee to get her opinion. [No]

3. You have a problem with your electric bill. The electric company customer-service office is only open during your working hours. [Yes]

4. You want to talk to a woman about wall papering your kitchen and you would rather not wait until after work. [No]

5. You want to call a friend to see what she did on the weekend. [No]

6. You aren't feeling well and want to cancel your after-work plans. [Yes]

Objective: Student will help decide which personal issues should be handled at work.

Subject: Expressive Literacy **Mode:** Discussion **Training Zone:** [C] Conscientiousness	**Readiness Factor:** [1] Career **Readiness Factor Category:** [b] Job Performance

EI 40: Handling unexpected or difficult situations

FUTR Tool: 122
PACT: yes

Supplies: None

Discuss these tips for handling unexpected or difficult situations:

1. Stay calm.
2. Ask questions.
3. Do not judge.
4. Listen.
5. Think before you speak.
6. Try to be fair to all.
7. Use logic.
8. Try to see others' points of view.
9. Be ready to compromise.

Objective: Student will discuss tips for handling unexpected or difficult situations.

Subject: Expressive Literacy **Mode:** Discussion **Training Zone:** [F] Flexibility	**Readiness Factor:** [3] Personal/Social **Readiness Factor Category:** [i] Relationships

EI 41: Having a conversation

FUTR Tool: no
PACT: yes

Supplies: None

Discuss that good conversations require effort and include involving all within the immediate group. Divide the class into groups of 6–8 students. Ask each group to work on having a conversation that includes the whole group. Afterwards, ask volunteers to share some of the conversation strategies used by their groups.

Objective: Student will take part in a group conversation that involves everyone within the group.

Subject: Expressive Literacy **Mode:** Discussion **Training Zone:** [Z] Socialization	**Readiness Factor:** [3] Personal/Social **Readiness Factor Category:** [i] Relationships

EI 42: Identifying interests and abilities

FUTR Tool: 140
PACT: yes

Supplies: None

As a group, brainstorm a list of at least 15 useful skills and write them in a column on the board. Turn the list into a chart by adding three columns to the right. Label the columns "Yes," "Not sure," and "No." Using tallies, survey the students to see who feels they have the different skills, who isn't sure, and who thinks they do not.

Objective: Student will help create a list of at least 15 useful skills and will then say whether or not she has each of the skills.

Subject: Expressive Literacy **Mode:** Graph or Chart **Training Zone:** [A] Analysis	**Readiness Factor:** [1] Career **Readiness Factor Category:** [a] Career Preparation

EI 43: Interviewing for a job

FUTR Tool: 128
PACT: yes

Supplies: None

As a group, choose a job from the want ads. (Try to pick a job for which at least some students in the class are qualified.) Ask for two volunteers and hold two short mock interviews. Include questions such as the following:

• What strengths do you bring to this job?
• Have you any related experiences?
• Do your high school records show you are reliable?

After the interviews, discuss the strengths and weaknesses in the interviews.

Objective: Student will participate in mock interviews and follow-up discussions.

Subject: Expressive Literacy **Mode:** Role Play **Training Zone:** [Z] Socialization	**Readiness Factor:** [1] Career **Readiness Factor Category:** [a] Career Preparation

EI 44: Introducing others

FUTR Tool: no
PACT: yes

Supplies: None

Discuss that, when you introduce someone, it is nice to have at least one statement to say along with the name. Point out that, in casual introductions, one statement can be how you know the person or it could be some interesting fact about the person that the person doesn't mind having shared. Ask students to each choose a partner. Then, have them role play introducing their partners to the class. Make sure they share both the person's name and at least one statement about the person.

Objective: Student will introduce someone to the rest of the class.

Subject: Expressive Literacy **Mode:** Action **Training Zone:** [Z] Socialization	**Readiness Factor:** [3] Personal/Social **Readiness Factor Category:** [i] Relationships

EI 45: Keeping an ongoing grocery list

FUTR Tool: no
PACT: yes

Supplies: None

Explain that there are two main ways to make a grocery list:

1. Sit down before you go to the store and think of what you want to get.
2. Keep an ongoing list that you add to each time you run out of something. Then, just before you go to the store, think about whether you want any additional things.

Ask students for ideas about why to choose one method over the other. Point out that, for most people, it is hard to remember everything you need to get if you try to make the list right before you go to the store, so the ongoing list method is usually the most reliable.

Objective: Student will discuss different methods of making a grocery list.

Subject: Expressive Literacy **Mode:** Discussion **Training Zone:** [O] Organization	**Readiness Factor:** [2] Daily Living **Readiness Factor Category:** [d] Household Care and/or Chores

EI 46: Keeping private information private

Supplies: None

Ask volunteers to choose answers to the these questions about keeping private information private:

1. Say you have some family information you want to keep private. Whom should you tell?
   a. Just your closest friend
   b. Just your parents
   c. No one

2. Which of these statements shows a safe, responsible way to handle your social security number?
   a. Feel free to give your social security number over the Internet if the site seems reliable.
   b. Feel free to give your social security number over the phone if the person sounds honest.
   c. Be reluctant to give out your social security number until you have personally checked into the credibility of the requester.

Objective: Student will answer questions about keeping private information private.

Subject: Expressive Literacy **Mode:** Oral Response **Training Zone:** [C] Conscientiousness	**Readiness Factor:** [3] Personal/Social **Readiness Factor Category:** [i] Relationships

EI 47: Knowing the front side of a piece of paper

Supplies: A 3-hole punched piece of paper for each student OR paper with a left margins but no holes

Discuss that the "front" side of a piece of paper is the one that is up when the holes or margin are on the left side. Tell them that they can remember which side is the "front" if they think about the paper being in a book and the holes or margin being in the binding—the "front" side would always come before the "back" side. Either have students take out a 3-hole punched piece of paper (or a piece of paper with a left margin) or pass out the pieces of paper. Ask students to hold the papers up so that the fronts are facing them. Then, ask them to hold them up so the backs are facing them.

Objective: Student will find the "front" side of a piece of paper.

Subject: Expressive Literacy **Mode:** Action **Training Zone:** [O] Organization	**Readiness Factor:** [1] Career **Readiness Factor Category:** [b] Job Performance

EI 48: Knowing when to use and avoid slang

Supplies: None

Discuss that, in some situations, slang is perfectly OK, but in other situations, it is out of place. Make a two-column chart on the board with these headings: Slang OK; Slang Not OK. As a group, brainstorm at least five examples for each column.

Answer:

• Some possible OKs—at home, out with friends, in school cafeteria, at a family gathering, when talking with friends at work

• Some possible Not OKs—in class, when talking to your boss at work, in a teacher or principal conference, when applying for a job, in a business letter

Objective: Student will help create a chart showing when slang use is OK and Not OK.

Subject: Expressive Literacy **Mode:** Graph or Chart **Training Zone:** [A] Analysis	**Readiness Factor:** [1] Career **Readiness Factor Category:** [a] Career Preparation

EI 49: Knowing when to use your signature

Supplies: None

Discuss that your signature is when you write your full name (or first name, middle initial, and last name) in cursive. Point out that, when you are directed to "sign your name" or "write your signature," you should always use the full-name, cursive version. Explain that, sometimes, you are simply directed to write or print your name, or you have blanks that are labeled first, middle, and last—and that these wordings do not require a signature. Tell students that, when a signature is not required, they can write their names as they wish unless they are specifically asked to print it. Ask students to print their names and then to write their signatures.

As a group, brainstorm situations that call for signatures.

Objective: Student will discuss when to use a signature and will practice writing his signature.

Subject: Expressive Literacy **Mode:** Written **Training Zone:** [R] Responsibility	**Readiness Factor:** [3] Personal/Social **Readiness Factor Category:** [k] Community Involvement and Responsibility

EI 50: Knowing your initials

FUTR Tool: no
PACT: yes

Supplies: None

Ask students to print their first and last initials. Then ask them to write them in cursive as an abbreviated signature.

Ask students to print their first, last, and middle initials. Then ask them to write them in cursive as an abbreviated signature.

Discuss that you can choose to use two or three initials (or more if you have them). Ask for a show of hands as to who would use two initials and who would use three (or more).

Objective: Student will print and write both her two and three-letter initials.

Subject: Expressive Literacy **Mode:** Written **Training Zone:** [S] Self-Awareness	**Readiness Factor:** [1] Career **Readiness Factor Category:** [a] Career Preparation

EI 51: Labeling files

FUTR Tool: no
PACT: no

Supplies: Enough file labels for each student to have two or three

Discuss that labels on files have to be written small or typed. Have students practice making hand-written labels. Have them make labels you can use in the classroom, or labels with general information such as their names. Remind them that labels often have to be read by people other than yourselves, so neat writing is an important factor.

Objective: Student will handwrite two or three file labels.

Subject: Expressive Literacy **Mode:** Written **Training Zone:** [O] Organization	**Readiness Factor:** [2] Daily Living **Readiness Factor Category:** [g] Time and Order

EI 52: Labeling moving boxes

FUTR Tool: no
PACT: no

Supplies: None

Point out that most people who move use a lot of boxes and that boxes that are packed to move to a new home will be easier to sort into the correct rooms in the new home if the room name is written on the outside of the box. In addition, point out that it also helps to write a one- to three-word summary of the contents of each box. Also, explain that labels should include specific things you will need right away. Ask volunteers to identify the relevant room and to provide a summary for boxes with the following contents:

1. Plates, bowls, glasses, and a few hot pads

2. A miscellaneous group of items—shoes, two backpacks, alarm clock, and cell phone charger

3. Pictures from the living room, kitchen, and bedroom walls; Two photo albums; kitchen clock

4. Two boxes of cereal, a bunch of canned food, some pasta, and three cake mixes

5. Magazine and newspapers you have not read; Mail from the last two days; New-home papers

6. Towels, shower curtain, soap dispenser, new soap bars; Bathroom-shelf knickknacks

Objective: Student will discuss information to use to label moving boxes.

Subject: Expressive Literacy **Mode:** Oral Response **Training Zone:** [O] Organization	**Readiness Factor:** [2] Daily Living **Readiness Factor Category:** [g] Time and Order

EI 53: Leaving a job

FUTR Tool: no
PACT: yes

Supplies: Calendar that is big enough for whole group to see

Discuss that, when you leave a job, you need to try to give a two-week notice so that the employer has a chance to try to replace you. Point out that a two-week notice typically means 10 business days. Using a calendar, ask a volunteer to tell when the two weeks would be up if you gave your notice today. Choose other dates and ask other volunteers to calculate the two-week point.

Objective: Student will calculate dates at the end of two-week work notices.

Subject: Expressive Literacy **Mode:** Calculation **Training Zone:** [C] Conscientiousness	**Readiness Factor:** [1] Career **Readiness Factor Category:** [b] Job Performance

EI 54: Leaving a message on a machine

FUTR Tool: 129
PACT: yes

Supplies: None

Discuss that using an answering machine is helpful to you as a caller so you do not have to remember to keep calling when someone isn't home. Also, point out that an answering machine is also helpful to you as the person being called so you can know what others are trying to tell you. Explain that, since answering machines are helpful in both directions, you should leave messages, even if you do not really like leaving messages.

Ask students to role play calling friends or relatives and leaving messages. Tell them to be sure to include their names, the time they called, and a brief message.

Objective: Student will role play leaving a message on an answering machine.

Subject: Expressive Literacy **Mode:** Role Play **Training Zone:** [Z] Socialization	**Readiness Factor:** [3] Personal/Social **Readiness Factor Category:** [k] Community Involvement and Responsibility

EI 55: Mailing a letter

FUTR Tool: 138
PACT: yes

Supplies: None

As a group, brainstorm places where you can mail a letter. Include ideas such as the following:

• Post Office
• School mail box
• Workplace mail box
• Street mail box
• Mail box in a shopping center
• A shipping store
• In a home or neighborhood mail box

Objective: Student will discuss places where he can mail a letter.

Subject: Expressive Literacy **Mode:** Brainstorming **Training Zone:** [M] Manipulation	**Readiness Factor:** [1] Career **Readiness Factor Category:** [a] Career Preparation

EI 56: Making a general shopping list

FUTR Tool: no
PACT: yes

Supplies: None

Discuss that general shopping lists include needed items other than groceries. As a group, brainstorm typical items that would show up on most people's general shopping lists. Make sure to include some of these items:

facial tissue	toilet paper	film
deodorant	soap	envelopes
shampoo	toothpaste	tape
garbage bags	dishwashing liquid	stamps
laundry detergent	computer paper	greeting cards

Objective: Student will help identify typical items that would show up on a general shopping list.

Subject: Expressive Literacy **Mode:** Brainstorming **Training Zone:** [O] Organization	**Readiness Factor:** [2] Daily Living **Readiness Factor Category:** [f] Shopping and Eating at Restaurants

EI 57: Making a grocery list

FUTR Tool: no
PACT: yes

Supplies: A collection of 10-20 empty food containers

Discuss that grocery lists help people remember to buy the grocery-store items they need. Point out that spelling isn't a major issue on grocery lists, but being able to read what you write is important. Ask each student to take out a piece of paper for a grocery list. Tell students you are going to randomly hold up grocery items and they are to add them to their grocery lists. One at a time, hold up the grocery items.

Objective: Student will identify food items and add them to her grocery list.

Subject: Expressive Literacy **Mode:** Hands-On, Written **Training Zone:** [U] Conclusion	**Readiness Factor:** [2] Daily Living **Readiness Factor Category:** [f] Shopping and Eating at Restaurants

EI 58: Making appointments

Supplies: None

Ask volunteers to role play making the following appointments:

1. a doctor's appointment for a sore throat

2. a meeting with your guidance counselor

3. an appointment to get your hair cut

4. 15 minutes to talk to your English teacher about an assignment you don't understand

Objective: Student will role play making an appointment.

Subject: Expressive Literacy **Mode:** Role Play **Training Zone:** [O] Organization	**Readiness Factor:** [2] Daily Living **Readiness Factor Category:** [g] Time and Order

EI 59: Making copies

FUTR Tool: no
PACT: yes

Supplies: Assorted messages copied from different screens on a copier machine

On the board, write messages from the screen on a copy machine and discuss what each means and how to handle it. (As an alternative, take a "field trip" to a copier in the school and read and discuss the screens that appear when making different choices.)

Objective: Student will discuss messages on copier screens that appear when making different choices.

Subject: Expressive Literacy **Mode:** Discussion **Training Zone:** [M] Manipulation	**Readiness Factor:** [1] Career **Readiness Factor Category:** [b] Job Performance

EI 60: Making restaurant reservations

FUTR Tool: 111
PACT: yes

Supplies: None

Ask volunteers to role play calling to make reservations at a restaurant. Make sure they include the following components:

1. Party name (usually a last name)

2. Time of day you want to eat

3. Number of people in party

4. Contact phone number

As a group, make a list of local restaurants that require reservations and some that do not.

Objective: Student will make mock restaurant reservation phone calls and will help make a list of local restaurants that require reservations and some that do not.

Subject: Expressive Literacy **Mode:** Role Play **Training Zone:** [O] Organization	**Readiness Factor:** [2] Daily Living **Readiness Factor Category:** [g] Time and Order

EI 61: Marking bills paid

FUTR Tool: no
PACT: yes

Supplies: None

On the board, use today's date to duplicate the "paid" markings below. Make sure to circle each "paid" mark. Explain that writing "paid" or its abbreviation "pd" and the date on a bill is a good way for you to remember that you paid it and exactly when you paid it. Adding "online," "Check #425," or "cash" under it lets you know how you made the payment. (Discuss that if you pay a bill in cash, you need to make sure you get a receipt since it will be your only record of having paid.)

```
   ( Pd )      ( Pd )      ( Pd )
 ( 12-10-06 )( 12-10-06 )( 12-10-06 )
  ( Online )   ( Chk )    ( Cash )
```

Objective: Student will watch as the teacher demonstrates how to mark a bill paid.

Subject: Expressive Literacy **Mode:** Demonstration **Training Zone:** [O] Organization	**Readiness Factor:** [2] Daily Living **Readiness Factor Category:** [c] Finances

---

EI 62: Naming cards in a card deck

FUTR Tool: no
PACT: no

Supplies: Several decks of cards—enough so that students can play simple card games

Randomly pull cards from a card deck and ask students to identify them. Have students practice recognizing the cards by playing simple card games such as the following:

- War
- Rummy
- Crazy 8
- Go Fish

Objective: Student will identify cards from a card deck and will play simple card games.

Subject: Expressive Literacy **Mode:** Hands-On **Training Zone:** [U] Conclusion	**Readiness Factor:** [3] Personal/Social **Readiness Factor Category:** [j] Leisure/Desires/Choices

---

EI 63: Negotiating a sale or purchase

FUTR Tool: no
PACT: no

Supplies: None

Discuss that negotiating a sale or purchase is sort of like compromising since those involved talk over different options until they arrive at one that satisfies everyone. Point out that, when negotiating, you should never say a price or condition that you are not ready to accept. For example, if you are selling a bike, and you would like to get $150, you should not say that you would like between $125 and $175 because as soon as you say $125, that is now the price you have said you will accept—so the buyer has no reason to offer anything higher.

Also, point out that you will likely often see your own things as being more valuable than they are in others' eyes. Explain that, if you want to sell something, you should try to get some impartial opinions about the value—perhaps by asking a couple friends or relatives who are not interested in buying the item.

Objective: Student will discuss issues involved in negotiating a sale or purchase.

Subject: Expressive Literacy **Mode:** Discussion **Training Zone:** [L] Logic	**Readiness Factor:** [2] Daily Living **Readiness Factor Category:** [f] Shopping and Eating at Restaurants

EI 64: Ordering form catalogs

FUTR Tool: no
PACT: yes

Supplies: Enough mail order catalogs for each group to have one (Can use the same catalogs and order forms for EI 66.)

Discuss that mail order catalogs usually offer ordering by mail, phone, or Internet. Divide the class into groups of four or five students. Give each group a catalog. Ask the groups to choose five things and fill out the order form. Ask groups to look for over-the-phone ordering numbers and show the class where in the catalogs they find them. Then, find at least one of the mail order companies on line and show students how to place an order online. Discuss that using the order form in the catalog is not just useful when ordering by mail—It is also very helpful when ordering online or over the phone since it is a way to collect needed information and it provides a record for you.

Discuss some of the pros and cons of mail order such as these: (Pros) can order from home, takes very little time, can buy 24-hours per day; (Cons) sometimes what you get is not what you expected, usually you have to pay for shipping, you have to pay to ship returns, it is too easy for people who are compulsive shoppers.

Objective: Student will explore catalog ordering options as well as some pros and cons of ordering by mail.

Subject: Expressive Literacy **Mode:** Action **Training Zone:** [M] Manipulation	**Readiness Factor:** [2] Daily Living **Readiness Factor Category:** [f] Shopping and Eating at Restaurants

EI 65: Ordering from menus

FUTR Tool: 137
PACT: yes

Supplies: Several menus from one of the local restaurants

Hand out menus so that every few students have one. Help students familiarize themselves with the menu by asking general questions such as the following:

1. What is the most expensive meal on the menu?
2. What is the least expensive meal on the menu?
3. Do they serve desserts?
4. Do they serve milk shakes?

Ask each team to choose two or three meals to share as a light snack. Have each team choose a representative to place its order.

Objective: Student will order from a menu.

Subject: Expressive Literacy **Mode:** Hands-On **Training Zone:** [M] Manipulation	**Readiness Factor:** [2] Daily Living **Readiness Factor Category:** [f] Shopping and Eating at Restaurants

EI 66: **Ordering items over the telephone**

FUTR Tool: no
PACT: yes

Supplies: Enough mail order catalogs for each group to have one (Can use the same catalogs and order forms from EI 64.)

Discuss that mail order catalogs usually offer ordering by mail, phone, or Internet. Divide the class into groups of four or five students. Give each group a catalog. Ask the groups to choose five things and fill out the order form. Ask each group to choose two people to role play placing a phone order—one person to place the order and one person to be a telephone order taker. Tell the order taker to make sure and collect all the areas of information that are on the order form.

Objective: Student will participate in an order-by-phone role play.

Subject: Expressive Literacy **Mode:** Role Play **Training Zone:** [M] Manipulation	**Readiness Factor:** [2] Daily Living **Readiness Factor Category:** [d] Household Care and/or Chores

EI 67: **Planning a surprise**

FUTR Tool: no
PACT: no

Supplies: None

Point out that some people love surprises and others do not, so you should plan surprises only for people you think will like them. Also, explain that some ways to make a surprise a success include the following:

1. Don't tell very many people
2. Don't start planning too far ahead of time
3. Keep the plans simple.

Objective: Student will discuss ways to make a surprise a success.

Subject: Expressive Literacy **Mode:** Discussion **Training Zone:** [Z] Socialization	**Readiness Factor:** [3] Personal/Social **Readiness Factor Category:** [i] Relationships

EI 68: **Reacting to mistakes**

FUTR Tool: no
PACT: no

Supplies: None

Share the following tips for reacting to mistakes:

1. Don't get down on yourself. Everyone makes mistakes!
2. Look at a mistake as a chance to learn. Make sure you find out why you were wrong and what you could have done or said to be right.
3. Don't let others make you feel embarrassed. They make mistakes, too!
4. Sometimes your mistakes cause problems for others. Make sure they know you are sorry for causing any inconveniences for them.
5. Be willing to go out of your way to correct mistakes.

Objective: Student will discuss tips for reacting to mistakes.

Subject: Expressive Literacy **Mode:** Discussion **Training Zone:** [A] Analysis	**Readiness Factor:** [3] Personal/Social **Readiness Factor Category:** [k] Community Involvement and Responsibility

EI 69: Recognizing slang

FUTR Tool: no
PACT: yes

Supplies: None

Discuss that we sometimes get so used to slang words that we don't realize they are not a part of the regular English language. As a group, brainstorm a list of slang words that students often use.

Objective: Student will help make a list of slang words that students often use.

Subject: Expressive Literacy **Mode:** Brainstorming **Training Zone:** [V] Observation	**Readiness Factor:** [1] Career **Readiness Factor Category:** [a] Career Preparation

EI 70: Recording an answering machine message

FUTR Tool: 118
PACT: yes

Supplies: A bell (optional)

Discuss that answering machine messages must usually be quite short, but that you want to be sure to include key ideas such as saying who you are and asking the callers to leave their names, numbers, and brief messages.

Divide the class into four teams. Ask each team to create a phone message that is 10 seconds or less. Then, ask them to share their messages and time them when they deliver them. If any go over 10 seconds, ring a bell or make a loud beeping sound to indicate the message has been cut off.

Objective: Student will help create a 10-second answering machine message.

Subject: Expressive Literacy **Mode:** Role Play **Training Zone:** [C] Conscientiousness	**Readiness Factor:** [2] Daily Living **Readiness Factor Category:** [d] Household Care and/or Chores

EI 71: Requesting adaptations/accommodations

FUTR Tool: 132
PACT: yes

Supplies: None

Discuss that some people require special adaptations or accommodations to take tests, get around a building, work at a job, and do other things. Ask volunteers to identify hypothetical situations and ask for needed adaptations or accommodations.

Objective: Student will ask for needed adaptations or accommodations for hypothetical situations.

Subject: Expressive Literacy **Mode:** Role Play **Training Zone:** [S] Self-Awareness	**Readiness Factor:** [1] Career **Readiness Factor Category:** [b] Job Performance

EI 72: Responding in your best interests when treated unfairly by a coworker

FUTR Tool: no
PACT: no

Supplies: None

Point out that people are sometimes treated unfairly, and that it is difficult to stay calm in unfair situations. Ask volunteers for ideas about reacting to the following unfair situations:

1. You did your homework, but a boy you don't know took it. Now your teacher thinks you didn't do your homework.

2. You are trying to impress a new friend when another student trips you and you fall flat on your face in front of the friend you want to impress.

3. Your favorite meal at school is lasagna, and today is lasagna day. You have to say after class because another student blamed you for making noises in class, but it wasn't you. By the time you leave class and get to the cafeteria, all the lasagna is gone.

Objective: Student will discuss ideas for reacting to some unfair situations.

Subject: Expressive Literacy **Mode:** Discussion **Training Zone:** [F] Flexibility	**Readiness Factor:** [1] Career **Readiness Factor Category:** [b] Job Performance

EI 73: Responding to strengths and weaknesses

FUTR Tool: 142
PACT: yes

Supplies: None

Discuss that everyone has strengths and weaknesses, and that it helps if you can "learn to play to your strengths." Tell students that, in other words, you should use your strengths to overcome your weaknesses. Ask volunteers to describe such a scenario for each of the following situations:

1. You have trouble remembering details. You are quite good at taking notes. You answer the phone and are asked to tell a family member to meet Joan at 4:30 at 514 W. Stone Ave.

2. You can't read. You are a good listener. You have heard that "Run, Sara, Run" is a good book and you want to read it.

3. You can't run very fast. Your arms are very strong. You are babysitting and the little girl tries to run past you to get outside where she is not safe.

Objective: Student will explain how to use strengths to overcome weaknesses in specific situations.

Subject: Expressive Literacy **Mode:** Oral Response **Training Zone:** [U] Conclusion	**Readiness Factor:** [1] Career **Readiness Factor Category:** [b] Job Performance

EI 74: **Returning an item you bought**

FUTR Tool: no
PACT: yes

Supplies: None

Discuss that sometimes you want to return perfectly good merchandise to a store because you changed your mind or found a better deal. Explain that, as long as you do not use or harm the merchandise in any way, returning it is just fine in most retail situations. Point out that, if you have the receipt, you can simply say that you changed your mind and that no other explanation is needed.

Objective: Student will discuss the process of returning an item to a store because she changed her mind.

Subject: Expressive Literacy **Mode:** Discussion **Training Zone:** [U] Conclusion	**Readiness Factor:** [2] Daily Living **Readiness Factor Category:** [f] Shopping and Eating at Restaurants

EI 75: **Saying thanks (orally or in writing)**

FUTR Tool: 127
PACT: yes

Supplies: None

Discuss that it is fine to say thank you in person to someone you know well after the person has done a small favor for you. Point out that thank yous for large favors or for people you do not know well should be given in writing.

Divide the class into four groups. Ask each group to write or say thank you for one of the following situations:

1. Thank your close friend, Jenny, for helping to make cookies for your party.
2. Thank your teacher, Ms. Johnson, for writing two references for you.
3. Thank Clement for welcoming you into his home for a month without even having met you.
4. Thank your mother for giving you a ride to your friend's house.

Objective: Student will help prepare a thank you note or in-person message.

Subject: Expressive Literacy **Mode:** Action **Training Zone:** [Z] Socialization	**Readiness Factor:** [3] Personal/Social **Readiness Factor Category:** [i] Relationships

EI 76: **Scheduling a job interview**

FUTR Tool: no
PACT: no

Supplies: None

Discuss that job hunters are almost always glad to get interviews. Point out that, when you are scheduling an interview, you should keep the following tips in mind:

1. Unless you have a very important conflict, agree to interview at the company's convenience.
2. If you are working at another job, tell the interviewing company how you can work around your existing job.
3. Write the time and date of the scheduled interview on your calendar. Don't risk forgetting the details.
4. Make sure you ask where the interview will be held and how to get there.
5. Make sure to find out where you can park or if taking a bus is an option.

Objective: Student will discuss tips for scheduling interviews.

Subject: Expressive Literacy **Mode:** Discussion **Training Zone:** [M] Manipulation	**Readiness Factor:** [1] Career **Readiness Factor Category:** [a] Career Preparation

EI 77: **Sending an e-mail**

Supplies: A computer with an e-mail program

Ask a volunteer to explain the step-by-step procedure for sending an e-mail. Write the steps on the board. Fill in any missed steps. Then go to a computer and demonstrate how to actually send an e-mail. Discuss each step from the board as you get ready to implement it.

Objective: Student will watch a step-by-step demonstration of sending an e-mail.

Subject: Expressive Literacy **Mode:** Demonstration **Training Zone:** [Z] Socialization	**Readiness Factor:** [3] Personal/Social **Readiness Factor Category:** [i] Relationships

EI 78: **Sending greeting cards**

FUTR Tool: no
PACT: yes

Supplies: None

Divide the class into six teams. Assign each team one of these special days:

- Valentine's Day
- Mother's Day
- Independence Day
- Christmas
- Wedding
- Birthday

Tell teams to imagine that they are sending a card for the assigned special day and to think of a short comment they could write on the cards before signing their names.

Objective: Student will help think of a short comment for a greeting card.

Subject: Expressive Literacy **Mode:** Written **Training Zone:** [Z] Socialization	**Readiness Factor:** [3] Personal/Social **Readiness Factor Category:** [i] Relationships

EI 79: **Setting goals**

FUTR Tool: 144
PACT: yes

Supplies: None

Discuss that a goal is like a plan that you work on to make it work out or a wish you focus on carefully so it will come true. Write these goals on the board and discuss them:

- Get a B in math
- Keep my room picked up
- Exercise three times a week

Ask each student to write one meaningful goal and then invite volunteers to share their goals.

Objective: Student will write one goal.

Subject: Expressive Literacy **Mode:** Written **Training Zone:** [U] Conclusion	**Readiness Factor:** [2] Daily Living **Readiness Factor Category:** [d] Household Care and/or Chores

EI 80: **Setting priorities**

FUTR Tool: 143
PACT: yes

Supplies: None

Point out that, even when a group of people agree that some issues are important, they are likely to have differences of opinions as to which of the issues are the most important. On the board, number from 1–10. Then, as a group, make a list of 10 things that are important to most teenagers. Ask students to use the numbers to individually put the list of things in order of importance to them. Ask volunteers to share their priority lists.

Objective: Student will help make a list of issues that are important to teenagers and will then personally prioritize the issues.

Subject: Expressive Literacy **Mode:** Graph or Chart **Training Zone:** [U] Conclusion	**Readiness Factor:** [2] Daily Living **Readiness Factor Category:** [d] Household Care and/or Chores

EI 81: **Solving problems**

FUTR Tool: 113
PACT: yes

Supplies: None

Discuss that most problems can be worked out if you think it through and make a plan. Divide the class into three teams. Ask each team to make a plan to solve one of these problems:

1. Spiral binders never seem to have enough pages for a whole class. [One solution: Use a 3-ring binder and looseleaf paper.]

2. Your socks pull inside your shoes when you walk. [One solution: Try a different brand of socks.]

3. Since you live alone, it takes you a while to eat a whole pound of hamburger and some of it always spoils. [One solution: Freeze part of it.]

Objective: Student will help to find a solution for a given problem.

Subject: Expressive Literacy **Mode:** Oral Response **Training Zone:** [L] Logic	**Readiness Factor:** [3] Personal/Social **Readiness Factor Category:** [i] Relationships

EI 82: **Sorting into categories**

FUTR Tool: no
PACT: yes

Supplies: A collection of at least 80 small items that students can sort into categories (books, rubberbands, paper clips, etc.)

Divide the class into four teams. Give each team a collection of at least 20 items. (Different teams can have like items or different items.) Ask teams to divide their items into three or four categories and to label each category. Invite teams to share their final categories with the group.

Objective: Student will help sort items into categories.

Subject: Expressive Literacy **Mode:** Hands-On **Training Zone:** [A] Analysis	**Readiness Factor:** [2] Daily Living **Readiness Factor Category:** [g] Time and Order

198 **Life Skill Lessons**

EI 83: Spelling names correctly

FUTR Tool: 115
PACT: yes

Supplies: None

Discuss that life is simpler when you are able to spell common names as well as the names of your peers. Ask students to number their papers so they have one number for each student in the class. Then, ask students to, one at a time, stand up and say their numbered first names. Have the rest of the class write the numbers and names as they are called out. Then, have students, one at a time, spell their names. Ask students to make corrections to their name lists as needed. Repeat the activity a few times for practice.

Objective: Student will spell first names of her peers.

Subject: Expressive Literacy **Mode:** Action **Training Zone:** [R] Responsibility	**Readiness Factor:** [3] Personal/Social **Readiness Factor Category:** [i] Relationships

EI 84: Spelling the days of the week correctly

FUTR Tool: no
PACT: yes

Supplies: None

Ask students to practice spelling the names of the days of the week by writing answers to these questions.

1. What day of the week was yesterday?
2. What day is today?
3. What day will it be tomorrow?
4. What day do you like the best?
5. What days do you not go to school?
6. What day was it two days ago?
7. What day will it be in two days?
8. What day was it two days ago?
9. What days, if any, haven't you written yet?

Objective: Student will spell the days of the week correctly.

Subject: Expressive Literacy **Mode:** Written **Training Zone:** [C] Conscientiousness	**Readiness Factor:** [2] Daily Living **Readiness Factor Category:** [g] Time and Order

EI 85: Summarizing movies and TV shows

FUTR Tool: no
PACT: yes

Supplies: None

Discuss that TV show and movie summaries can be long or short. Explain that long summaries are best to share with individuals who are specifically interested in the show or movie. Explain that short summaries are best for groups, casually-interested individuals, and people who plan to see the show or movie themselves. Point out that, when talking to people who plan to see a show or movie, summaries should not include the ending nor other key surprise details. Ask volunteers to summarize favorite TV shows or movies in one minute or less.

Objective: Student will summarize a favorite TV show or movie in one minute or less.

Subject: Expressive Literacy **Mode:** Oral Response **Training Zone:** [V] Observation	**Readiness Factor:** [3] Personal/Social **Readiness Factor Category:** [j] Leisure/Desires/Choices

EI 86: Taking notes

FUTR Tool: no
PACT: yes

Supplies: A textbook for each student or for every two students

Discuss that one way to take notes is by using the "folded paper/left–right column" method. Ask students to fold a piece of paper lengthwise. Then, have them open a textbook they all have (or have them join in groups to share textbooks). As a group, take notes from one or two pages. Have students write a subheading in the left column. In the right column, have them take notes that relate to the subheading. Then, have them draw a horizontal line to mark the end of that subheading and repeat with the next subheading.

Objective: Student will take a few notes using the "folded paper/left-right column" method.

Subject: Expressive Literacy **Mode:** Hands-On **Training Zone:** [U] Conclusion	**Readiness Factor:** [3] Personal/Social **Readiness Factor Category:** [k] Community Involvement and Responsibility

EI 87: Talking in simple sentences

FUTR Tool: no
PACT: no

Supplies: None

Point out that sometimes people get into the habit of talking fast and in phrases instead of sentences or in very long, wordy sentences. Explain that talking in simple, complete sentences makes it easy for others to understand what you are saying. Ask students to reword the following comments into simple, complete sentences:

1. Ah, food. Looks good. You? Alright, chow time! Share? Thanks! Yo, good stuff!

2. You can come with us if you want as long as it is OK with Lenny and his brother—you know the guy who always wears the black vest—and as long as you don't mind if we get home late and maybe even stop at Lenny's house for a while.

3. Hey, you! Coming? Now! Gotta go. Now. Not later.

Objective: Student will reword some comments into simple sentences.

Subject: Expressive Literacy **Mode:** Oral Response **Training Zone:** [O] Organization	**Readiness Factor:** [3] Personal/Social **Readiness Factor Category:** [i] Relationships

EI 88: Talking on the phone with someone you do not know

FUTR Tool: no
PACT: yes

Supplies: None

Point out that, if you answer the phone at home, you will sometimes talk to people you do not know. Tell students to use these tips when talking to strangers on the phone:

1. Always be polite.

2. If the call is for someone else, write a message.

3. If you can tell you are talking to a computer instead of a real person, hang up.

4. If the caller is rude, hang up. [Rude includes actions such as using swear words or refusing to stop talking to let you ask a question.]

Objective: Student will discuss tips to use when talking to strangers on the phone.

Subject: Expressive Literacy **Mode:** Discussion **Training Zone:** [L] Logic	**Readiness Factor:** [2] Daily Living **Readiness Factor Category:** [e] Safety and Security

EI 89: Talking to a Supervisor about personal problems

FUTR Tool: no
PACT: no

Supplies: None

Explain that personal difficulties can cause problems with your work schedule or work performance. Point out that, rather than being seen as a poor worker, you should talk to your supervisor about your problems. Make sure students understand to only choose this path for serious issues. Model the following conversation as an example:

You: I'm going to be late for a few days because my daughter broke her leg, and I have to drive her to school until the permanent cast goes on.

Supervisor: How late?

You: About 30 minutes.

Supervisor: When will the cast go on?

You: In about five days.

Supervisor: OK, get here as quickly as you can.

You: Thanks!

Objective: Student will discuss talking to a supervisor about personal problems and will listen to a modeled employee-supervisor conversation.

Subject: Expressive Literacy **Mode:** Demonstration **Training Zone:** [C] Conscientiousness	**Readiness Factor:** [1] Career **Readiness Factor Category:** [b] Job Performance

EI 90: Talking to authority figures

FUTR Tool: no
PACT: yes

Supplies: None

Point out that authority figures have some control over the choices you will be allowed to make. Explain that, for this reason, you should try to be extra polite and respectful around authority figures in an effort to make a good impression. As a group, make a list of authority figures.

Answer: Some possibilities include parent, teacher, principal, minister, boss, police officer, and mayor

Objective: Student will discuss talking with authority figures and will help make a list of authority figures.

Subject: Expressive Literacy **Mode:** Discussion, Brainstorming **Training Zone:** [C] Conscientiousness	**Readiness Factor:** [1] Career **Readiness Factor Category:** [b] Job Performance

EI 91: Talking to children

FUTR Tool: no
PACT: yes

Supplies: None

Ask four volunteers to role play the differences between talking to teens or adults and talking to children. Ask three of the volunteers to be themselves and the fourth one to be a five-year-old child. Divide them up into two groups of two. Ask each group to discuss some favorite movies. Point out to the "teenager" who is talking to the "child" that it is up to the older person in the conversation to bring the conversation down to the level of the child. Make sure the teenager talks to the child about a children's movie and in a way that a five-year-old can understand. Ask students who are watching and listening to the two conversations to take notes so the group can discuss the differences in the two conversations.

Objective: Student will take part in a role play of a conversation between a teenager and a child.

Subject: Expressive Literacy **Mode:** Role Play **Training Zone:** [R] Responsibility	**Readiness Factor:** [3] Personal/Social **Readiness Factor Category:** [i] Relationships

EI 92: Telling jokes

FUTR Tool: no
PACT: no

Supplies: None

Discuss the following tips for telling jokes successfully:

1. Match your jokes to your audience. In other words, try to choose jokes that you think those listening to you will find funny.
2. Try not to laugh when you tell a joke.
3. Make sure you remember the whole joke before you start to tell it.
4. Make sure you do not tell a joke that will offend even one person in the group.

Ask volunteers to tell jokes that are appropriate for a classroom audience.

Objective: Student will discuss tips for telling jokes successfully and will tell a joke.

Subject: Expressive Literacy **Mode:** Discussion **Training Zone:** [Z] Socialization	**Readiness Factor:** [3] Personal/Social **Readiness Factor Category:** [j] Leisure/Desires/Choices

EI 93: Using a calendar to keep a schedule

FUTR Tool: 110
PACT: yes

Supplies: Calendar page(s) for the next 30 days

Discuss that writing on a calendar is a good way to stay organized and make sure you do not forget activities and responsibilities. Give each student a copy of a calendar page(s) for the next 30 days. Have them record personal, family, and school activities and responsibilities that they know are coming up.

Objective: Student will record upcoming activities on a calendar.

Subject: Expressive Literacy **Mode:** Hands-On **Training Zone:** [O] Organization	**Readiness Factor:** [2] Daily Living **Readiness Factor Category:** [g] Time and Order

EI 94: Using a computer for basic needs

FUTR Tool: 136
PACT: yes

Supplies: A computer with basic software and Internet service

Demonstrate how to implement one or more of the following examples of ways to use a computer for basic needs:

1. Make a grocery list
2. Communicate with a friend
3. Check your bank balance
4. Pay bills
5. Set an alarm
6. Watch a movie
7. Buy an airline ticket

Objective: Student will watch a demonstration of using a computer for basic needs.

Subject: Expressive Literacy **Mode:** Demonstration **Training Zone:** [M] Manipulation	**Readiness Factor:** [1] Career **Readiness Factor Category:** [a] Career Preparation

EI 95: Using a confident voice

Supplies: None

Make a circle on the board and in the center, write "Using a confident voice." Out from the circle, draw four lines leading to boxes with these phrases in the boxes:

1. Use good posture with head held high

2. Use eye contact

3. Speak loudly enough to be easily heard

4. Know what you want to say

Discuss that these four points can help you speak confidently. Ask your students to practice talking in front of the class using these four steps.

Objective: Student will practice speaking confidently using four defined steps.

Subject: Expressive Literacy	**Readiness Factor:** [1] Career
Mode: Action	**Readiness Factor Category:** [b] Job Performance
Training Zone: [Z] Socialization	

EI 96: Using a planner

FUTR Tool: no
PACT: no

Supplies: A daily planner

Discuss that a planner is a small booklet with one page or space for each day. Explain that people who have a lot of activities to keep track of often use a planner. Show your students a planner and show how it is laid out. Discuss that different planners vary in amount of space given to write, number of days included on a page, extra information that is provided, and overall set-up.

As a group, brainstorm things you might write in a planner.

Objective: Student will discuss characteristics of planners and will help make a list of things he might write in a planner.

Subject: Expressive Literacy	**Readiness Factor:** [2] Daily Living
Mode: Demonstration	**Readiness Factor Category:** [g] Time and Order
Training Zone: [O] Organization	

EI 97: Using abbreviations

FUTR Tool: no
PACT: yes

Supplies: None

As a group, brainstorm a list of abbreviations. Make sure to include abbreviations such as these:

A.M.	P.M.	Ave.	Blvd.	Rd.	lb.	M.D.	R.N.	R.S.V.P.
Dr.	Mr.	Mrs.	Ms.	Jr.	Sr.	TBA	DBA	C.O.D.
ID	pd.	ATM	ASAP	misc.	TLC	TOC	U.S.	FWD

Then, ask each student to write ten sentences using as many of the abbreviations from the list as they can work in.

Objective: Student will help to make a list of abbreviations and will then write ten sentences using many of the abbreviations.

Subject: Expressive Literacy	**Readiness Factor:** [3] Personal/Social
Mode: Brainstorming, Written	**Readiness Factor Category:** [j] Leisure/Desires/Choices
Training Zone: [L] Logic	

EI 98: Using appropriate tones and volume levels

FUTR Tool: no
PACT: yes

Supplies: None

Discuss that tone and volume are two traits that determine the effect a person's voice has on others. Explain that tone is altered when emotion enters a voice, hence a person can sound happy, scared, or angry. Point out that volume is the loudness or softness of a voice, and that a person chooses a volume based on choices such as wanting to talk louder so a whole group can hear and wanting to talk very softly to prevent nearby people from hearing.

Divide the class into six teams. Ask teams to role play examples of situations where the following voice volumes and tones would be appropriate:

1. Loud volume, happy tone

2. Regular volume, excited tone

3. Low volume, frightened tone

4. Loud volume, angry tone

5. Low volume, guilty tone

6. Regular volume, confused tone

Objective: Student will role play using a specific voice volume and tone.

Subject: Expressive Literacy **Mode:** Role Play **Training Zone:** [S] Self-Awareness	**Readiness Factor:** [1] Career **Readiness Factor Category:** [b] Job Performance

---

EI 99: Using change-of-address forms

FUTR Tool: no
PACT: no

Supplies: A change-of-address form for each student (copies are fine)

Discuss that change-of-address forms are used by the post office to reroute your mail from your old address to your new address. Point out that you should still give your new address to friends, relatives, and businesses you frequent and let the change-of-address forms catch the people you miss. Explain that the way change-of-address forms work is that the post office puts a forwarding address (your new address) on each piece of mail that is addressed with your name and old address, and that they will usually do this forwarding for six months. Also, let students know that, when you receive letters with forwarding stickers on them, you should contact the senders and give them your new address (unless you do not want them to have your address).

Give each student a change-of-address form. Ask them to fill out the forms using their current addresses as the "current" address and the school address as the 'new' address.

As a group, brainstorm a list of people and places that you would need to notify of your new address.

Objective: Student will fill out and discuss change-of-address forms.

Subject: Expressive Literacy **Mode:** Hands-On **Training Zone:** [O] Organization	**Readiness Factor:** [2] Daily Living **Readiness Factor Category:** [g] Time and Order

EI 100: **Using effective phone skills**

Supplies: None

Discuss that even everyday skills, like talking on the telephone, have "rules." Ask students to brainstorm a list of telephone rules such as the following:

1. Talk loudly enough to be heard, but don't yell. Yelling can hurt the ears of the person on the other end.
2. When you call someone, identify yourself right away unless you know for sure that the person who answered already knows who you are.
3. Be sensitive to other peoples' time. Say goodbye when you sense that a person wants to hang up or that a conversation has wound down.
4. If you get a wrong number, apologize and hang up.

Objective: Student will help make a list of telephone rules.

Subject: Expressive Literacy **Mode:** Brainstorming **Training Zone:** [C] Conscientiousness	**Readiness Factor:** [1] Career **Readiness Factor Category:** [a] Career Preparation

EI 101: **Using eye contact**

Supplies: None

Discuss that it is always best to look someone in the eye when talking to him or her. Ask your students to move around the room talking to each other and practicing using eye contact. Discuss that, although eye contact is almost always a wise choice in a conversation, there are times when it is very critical and times when it should be avoided:

1. Eye contact is very critical during a job interview.
2. Eye contact is very critical when trying to convince someone to see your point of view.
3. Eye contact is very critical when trying to convince someone you are honest.
4. Eye contact should be avoided with shady characters you meet on a sidewalk or in a park.
5. Eye contact should be avoided with someone who is likely to make you laugh or cry while talking in front of a group.

Objective: Student will practice using eye contact and will discuss some eye-contact issues.

Subject: Expressive Literacy **Mode:** Action **Training Zone:** [Z] Socialization	**Readiness Factor:** [3] Personal/Social **Readiness Factor Category:** [i] Relationships

EI 102: Using good judgment when talking to strangers

FUTR Tool: no
PACT: yes

Supplies: None

Discuss that there are times when it is OK to speak to strangers and times when you should completely stay away from them. Discuss the following examples:

1. It is OK to have casual conversation with a stranger sitting next to you on an airplane.
2. It is OK to talk with and get to know a stranger who is with your friends or relatives.
3. Never talk to a stranger when you are outside at night.
4. Never talk to a stranger in a car who calls out and offers you a ride.
5. Never talk to a stranger who makes you uncomfortable.

Objective: Student will discuss when to talk to and not talk to strangers.

Subject: Expressive Literacy **Mode:** Discussion **Training Zone:** [E] Exploration	**Readiness Factor:** [3] Personal/Social **Readiness Factor Category:** [k] Community Involvement and Responsibility

EI 103: Using manners in conversations

FUTR Tool: 119
PACT: yes

Supplies: None

As a group, brainstorm two or three answers for each of the following questions:

1. When should you keep listening to someone tell a long story even if you think it is boring? [Two possible answers: Senior citizen, teacher]
2. When should you say "excuse me," and walk away from a conversation? [Two possible answers: Sick, someone you need to see is leaving]
3. When should you try to change the topic of conversation? [Two possible answers: Is offensive, has run its course]
4. When should you hold back an inclination to laugh during a conversation? [Two possible answers: When might hurt someone's feelings, when it would appear that you are laughing at someone.]

Objective: Student will help give answers to questions about manners in conversations.

Subject: Expressive Literacy **Mode:** Brainstorming **Training Zone:** [C] Conscientiousness	**Readiness Factor:** [3] Personal/Social **Readiness Factor Category:** [i] Relationships

EI 104: Using TO DO lists

FUTR Tool: no
PACT: no

Supplies: None

Discuss that TO DO lists are simply lists of things that you plan to do. Tell your students that, by writing the things you have to do, you will have an easier time remembering all of them. Also, point out that checking them off as you complete them is sort of like giving yourself a little reward.

Explain that TO DO lists help many people keep themselves organized. Ask students to take a sheet of paper and create a decorative "TO DO" at the top. Then, have make lists of things they have to do that day. Tell them to check them off as they do them.

Objective: Student will create a TO DO list heading and make a TO DO list for the day.

Subject: Expressive Literacy **Mode:** Drawing **Training Zone:** [O] Organization	**Readiness Factor:** [2] Daily Living **Readiness Factor Category:** [g] Time and Order

EI 105: **Volunteering to help a friend or neighbor**

FUTR Tool: no
PACT: yes

Supplies: None

Discuss that one of the most neighborly things you can do is to volunteer to help a neighbor in need. As a group, make a list of situations where a neighbor might need help. Include ideas such as the following:

1. Help to hold bags while he bags his leaves
2. Pick up his newspaper when he is out of town
3. Take a delivery when he is not home
4. Give him a ride when he needs to pick up his car at the repair shop

Objective: Student will help make a list of situations where a neighbor might need help.

Subject: Expressive Literacy **Mode:** Brainstorming **Training Zone:** [F] Flexibility	**Readiness Factor:** [3] Personal/Social **Readiness Factor Category:** [k] Community Involvement and Responsibility

EI 106: **Writing a basic resume**

FUTR Tool: no
PACT: no

Supplies: Computers for students to use (optional)

Discuss that most resumés include these basic parts: name, address, phone number, education (levels and schools), jobs you have held (titles of jobs, names and addresses of companies). Ask students to hand write (or do in computers if feasible) very basic resumes. If you run out of time, have them finish them as homework assignments.

Objective: Student will write a basic resume.

Subject: Expressive Literacy **Mode:** Written **Training Zone:** [U] Conclusion	**Readiness Factor:** [1] Career **Readiness Factor Category:** [a] Career Preparation

EI 107: **Writing a business letter**

FUTR Tool: no
PACT: no

Supplies: Mailing envelopes (optional)

Discuss that business letters are formal letters which means they have features such as these: they are typed; they do not discuss personal issues; they are direct and to the point; they have the business name/contact name/address before the greeting; the greeting is either Dear Sir(s), Dear Madam, or Dear (specific contact name); the salutation is either "Thank you" or "Sincerely"; the person writing the letter leaves space before typing his name and writes his signature in the space; the address of the person writing the letter follows the typed name. Ask students to choose products they particularly like or dislike and to write letters to the companies that manufacture the products sharing their opinions and the reasons behind them. You can choose to mail the letters or have them simply be a practice exercise.

Objective: Student will write a business letter.

Subject: Expressive Literacy **Mode:** Written **Training Zone:** [R] Responsibility	**Readiness Factor:** [1] Career **Readiness Factor Category:** [a] Career Preparation

EI 108: Writing a friendly letter

FUTR Tool: no
PACT: no

Supplies: Mailing envelopes (optional)

Discuss that, in today's world, people often send e-mails rather than writing letters. Point out that some people do not have e-mail, especially some elderly people. Have students write letters to friends or relatives. For those who have elderly people in their lives, suggest they write to them. Tell students to make sure to include these parts in their letters: date, greeting, introductory paragraph, body of the letter, conclusion, friendly closing, and casual signature.

Actually mail the letters of those students who wish to do so.

Objective: Student will write a friendly letter.

Subject: Expressive Literacy **Mode:** Written **Training Zone:** [Z] Socialization	**Readiness Factor:** [1] Career **Readiness Factor Category:** [a] Career Preparation

EI 109: Writing e-mail subject lines

FUTR Tool: 141
PACT: yes

Supplies: None

Discuss that e-mail subject lines should be short so they show up in their entirety. Also, point out that e-mail subject lines should relate to the main idea in the e-mail so they can be used to easily sort e-mails.
Divide the class into four teams. Ask each team to hand-write a short e-mail and to create a short, meaningful subject line to go with it.

Objective: Student will help write an e-mail and a subject line that is short and meaningful.

Subject: Expressive Literacy **Mode:** Written **Training Zone:** [A] Analysis	**Readiness Factor:** [1] Career **Readiness Factor Category:** [b] Job Performance

EI 110: Writing For Sale ads

FUTR Tool: no
PACT: yes

Supplies: "For Sale" ads from several different days of local newspapers

Discuss that one easy way to write For Sale ads is to find an ad in the paper that is similar to what you have to sell, and then pattern your ad after it. Have students each choose a For Sale ad from the newspaper. Then, have them choose a household item and write a similar For Sale ad for the item.

Objective: Student will use an existing For Sale ad as a pattern for writing a new For Sale ad.

Subject: Expressive Literacy **Mode:** Hands-On **Training Zone:** [A] Analysis	**Readiness Factor:** [2] Daily Living **Readiness Factor Category:** [f] Shopping and Eating at Restaurants

EI 111: Writing on a gift tag

FUTR Tool: no
PACT: yes

Supplies: Several pieces of unlined paper, scissors

Discuss that most gift tags are quite small, so you cannot write much and what you do write must be small. Cut several pieces of unlined paper into one inch by two inch rectangles and give each student one of these "gift tags." Ask students to write gift tags to the students on their left and to use their own names as the givers of the gifts. Have them use these formats "To Name" and "From Name." Discuss that, when you know the person well, last names need not be used.

Objective: Student will write a gift tag.

Subject: Expressive Literacy **Mode:** Hands-On, Written **Training Zone:** [O] Organization	**Readiness Factor:** [3] Personal/Social **Readiness Factor Category:** [i] Relationships

EI 112: Writing phone messages

FUTR Tool: 109
PACT: yes

Supplies: None

Pair students up with partners. Ask them to role play being a phone caller and a phone answerer/message taker using this general format:

1. The phone caller asks to talk to someone other than the phone answerer.
2. The phone answerer says the requested person is not present and offers to take a message.
3. The phone caller says thanks and leaves a message.
4. The phone answerer writes the message while the caller is still on the phone.
5. The phone answerer reads the message to the caller to verify that it is correct.
6. Both parties say goodbye.

Have partners change roles and repeat.

Objective: Student will role play a phone message situation.

Subject: Expressive Literacy **Mode:** Role Play **Training Zone:** [O] Organization	**Readiness Factor:** [3] Personal/Social **Readiness Factor Category:** [i] Relationships

EI 113: **Writing school excuses**

FUTR Tool: no
PACT: yes

Supplies: None

Ask students how many of them have ever missed school and had to get a note from their parents when they went back to school. Explain that you need to know how to write school excuses in case you ever have children of your own. Divide the class into four teams. To each team, assign one of the following reasons for missing school.

1. A doctor's appointment at 1:00—need to leave at 12:30

2. Has the flu

3. Has a bad cold

4. Grandmother died

Ask each team member to write a school excuse for "Ali." Ask volunteers to share their excuses.

Objective: Student will write a school excuse for a specific reason to miss school.

Subject: Expressive Literacy **Mode:** Written **Training Zone:** [R] Responsibility	**Readiness Factor:** [3] Personal/Social **Readiness Factor Category:** [k] Community Involvement and Responsibility

EI 114: **Writing within given space**

FUTR Tool: 139
PACT: yes

Supplies: A sheet of unlined paper for each student

Discuss that sometimes you have to change the size of your writing to fit in the space you have. Ask each student to fold a piece of unlined paper in half and tear it in two. Have them save one of the 8 1/2 x 5 1/2 pieces and fold the other one in half. Have them tear the paper on the fold, and save one of the 4 1/4 x 5 1/2 pieces. Have them fold the other piece of paper in half and tear on the fold. Have them save one of the 4 1/4 x 2 3/4 pieces and tear the other one in half. Have them tear on the fold and discard one of the pieces and keep the other which should be about 2 1/8 x 2 3/4. Then, on each of their four pieces of paper, have them write the ABCs so that they fill the page, but all fit on.

Objective: Student will write the ABCs four times so that they fit in four different-size spaces.

Subject: Expressive Literacy **Mode:** Action **Training Zone:** [A] Analysis	**Readiness Factor:** [1] Career **Readiness Factor Category:** [a] Career Preparation

EI 115: **Zigzagging through a crowd**

FUTR Tool: no
PACT: no

Supplies: None

Discuss that working your way through a thick crowd is not always easy, and if you kind of zigzag back and forth, you can find small openings to squeeze through. Also, point out that it is helpful to offer ongoing polite "let me through" requests such as the following:

• Excuse me

• Pardon me

• Can I squeeze through here, please?

• Hi. Can I please get through?

• I'm sorry, I didn't mean to bump you.

Objective: Student will discuss techniques for getting through a thick crowd.

Subject: Expressive Literacy **Mode:** Discussion **Training Zone:** [Z] Socialization	**Readiness Factor:** [3] Personal/Social **Readiness Factor Category:** [k] Community Involvement and Responsibility

Receptive
Literacy

Life Skill Lessons

Table of Contents: *Receptive Literacy*

RI 1: Accepting compliments

FUTR Tool: 163
PACT: yes

Supplies: None

Discuss that, when someone gives you a compliment, you should say "Thank you." Point out that sometimes you might feel embarrassed and want to discount the compliment, but that it is impolite not to accept a genuine compliment. Explain to the students that you are going to give them some compliments, you want them to say "Thanks"—and you want them to mean it. Point out that, as long as you do not try to diminish the compliment, you can say additional words such as "Thanks, I'm glad you like it" or "Thanks, it's a family trait" or "Thanks, it's my creative side showing through" or "Thanks, I really tried hard." Either after or during the discussion, randomly give out compliments to different students.

Objective: Student will accept a compliment with a "Thank you."

Subject: Receptive Literacy **Mode:** Oral Response **Training Zone:** [Z] Socialization	**Readiness Factor:** [3] Personal/Social **Readiness Factor Category:** [i] Relationships

RI 2: Asking for reading help if needed

FUTR Tool: 167
PACT: yes

Supplies: None

Discuss that not being able to read is a problem, but being an adult trying to get by without knowing what any written material says is even a bigger problem. Explain that struggling adult readers should have one or two people they can regularly turn to for reading help. Suggest the following possibilities for reading helpers:

1. parent
2. sibling
3. spouse
4. close friend
5. neighbor
6. child

Objective: Student will discuss the importance for struggling readers to have a reading helper and will go over a list of people who are possible reading helpers.

Subject: Receptive Literacy **Mode:** Discussion **Training Zone:** [S] Self-Awareness	**Readiness Factor:** [1] Career **Readiness Factor Category:** [b] Job Performance

RI 3: Asking for verbal clarification

FUTR Tool: 156
PACT: yes

Supplies: None

Discuss that, when speaking over the phone, some letters require clues because it is hard to hear the difference between like-sounding letters. Point out that the following letters are commonly misheard:

f   s   m   n   p   g   t   v   b   d

Explain that, when someone says a name or word and you are not sure what was said, you should ask for verbal clarification by asking, for example, is that M as in Mary. Point out that you can use any name or word as long as it clarifies the confusion.

Ask students to role play asking for verbal clarification by having Student A stand with her back to the class while Student B spells a last name with at least one confusing letter. Have Student A ask for clarification by using a word clue such as M as in Mary.

Objective: Student will discuss and role play asking for letter clues for verbal clarification.

Subject: Receptive Literacy **Mode:** Role Play **Training Zone:** [C] Conscientiousness	**Readiness Factor:** [1] Career **Readiness Factor Category:** [b] Job Performance

RI 4: **Blocking out distracting background noise**

FUTR Tool: no
PACT: no

Supplies: Two different music players so you can play two different songs at once

Discuss that background noises can be frustrating when you are trying to listen to something of your choosing. Review the following tips for blocking out background noise:

1. Keep your eyes focused on the source of what you are trying to hear.

2. If you are talking to someone, watch his mouth to help you understand the words.

3. Actually participate in what you are trying to hear. For example, talk to the person, take notes, get closer.

Play two different songs in the background. Ask students to block out the background and have a conversation.

Objective: Student will discuss tips for blocking out background noise and will then practice using the tips.

Subject: Receptive Literacy **Mode:** Action **Training Zone:** [A] Analysis	**Readiness Factor:** [2] Daily Living **Readiness Factor Category:** [g] Time and Order

RI 5: **Buying an airline ticket online**

FUTR Tool: no
PACT: no

Supplies: Computer with Internet service

Go online and demonstrate the steps to buying an airline ticket including the following:

1. Find an airline ticket site.

2. Put in flight dates, your local airport, and a destination.

3. Discuss the available flight times and prices.

4. Select a flight.

5. When you come to the "pay" screen, discuss the different options and then cancel out (unless you actually want to buy a ticket).

6. Explain that, after you pay, you will get a confirmation screen with your e-ticket. Point out that you are to print the e-ticket and take it to the airport (along with a picture ID) on your flight date.

Objective: Student will watch a demonstration of buying an airline ticket online.

Subject: Receptive Literacy **Mode:** Demonstration **Training Zone:** [E] Exploration	**Readiness Factor:** [2] Daily Living **Readiness Factor Category:** [h] Transportation/Travel/Worldliness

RI 6: **Choosing e-mail options**

FUTR Tool: no
PACT: no

Supplies: Computer with Internet service

Discuss that e-mail programs offer a variety of options. Open an e-mail program and show students how to change options such as how the screen looks, how the text looks, what noise (if any) you hear when an e-mail arrives. Ask volunteers to share how their e-mail screens are like or different from the one you are showing them.

Objective: Student will watch a demonstration showing how to chose different e-mail options.

Subject: Receptive Literacy **Mode:** Demonstration **Training Zone:** [U] Conclusion	**Readiness Factor:** [2] Daily Living **Readiness Factor Category:** [h] Transportation/Travel/Worldliness

RI 7: Choosing papers and things to keep

FUTR Tool: 146
PACT: yes

Supplies: None

Point out that you should throw some papers and things away after having seen or used them once, and you should keep some other papers and things. Ask volunteers to say "Keep" or "Throw or give away" for each of these items:

1. Warranty for a new camera [keep]
2. Receipt for a candy bar [throw]
3. Apartment rental agreement [keep]
4. Graduation diploma [keep]
5. A sales flyer [throw]
6. Directions for your blender [keep]
7. Last month's newspapers [throw]
8. Birth certificate [keep]
9. Political advertisement [throw]
10. Letter from your grandmother [keep]

Objective: Student will help decide whether items should be kept or thrown away.

Subject: Receptive Literacy **Mode:** Oral Response **Training Zone:** [O] Organization	**Readiness Factor:** [2] Daily Living **Readiness Factor Category:** [g] Time and Order

RI 8: Choosing possible jobs through help-wanted ads

FUTR Tool: no
PACT: yes

Supplies: A set of job ads and a highlighter for each student

Give each student the job ads from one day's newspaper. Have them use a highlighter to mark the jobs as follows:

1. Put an X over job ads that are of no interest.
2. Circle the jobs that sound fairly good.
3. Circle and star the jobs that sound the best.
4. Leave the not-good-but-not-bad jobs unmarked.

Objective: Student will use a highlighter to mark possible jobs in the newspaper job ads.

Subject: Receptive Literacy **Mode:** Drawing **Training Zone:** [U] Conclusion	**Readiness Factor:** [1] Career **Readiness Factor Category:** [a] Career Preparation

RI 9: Choosing recipes for a meal

FUTR Tool: no
PACT: yes

Supplies: A cookbook for each team

Divide the class into teams of three to five students. Give each team a cookbook. Ask teams to choose the following items to make a well-balanced meal:

1. salad and/or hors d'oeuvres
2. drinks
3. meat
4. vegetable #1
5. vegetable #2
6. bread
7. potato
8. dessert

Ask teams to share their meal plans.

Objective: Student will help choose recipes for a meal.

Subject: Receptive Literacy **Mode:** Hands-On **Training Zone:** [V] Observation	**Readiness Factor:** [2] Daily Living **Readiness Factor Category:** [d] Household Care and/or Chores

RI 10: Dealing with criticism

Supplies: None

Ask students to choose the best response for each of these criticism situations:

1. Your friend says, "That shirt is too worn out to wear."

    a. Shut up.

    b. Do you really thinks so?

    c. Like your shirt is so great.

2. A teacher says, "I really think you can do better than this."

    a. No, I can't.

    b. You don't know anything about me.

    c. Why do you think that?

3. Your brother says, "You need to wash your hair."

    a. I will tonight.

    b. Right, freak. Like you are Mr. Clean.

    c. Don't tell me what to do.

Objective: Student will choose the best response for several criticism situations.

Subject: Receptive Literacy **Mode:** Oral Response **Training Zone:** [Z] Socialization	**Readiness Factor:** [3] Personal/Social **Readiness Factor Category:** [i] Relationships

RI 11: Dealing with speeding tickets

Supplies: None

Discuss that speeding tickets have a lot of information given in a little space. Point out that, even though the print is very small, you want to be sure to read it all. Explain that some of the information tells these details:

1. What you should do if you want to plead guilty.

2. What you should do if you if you want to plead innocent.

3. What will happen if you do not follow the instructions.

4. Deadlines for different options.

5. A number to call if you have questions.

Objective: Student will discuss the information included on a speeding ticket.

Subject: Receptive Literacy **Mode:** Discussion **Training Zone:** [R] Responsibility	**Readiness Factor:** [2] Daily Living **Readiness Factor Category:** [h] Transportation/Travel/Worldliness

RI 12: **Feeding parking meters**

FUTR Tool: no
PACT: yes

Supplies: None

Discuss the following facts about parking meters:

1. Parking meters almost always require coins.
2. Meters usually require a set amount of money for a set amount of time such as 25¢ or 50¢ for 10 minutes, 15 minutes, 20 minutes, or 30 minutes.
3. Sometimes a meter has paid-up time when you arrive because the last person paid for more time than she used. You can use the time if it is enough or add more time if needed.
4. If you run out of paid-up-time, an out-of-time signal such as a red circle, will show in the meter window to signal the parking police to give you a ticket.
5. In many places, parking is free on week-ends, so you do not have to put money in the meters from Friday night through Sunday night.

Objective: Student will discuss facts about parking meters.

Subject: Receptive Literacy **Mode:** Discussion **Training Zone:** [A] Analysis	**Readiness Factor:** [2] Daily Living **Readiness Factor Category:** [c] Finances

RI 13: **Filing papers and bills**

FUTR Tool: 145
PACT: yes

Supplies: None

On the board, draw six "file folders" labeled as follows: phone bills, report cards, reference letters, memories, class ring, community service. Call out papers to file, such as those listed below, and have students "add" them to the correct files.

1. 9-weeks grades
2. Thank you from nursing home for helping at craft time
3. A program from a play you were in
4. A note from a teacher saying he appreciates all the effort you put into your work
5. Your October cell phone bill
6. A copy of your class ring order form

Objective: Student will determine which papers to file into which file folders.

Subject: Receptive Literacy **Mode:** Action **Training Zone:** [O] Organization	**Readiness Factor:** [2] Daily Living **Readiness Factor Category:** [d] Household Care and/or Chores

RI 14: Finding a book in the library

FUTR Tool: no
PACT: no

Supplies: Two library books with shelving information on the spine—one fiction and one nonfiction

Discuss that library books have categorizing information on their spines that give the books a place to be shelved. Show students a nonfiction book and point out the Dewey Decimal Code on the spine. Explain that nonfiction books are on the shelves by topic. Show students a fiction book and point out the first letters of the author's last name on the spine. Explain that fiction books are on the shelves in ABC order by authors' last names. Point out that you can use one of two ways to find a book:

1. Look on the shelves—If you know the author of a fiction book, simply look it up on the shelf. If you know the Dewey Decimal number for the topic, go to that area and browse through books on the topic.
2. Search by computer—Libraries have computers with search programs. You can enter the title, author, or subject and find the author or Dewey Decimal Code as well as whether or not the book is checked out.

Objective: Student will discuss how to find a book in a library.

Subject: Receptive Literacy Mode: Hands-On Training Zone: [E] Exploration	Readiness Factor: [2] Daily Living Readiness Factor Category: [g] Time and Order

RI 15: Finding a file in a computer or on a CD

FUTR Tool: no
PACT: no

Supplies: A computer with a CD drive; a CD

On a computer, show students how to find a file in a computer. Identify a specific file you are looking for. Then, start at the desktop and explain what you are doing as you search through the layers of folders. Repeat the process with a CD.

Let students take turns searching for files.

Objective: Student will search for files on a computer or CD.

Subject: Receptive Literacy Mode: Action Training Zone: [L] Logic	Readiness Factor: [1] Career Readiness Factor Category: [b] Job Performance

RI 16: Finding appliance repair numbers and addresses

FUTR Tool: no
PACT: yes

Supplies: One appliance repair manual for every four or five students

Divide the class into teams of four or five students. Give each team an appliance repair manual. Tell teams to try to find a phone number to use to talk to a technical support or repair department and an address where you can send a product for repairs.

Also, go online and search for a company and product to see if you can also find the phone number and address online.

Objective: Student will find the phone number and address for a certain appliance repair.

Subject: Receptive Literacy Mode: Action Training Zone: [E] Exploration	Readiness Factor: [2] Daily Living Readiness Factor Category: [d] Household Care and/or Chores

RI 17: Finding emergency numbers

FUTR Tool: 171
PACT: yes

Supplies: Several phone books

Discuss that 9-1-1 is the emergency number to use whenever you have a serious emergency. Point out that, when you have a need that is not such a serious emergency, you can call other secondary-level emergency numbers. Explain that these numbers are often listed under local, state, and national government. Divide the class into small groups and give each group a phone book. Ask teams to find the following emergency phone numbers:

1. fire department
2. police department
3. animal control
4. ambulance service
5. child protection agency
6. poison control center

Objective: Student will find phone numbers for secondary-level emergency situations.

Subject: Receptive Literacy **Mode:** Action **Training Zone:** [E] Exploration	**Readiness Factor:** [2] Daily Living **Readiness Factor Category:** [e] Safety and Security

RI 18: Finding ways to remember facts

FUTR Tool: no
PACT: no

Supplies: None

Discuss that it is not always easy to remember things you hear. Explain that one way you can help yourself remember is by creating memory clues such as these two: ROY G BIV for the order of the colors in the rainbow and Mad Wish to remember that Madison is the capital of Wisconsin. Choose a few facts that the students are currently studying and ask students to think of word clues to help remember them.

Objective: Student will create memory clues to help remember study details.

Subject: Receptive Literacy **Mode:** Oral Response **Training Zone:** [E] Exploration	**Readiness Factor:** [2] Daily Living **Readiness Factor Category:** [g] Time and Order

RI 19: Following multiple oral directions

FUTR Tool: 175
PACT: yes

Supplies: A book with at least 79 pages

Explain that there are many times in life when it is helpful to be able to follow multiple directions at a time. Ask a volunteer to follow the four directions below, but not to start until you have given all four directions. Hand the student the book as you give these four directives:

1. Open the book.

2. Turn to page 42.

3. Turn to page 79.

4. Touch your chin.

Repeat with similar directions and other volunteers.

Objective: Student will follow multiple oral directions.

Subject: Receptive Literacy **Mode:** Action **Training Zone:** [A] Analysis	**Readiness Factor:** [1] Career **Readiness Factor Category:** [b] Job Performance

RI 20: **Following written directions**

FUTR Tool: no
PACT: yes

Supplies: None

Write these directions on the board and ask students to follow them:

1. Get out a piece of paper.

2. Put your name in the upper right corner.

3. Draw a large "S" in the middle of the page.

4. Put an "X" in the top half of the "S."

5. Put a circle in the bottom half of the "S."

6. Draw a box around the "X."

7. Draw a squiggly line around the "S."

8. Draw a smiley face inside the circle.

9. Fold your paper in half.

10. Turn your paper in.

Objective: Student will follow a set of written directions.

Subject: Receptive Literacy **Mode:** Action **Training Zone:** [A] Analysis	**Readiness Factor:** [1] Career **Readiness Factor Category:** [b] Job Performance

RI 21: **Handling an automated phone system**

FUTR Tool: 149
PACT: yes

Supplies: None

Discuss that automated phone systems have several basic functions such as those below:

1. You have to listen and choose from given choices by pushing numbers.

2. You can almost always choose to listen to the choices again.

3. If you make no choice, you will either get locked into a loop that lists the choices, be disconnected, or get rerouted to a live attendant.

4. Sometimes you have a choice to go to a company directory where you are asked to punch in an employee's identity such as the first three letters of the person's last name.

5. Sometimes you can't seem to get to the person you need. When this happens, you can try different options, even though they are not what you want, until you get to a live person. Then, you can ask the live person to help route you to the desired person.

Objective: Student will discuss some basic functions of automated phone systems.

Subject: Receptive Literacy **Mode:** Discussion **Training Zone:** [L] Logic	**Readiness Factor:** [1] Career **Readiness Factor Category:** [a] Career Preparation

RI 22: **Handling gossip**

FUTR Tool: 166
PACT: yes

Supplies: None

Discuss that gossip can be destructive to both the person doing the gossiping and to the person being gossiped about. As a group, brainstorm some destructive features of gossiping. Include ideas such as the following:

1. Unfairly gives people bad reputations
2. Spreads negative attitudes
3. Gives gossipers busy-body reputations
4. Ruins friendships
5. Takes time away from productive activities

Objective: Student will help list some destructive features of gossiping.

Subject: Receptive Literacy **Mode:** Brainstorming **Training Zone:** [S] Self-Awareness	**Readiness Factor:** [3] Personal/Social **Readiness Factor Category:** [i] Relationships

RI 23: **Identifying sources of occupational training**

FUTR Tool: 151
PACT: yes

Supplies: Yellow pages and/or computer with Internet service

Using either the yellow pages, the Internet, or both, work together to find sources of occupational training for jobs such as the following:

1. plumber
2. mechanic
3. construction worker
4. nursing assistant
5. brick layer
6. electrician
7. concrete layer
8. heating/air conditioning technician
9. computer technician

Objective: Student will help find sources of occupational training for a variety of jobs.

Subject: Receptive Literacy **Mode:** Action **Training Zone:** [R] Responsibility	**Readiness Factor:** [1] Career **Readiness Factor Category:** [a] Career Preparation

RI 24: Interpreting idioms

FUTR Tool: no
PACT: no

Supplies: None

Discuss that idioms are slang phrases that come and go in popularity. Explain that you can usually figure out the meaning of idioms by looking at the rest of the sentence, the tone of voice, and things going on at the time. Use some idioms such as those below and ask volunteers to explain them.

1. This is going to be a piece of cake. [This is going to be easy.]

2. You're going to have to burn the midnight oil. [You will have to work late.]

3. Don't count your chickens before they hatch. [Don't assume until you have proof.]

4. I'm as happy as a pig in a poke. [I'm very happy.]

5. I can talk until I'm blue in the face, but it won't make any difference. [It will not matter what I say.]

6. Don't toot your own horn. [Don't brag.]

7. Birds of a feather flock together. (People with the same interests tend to spend time together.)

8. Knock it off, Terry. [Stop it, Terry.]

Objective: Student will interpret some idioms.

Subject: Receptive Literacy **Mode:** Oral Response **Training Zone:** [A] Analysis	**Readiness Factor:** [3] Personal/Social **Readiness Factor Category:** [j] Leisure/Desires/Choices

RI 25: Interpreting what people say

FUTR Tool: 177
PACT: yes

Supplies: None

Explain that, to understand what others are saying, you have to listen to both the words and the tone of voice. Also, point out that you have to decide if things others say are facts or opinions and whether they said exactly what they meant. Ask students to keep these ideas in mind while answering the following questions:

1. Is this comment a fact or an opinion?—Horses make great pets. [opinion]

2. Is this comment a fact or an opinion?—Apples and pears are both fruits. [fact]

3. Lyle said, "I'm so thirsty, I could eat three cheeseburgers." What do you think Lyle meant to say? [I'm so hungry, I could eat three cheeseburgers.]

4. Kelly said, "(Roll your eyes and chuckle) I think that it is great idea."—What do you think Kelly meant? [She doesn't think it is a good idea.]

Objective: Student will interpret facts and opinions, misspeaks, and voice intonations.

Subject: Receptive Literacy **Mode:** Oral Response **Training Zone:** [A] Analysis	**Readiness Factor:** [3] Personal/Social **Readiness Factor Category:** [k] Community Involvement and Responsibility

RI 26: **Keeping up with the news**

FUTR Tool: no
PACT: yes

Supplies: None

Ask students to brainstorm a list of ways that they can keep up with the news. Include ideas such as the following:

1. Watch the news on TV.
2. Read the newspaper.
3. Listen to the radio.
4. Read news magazines.
5. Read online news.
6. Talk to people who read or hear the news.
7. Pay close attention in classes where current events are discussed.

Objective: Student will help make a list of ways to keep up with the news.

Subject: Receptive Literacy **Mode:** Brainstorming **Training Zone:** [R] Responsibility	**Readiness Factor:** [2] Daily Living **Readiness Factor Category:** [h] Transportation/Travel/Worldliness

RI 27: **Knowing basis for voting decisions**

FUTR Tool: no
PACT: yes

Supplies: None

Point out that making an educated decision about who to vote for takes effort. Discuss that the following options can help a person become educated about a candidate:

1. Listen to the news.
2. Listen to political ads on TV.
3. Read newspapers.
4. Watch debates on TV.
5. Read flyers.
6. Accept that you probably will not agree with everything any one politician says.
7. Decide what you think is true based on the news, ads, newspaper, debates, and flyers.
8. Decide with which candidate's points of view you most agree.

Objective: Student will discuss options that can help her become educated about a political candidate.

Subject: Receptive Literacy **Mode:** Discussion **Training Zone:** [R] Responsibility	**Readiness Factor:** [2] Daily Living **Readiness Factor Category:** [h] Transportation/Travel/Worldliness

RI 28: Knowing what type of material you like to read or watch

FUTR Tool: no
PACT: yes

Supplies: None

Make a two-column, five-row chart on the board with these headings:

- Find interesting to read
- Do not find interesting to read

Label the rows with the following book types:

- Mysteries
- Fantasy
- Horrow
- Dramas
- Love Stories
- Use tallies to mark students' opinions about each type of book.

Objective: Student will help create a chart showing types of material the class likes to read.

Subject: Receptive Literacy **Mode:** Graph or Chart **Training Zone:** [S] Self-Awareness	**Readiness Factor:** [3] Personal/Social **Readiness Factor Category:** [j] Leisure/Desires/Choices

RI 29: Knowing where to turn for advice

FUTR Tool: no
PACT: yes

Supplies: None

As a group, brainstorm a list of people you might be able to turn to for advice. Make sure to include people such as the following:

- parents
- aunts and uncles
- school counselors
- co-workers
- grandparents
- neighbors
- friends' parents
- bosses
- older siblings
- teachers
- friends

Objective: Student will help make a list of people she might be able to turn to for advice

Subject: Receptive Literacy **Mode:** Brainstorming **Training Zone:** [Z] Socialization	**Readiness Factor:** [3] Personal/Social **Readiness Factor Category:** [i] Relationships

RI 30: Listening actively

FUTR Tool: no
PACT: yes

Supplies: None

Discuss that active listening leads to interesting conversations and involves the following behaviors:

1. Listen to others talk and take an interest in their feelings and ideas.
2. Ask questions to encourage others to continue to share.
3. At times, repeat your understanding of others' comments. Example: I think you are saying that you like unsweetened rhubarb.
4. Imagine the experiences others describe.
5. Listen to understand, not to critique or change.
6. Show warmth and caring.

Ask students to use the six behaviors to practice really listening and caring about what others have to say.

Objective: Student will discuss behaviors that promote active listening and will then practice using them.

Subject: Receptive Literacy **Mode:** Action **Training Zone:** [Z] Socialization	**Readiness Factor:** [3] Personal/Social **Readiness Factor Category:** [i] Relationships

RI 31: Listening to an interviewer

FUTR Tool: no
PACT: no

Supplies: None

Discuss that when you interview for a job, you need to be careful to listen to the interviewer closely so you can answer questions correctly and pick up other helpful clues. Point out that you can be honest and still choose your words carefully. Ask volunteers to identify interviewing clues in these interviewer questions:

1. Would you consider yourself a talker? [The interviewer might be trying to decide if you can work quietly and get your work done OR if you will talk freely with customers OR both.]
2. Would you be willing to walk out of your job today and start here tomorrow? [The interviewer might be checking your loyalty level.]
3. Do you think workers with colds should be at work? [The interviewer might be checking your dedication level in the face of minor discomfort.]

Objective: Student will listen for clues from an interviewer.

Subject: Receptive Literacy **Mode:** Oral Response **Training Zone:** [V] Observation	**Readiness Factor:** [1] Career **Readiness Factor Category:** [b] Job Performance

RI 32: Listening to others' opinions

FUTR Tool: no
PACT: no

Supplies: None

Discuss that listening to others' opinions is a way of showing respect as well as a way to expose yourself to others' ideas. Ask students to think about their opinions on this topic:

Should schools give students personal holidays on their birthdays?

Ask volunteers to share their opinions. Tell other students they are to listen to opinions without interrupting, but tell them they can ask questions following each opinion. Throughout the process, make sure students respect others' opinions and exhibit an understanding that opinions are neither right nor wrong.

Objective: Student will listen to others' opinions.

Subject: Receptive Literacy **Mode:** Action **Training Zone:** [Z] Socialization	**Readiness Factor:** [3] Personal/Social **Readiness Factor Category:** [i] Relationships

RI 33: Listening when others talk

FUTR Tool: 159
PACT: yes

Supplies: None

Discuss that active listening is very focused on the other person whereas simple polite listening is more of a give and take. Discuss the following polite choices for listening when others talk:

1. Maintain eye contact.

2. Don't interrupt.

3. Show interest with your facial expressions.

4. Keep your mind from wandering by thinking about what the person is saying.

5. When the person comes to a natural break, ask a question or share a related comment.

Ask students to have conversations and practice being polite listeners.

Objective: Student will practice being a polite listener.

Subject: Receptive Literacy **Mode:** Action **Training Zone:** [F] Flexibility	**Readiness Factor:** [3] Personal/Social **Readiness Factor Category:** [i] Relationships

RI 34: Making choices based on advertising

FUTR Tool: 178
PACT: yes

Supplies: A collection of advertisements from magazines and newspapers

Discuss that advertisements use emotional tactics to try to attract customers. Point out that some common tactics include suggesting you should use the product because:

1. a famous person does.

2. beautiful people do, and it will make you like them.

3. it will make other people want to be around you.

4. it is a choice that people with money make.

5. it is associated with a perfect life full of happiness.

Divide the class into five or six teams. Give each team two or more advertisements. Ask teams to study their advertisements and tell the class what emotional tactics the advertisements are using to try to attract customers.

Objective: Student will look for emotional tactics used in advertisements.

Subject: Receptive Literacy **Mode:** Hands-On **Training Zone:** [U] Conclusion	**Readiness Factor:** [2] Daily Living **Readiness Factor Category:** [f] Shopping and Eating at Restaurants

RI 35: Making conclusions about what you hear

Supplies: Bell, book, scissors, clothing item with a zipper, stapler, cell phone, push pen, whistle, box of paper clips (or substitutes of your choosing)

Ask students to number their papers from 1–10. Making certain students cannot see the sources of the sounds, make the following sounds and ask students to identify them:

1. Ring a bell
2. Open and shut a pair of scissors
3. Use a stapler
4. Clap your hands
5. Blow a whistle

6. Shut a book loudly
7. Zip a zipper
8. Dial a cell phone
9. Push a push pen in and out
10. Shake a box of paper clips

Objective: Student will identify common sounds without seeing the sources of the sounds.

Subject: Receptive Literacy **Mode:** Oral Response **Training Zone:** [U] Conclusion	**Readiness Factor:** [2] Daily Living **Readiness Factor Category:** [k] Community Involvement and Responsibility

RI 36: Making insurance choices

Supplies: None

Point out that insurance is sometimes an option and other times not. Explain that, if you buy a house, your bank can require that you have some insurance, and if you own a car, the state can require that you have some basic insurance. Tell students that, in most situations, you can choose whether or not to buy insurance and which features you want the insurance to have. Discuss the following types of insurances and some of the available choices:

1. Life insurance [Might offer retirement pay, pays for funeral, pays beneficiary when you die]
2. Health insurance [Often through job, often can choose amount of deductibles and co-pays]
3. Car insurance [State probably requires liability coverage, can choose comprehensive, can choose deductibles]
4. Home owners or renters insurance [Might be required, can choose deductibles, can set replacement value, can choose specialty insurance like hail or flood]

Objective: Student will discuss types and of insurance and some available insurance choices.

Subject: Receptive Literacy **Mode:** Discussion **Training Zone:** [U] Conclusion	**Readiness Factor:** [2] Daily Living **Readiness Factor Category:** [e] Safety and Security

RI 37: Making leisure choices from the newspaper

Supplies: Newspaper pages with local activities and movies (Pages do not have to be current.)

Divide the class into teams. Give each team at least one newspaper activity page and tell them to find some fun things that are going on in the local area. Ask teams to choose one expensive activity, one medium-expense activity, and one inexpensive activity and share their choices with the class.

Objective: Student will choose leisure activities from those advertised in the local newspaper.

Subject: Receptive Literacy **Mode:** Hands-On **Training Zone:** [Z] Socialization	**Readiness Factor:** [3] Personal/Social **Readiness Factor Category:** [j] Leisure/Desires/Choices

RI 38: Managing your mail

Supplies: None

Discuss the following tips for managing your mail:

1. Look at each piece of mail the day that it arrives.
2. Have a wastebasket nearby so you can look at junk mail and then throw it out without ever putting it back down.
3. Determine a place to keep all unpaid bills such as a shelf or drawer. When a bill arrives, write the due date on the calendar and place the bill in the unpaid bill location.
4. Read all personal mail and then either throw it away or file it with your keepsakes.
5. Choose a place to keep all invitations. When an invitation arrives, read it and write the date on the calendar. Then place the invitation in the invitation place.
6. When you receive mail that requires a response, either respond immediately or put it where you will see it so you can do it within a day or two.

Objective: Student will discuss tips for managing mail.

Subject: Receptive Literacy **Mode:** Discussion **Training Zone:** [C] Conscientiousness	**Readiness Factor:** [2] Daily Living **Readiness Factor Category:** [d] Household Care and/or Chores

RI 39: Monitoring your academic progress

Supplies: Make the computer-created chart described below and print a copy for each student.

In the computer, create a horizontal chart with nine columns and six rows. Label the columns Week 1, Week 2.... Week 9. Give each student a copy of the chart and ask them to list their classes to the left of the first column—one in each row. Then, tell them that you want them to use the chart to keep track of grades they receive during the nine-weeks term so they know how they are doing with their grades. (If your school is not on a 9-week plan, alter the chart to fit your needs.) Either decide on a method for students to keep the charts without losing them or keep the charts in your classroom where students can find them and update them each week.

Objective: Student will create a chart to keep track of weekly progress in his classes.

Subject: Receptive Literacy **Mode:** Action **Training Zone:** [V] Observation	**Readiness Factor:** [3] Personal/Social **Readiness Factor Category:** [j] Leisure/Desires/Choices

RI 40: Paying attention to noises and comments around you

FUTR Tool: no
PACT: yes

Supplies: A cassette recorder with these comments and noises in this order: A muffled call for help, breaking glass, a cat meowing loudly as if in trouble

Discuss that, even though you typically try to avoid background noise, (As you are talking, subtly push the recorder to play the muffled "Help Me.") you should pay attention to important noises and comments. Look around to see who reacts to the "Help Me" call and then ask who all heard the call for help. Point out that, even if you are involved in a (As you are talking, subtly push the recorder to play the breaking glass sound.) conversation or watching TV, you can let some sounds into your consciousness. Look around to see who reacts to the broken glass sound and then ask who all heard the glass break. Explain that the sound of breaking glass can be caused by many different things, but that none of them (As you are talking, subtly push the recorder to play the cat sound) are good, so you always want to follow-up on a such a sound. Look around to see who reacts to the cat sound. Point out that cries for help, breaking glass, and cat sounds are all sounds that you might typically not want to ignore.

Objective: Student will discuss and pay attention to background noises.

Subject: Receptive Literacy **Mode:** Hands-On **Training Zone:** [E] Exploration	**Readiness Factor:** [1] Career **Readiness Factor Category:** [b] Job Performance

RI 41: Paying attention to written notes and signs

FUTR Tool: 155
PACT: yes

Supplies: None

Ask volunteers to describe signs they have seen somewhere around the school. After each description, ask for a show of hands from other students who have seen the sign. Discuss that, especially within a familiar environment where you are relaxed and not necessarily paying much attention, you need to make an effort to pay attention to notes and signs that are put up since they might contain information you want to know. Ask students to specifically look for the signs that you discussed in class.

Objective: Student will describe a sign he has seen around the school.

Subject: Receptive Literacy **Mode:** Discussion **Training Zone:** [C] Conscientiousness	**Readiness Factor:** [1] Career **Readiness Factor Category:** [b] Job Performance

RI 42: Programming a VCR or DVD player

FUTR Tool: no
PACT: yes

Supplies: None

Ask a volunteer to list the steps involved in programming a VCR or DVD player to record a TV show. Invite others to discuss how programming their VCR or DVD players is like or different from the list.

Objective: Student will discuss the steps involved in programming a VCR or DVD player to record a show.

Subject: Receptive Literacy **Mode:** Discussion **Training Zone:** [M] Manipulation	**Readiness Factor:** [3] Personal/Social **Readiness Factor Category:** [j] Leisure/Desires/Choices

RI 43: Proofreading for others

FUTR Tool: no
PACT: yes

Supplies: None

Discuss that you will often have trouble seeing mistakes in your own writing, so it is helpful to have someone else proofread for you. Point out that, the flip side of that situation is that others might ask you to proofread what they have written, and you should be willing to help out when you can.

Ask each student to write a paragraph about a talking stuffed tiger. Then, have students exchange papers with a classmate and proofread each other's work.

Objective: Student will proofread a classmate's work.

Subject: Receptive Literacy **Mode:** Action **Training Zone:** [F] Flexibility	**Readiness Factor:** [3] Personal/Social **Readiness Factor Category:** [i] Relationships

RI 44: Proofreading your writing

FUTR Tool: no
PACT: no

Supplies: None

Discuss that all people—kids and adults—should read over everything they write to make sure it says what they mean it to say. Explain that this proofreading includes everything from short notes to long papers. Discuss that, following proofreading, you can make some changes to correct errors and other changes because you just want to say something differently and that both types of changes usually make a piece of writing better. Ask students to write a short paragraph describing what they are wearing today. Then, have them proofread it and make any needed or desired changes.

Objective: Student will write a paragraph and then will proofread and make changes as needed or desired.

Subject: Receptive Literacy **Mode:** Written **Training Zone:** [V] Observation	**Readiness Factor:** [3] Personal/Social **Readiness Factor Category:** [j] Leisure/Desires/Choices

RI 45: Putting files in order

FUTR Tool: no
PACT: yes

Supplies: Three or more sets of manila folders as follows—15 files, each labeled with a number followed by a dash and the last name of a student (Make name ABC order and number order different)

Discuss that files can be put in different orders such as ABC order, numerical order, or date order—but the most common order is ABC order.

Ask for volunteers to put the stacks of files in ABC order. Then, ask them to reorder them in numerical order. Repeat with other volunteers. Continue until all students have had a turn.

Objective: Student will put a set of files in ABC-order.

Subject: Receptive Literacy **Mode:** Hands-On **Training Zone:** [O] Organization	**Readiness Factor:** [2] Daily Living **Readiness Factor Category:** [g] Time and Order

RI 46: Reacting to others' moods

FUTR Tool: 165
PACT: yes

Supplies: None

Discuss that all people have good and bad moods and that some people are much more moody than others. Point out that, one key tactic in getting along with people is to be flexible with their moods. Ask volunteers to tell how they would react to each of the mood situations below:

1. You go to your boss's office to ask for a day off, but just as you get to the door, you see her throw a book across the room in anger. What will you do?

2. You come home after a ball game and start to tell your mother about the game, but everything you say seems to make her angry. What will you do?

3. You plan to wait until after class to ask your teacher if you can do some extra credit. When he comes into the room before class, he is in a cheery, talkative mood. What will you do?

Objective: Student will react to situations involving moods of others.

Subject: Receptive Literacy **Mode:** Oral Response **Training Zone:** [Z] Socialization	**Readiness Factor:** [3] Personal/Social **Readiness Factor Category:** [i] Relationships

RI 47: Reading a movie schedule

FUTR Tool: no
PACT: yes

Supplies: Copies of a movie schedule from the newspaper

Discuss that movie schedules give people lots of options, but it can still be difficult to choose a movie and a time that works for all members of a group. Divide the class into groups of five or six students. Give each group a copy of the movie schedule. Ask groups to find a movie that they would all like to see and a time when they could see it together.

Objective: Student will choose a movie and a movie time that will work for a group.

Subject: Receptive Literacy **Mode:** Hands-On **Training Zone:** [E] Exploration	**Readiness Factor:** [3] Personal/Social **Readiness Factor Category:** [j] Leisure/Desires/Choices

RI 48: Reading abbreviations

FUTR Tool: 148
PACT: yes

Supplies: None

Write the following list of abbreviations on the board and ask students to read them using the full name for each abbreviation.

1. NV [Nevada]
2. Ave. [Avenue]
3. C.O.D. [Cash on Delivery]
4. Dec. [December]
5. ASAP [as soon as possible]
6. Mr. [Mister]
7. N. [North]
8. etc. [etcetera]
9. Blvd [boulevard]
10. @ [at]
11. ID [identification]
12. "L" on elevator pad [lobby]
13. lb. [pound]
14. "Gar" on elevator pad [garage]
15. M.D. [medical doctor]
16. ¢ [cents]
17. RSVP [let me know if you can come]
18. P.O. Box [post office box]

Objective: Student will write meanings for a group of abbreviations.

Subject: Receptive Literacy **Mode:** Written **Training Zone:** [L] Logic	**Readiness Factor:** [1] Career **Readiness Factor Category:** [a] Career Preparation

RI 49: Reading arrows

FUTR Tool: no
PACT: yes

Supplies: None

Discuss that arrows are a visual way to direct a person's attention and that arrows are usually easier to follow than words. Write the story below on the board, but put each sentence on a different part of the board with some sideways and some upside down. Use arrows to show the order in which students are to read the pieces. Have students follow the arrows and read the story.

A little boy was walking down the street one day. As he walked, he nodded his head to people he passed and two people nodded back. Then a top hat fell out of the sky and landed on his head. He kept walking. As he walked, he tipped his new hat to people he passed, and 20 people nodded back at him. Then a gust of wind came up and whipped the hat off his head. A crown fell out of the windy sky and landed on his head. He kept walking, slightly tipping his crown to people he passed, and almost everyone stopped to talk to him. At the end of the day, he noted that he was lucky to have met two genuine friendly people that day.

Objective: Student will follow arrows to read a spread-out story.

Subject: Receptive Literacy Mode: Action Training Zone: [L] Logic	Readiness Factor: [2] Daily Living Readiness Factor Category: [g] Time and Order

RI 50: Reading cash register receipts

FUTR Tool: no
PACT: no

Supplies: Copies of a cash register receipt (one per student) (Make sure to choose a receipt that has the parts listed below.)

Ask students to number their papers from 1–7. Pass out copies of the cash register receipt and ask these questions:

1. From what store did this receipt come?
2. On what date was the purchase made?
3. What was the total amount of the bill?
4. How much tax was charged?

5. Was the bill paid for with cash or charge?
6. What is one item that was bought?
7. What is the phone number of the store?

Objective: Student will read a cash register receipt to answer questions.

Subject: Receptive Literacy Mode: Hands-On Training Zone: [A] Analysis	Readiness Factor: [2] Daily Living Readiness Factor Category: [f] Shopping and Eating at Restaurants

RI 51: Reading clothing labels

FUTR Tool: no
PACT: yes

Supplies: Enough clothing items (with label tags) to have one per student or one for every two students

Copy two or three clothing labels onto the board and ask volunteers to read them. Discuss what each of them means. Pass out the clothing items and ask students to read the labels and answer the following questions:

1. Who has something that can be washed in a washing machine?
2. Who has something that must be dry cleaned?
3. Who has something that was made in the U.S.A.?

4. Who has something that is a size large?
5. Who has something that is made of 100% cotton?
6. Who has something with lycra in it?

Objective: Student will read clothing labels to answer questions.

Subject: Receptive Literacy Mode: Hands-On Training Zone: [V] Observation	Readiness Factor: [2] Daily Living Readiness Factor Category: [f] Shopping and Eating at Restaurants

RI 52: **Reading food nutrition labels**

FUTR Tool: no
PACT: yes

Supplies: An overhead with an enlarged nutrition label OR copies of an enlarged nutrition label

Ask students to look at the enlarged nutrition label and answer the following questions:

1. What ingredients have you heard of before?
2. Are there some ingredients you have not heard of before?
3. How many calories are in a serving?
4. How big is a serving?
5. What vitamin(s) will you get the most of when eating this food?
6. Do you think this food item is healthy to eat?
7. Where was this product prepared and packaged?

Objective: Student will read a nutrition label to answer some questions.

Subject: Receptive Literacy **Mode:** Oral Response **Training Zone:** [V] Observation	**Readiness Factor:** [3] Personal/Social **Readiness Factor Category:** [l] Health, Diet, and Appearance

RI 53: **Reading food preparation charts**

FUTR Tool: no
PACT: yes

Supplies: Five copies of a meat preparation chart from a cookbook

Divide the class into five teams. Give each team a food preparation chart. Assign teams one of the following meat products and ask them to tell the class how long it needs to cook.

1. 14-pound turkey
2. 10-pound ham
3. 7 pound rib roast
4. 4 pound pork roast
5. 4 pound whole chicken

Objective: Student will use a meat preparation chart to determine time needed to cook a piece of meat.

Subject: Receptive Literacy **Mode:** Role Play **Training Zone:** [V] Observation	**Readiness Factor:** [2] Daily Living **Readiness Factor Category:** [d] Household Care and/or Chores

RI 54: **Reading job ads**

FUTR Tool: 169
PACT: yes

Supplies: For each student: A copy of a piece of paper that has several newspaper job ads attached to it

Pass out the job ads. Ask specific questions similar to those below and ask students to find the answers.

1. Which job is located on Cherry Street?
2. Which job requires an experienced waitress?
3. How should you apply for the mechanic job?
4. Where should you send your resumé for the security guard job?
5. How long do you have to submit an application for the secretary job?
6. Which job does not require any experience?
7. Which job is looking for people to start tomorrow?

Objective: Student will read job ads to answer questions.

Subject: Receptive Literacy **Mode:** Hands-On **Training Zone:** [E] Exploration	**Readiness Factor:** [1] Career **Readiness Factor Category:** [a] Career Preparation

RI 55: Reading medicine labels

FUTR Tool: 152
PACT: yes

Supplies: Several empty over-the-counter medicine containers

Have students gather in teams so that each team has one medicine container. Ask students to read their labels and answer these questions:

1. How much should teenagers take at once?
2. What symptoms does the medicine take care of?
3. Can you drive while taking this medicine?
4. Do the directions say to take the medicine with food or drink?
5. How many times a day do you take this medicine?
6. Are there any people who should not take this medicine?

Objective: Student will read medicine labels to answer questions.

Subject: Receptive Literacy **Mode:** Hands-On **Training Zone:** [R] Responsibility	**Readiness Factor:** [3] Personal/Social **Readiness Factor Category:** [l] Health, Diet, and Appearance

RI 56: Reading menus

FUTR Tool: 170
PACT: yes

Supplies: None

Write these menu vocabulary words on the board and ask volunteers to explain what each means:

filet	side dishes	starters	free refills	a la mode	specials	complete dinner
Cajun	T-bone	ribeye	home style	blackened	Southwest	a la carte
fried	broiled	baked	boiled	charcoaled	grilled	hors d'oeuvres

Objective: Student will explain the meanings of some menu vocabulary words.

Subject: Receptive Literacy **Mode:** Oral Response **Training Zone:** [E] Exploration	**Readiness Factor:** [2] Daily Living **Readiness Factor Category:** [f] Shopping and Eating at Restaurants

RI 57: Reading non-edible product labels

FUTR Tool: no
PACT: no

Supplies: Non-edible products with labels of some type

Discuss that, unlike food products, non-edible product labels are often only on an outer package and are usually thrown away once the item is opened. Divide the class into teams so that each team has one product to study. Ask teams to find the labels on their products and share with the class what the labels say.

Objective: Student will find labels on non-edible food products and will share the label information with the class.

Subject: Receptive Literacy **Mode:** Hands-On **Training Zone:** [V] Observation	**Readiness Factor:** [2] Daily Living **Readiness Factor Category:** [f] Shopping and Eating at Restaurants

RI 58: Reading pictures

Supplies: Photographs or pictures from magazines—one per student or one for every two students

Discuss that, by studying pictures carefully, you can learn more than is initially obvious. Pass out the pictures and encourage students to study parts such as the backgrounds, clothing people are wearing, items people are holding, signs of weather, and clues about the setting. Ask volunteers to share information they have gathered from their pictures including the obvious up front point of the picture as well as other details that can be learned from studying the picture. (Example: a family group picture—Obvious: A picture of everyone who attended the family gathering. Other details: Martha and Sam must have been sharing a joke because you can see that they are both kind of laughing. It must have been cold because everyone has a sweater on. It was night time because the window in the background shows and it is black.)

Objective: Student will study a picture to find obvious and not-so-obvious details.

Subject: Receptive Literacy **Mode:** Hands-On **Training Zone:** [V] Observation	**Readiness Factor:** [2] Daily Living **Readiness Factor Category:** [h] Transportation/Travel/Worldliness

RI 59: Reading signs

Supplies: Sign flash cards or pictures of signs from sources such as a driver's handbook and a factory safety manual

Show flash cards or pictures to students and ask a volunteer to read each sign, tell what the sign means, and why the sign is needed. Include signs such as the following:

1. Closed	5. Fragile	9. (Curved arrow)	13. No trespassing	17. Deer Crossing
2. Don't Walk	6. Rest Room	10. Exit	14. Slippery When Wet	18. Emergency Exit Only
3. Information	7. Stop	11. Elevator	15. Wet Floor	
4. Wrong Way	8. Yield	12. Beware of Dog	16. Employees Only	

Objective: Student will look at signs, read them, tell what they mean, and explain why the signs are needed.

Subject: Receptive Literacy **Mode:** Hands-On **Training Zone:** [V] Observation	**Readiness Factor:** [2] Daily Living **Readiness Factor Category:** [e] Safety and Security

RI 60: Reading symbols and icons

Supplies: None

Discuss that symbols and icons are commonly used and knowing some common ones makes it easier to understand what is going on around you. Ask volunteers to explain what each of these signs or icons means:

$ [dollar]	¢ [cents]	% [percent]	@ [at]	& [and]
+ [plus]	= [equal]	≠ [not equal]	< [less than]	> [greater than]
™ [trade mark]	® [trade mark]	© [copyright]	° [degrees]	# [pound or number]
÷ [divide]	Ø [Do not/No]	? [question]	√ [check]	± [plus or minus]
" [inches]	' [feet]	! [surprise]	• [bullet]	( ) [parentheses]

Objective: Student will tell the meanings of different symbols and icons.

Subject: Receptive Literacy **Mode:** Oral Response **Training Zone:** [A] Analysis	**Readiness Factor:** [1] Career **Readiness Factor Category:** [b] Job Performance

RI 61: Recognizing and accepting authority

FUTR Tool: 158
PACT: yes

Supplies: None

Ask volunteers to identify authority figures in each of these settings:

- School [staff]
- At a fire in the neighborhood [firemen]
- Around the city [police]
- At a friend's home [Friend's parents]
- Church [minister]

- In a private business [owner or manager]
- At work [boss]
- At a meeting [person running the meeting]
- Home [parents]
- At a road construction site you are driving by [all the workers]

Objective: Student will identify authority figures in different areas of her life.

Subject: Receptive Literacy **Mode:** Discussion **Training Zone:** [F] Flexibility	**Readiness Factor:** [1] Career **Readiness Factor Category:** [b] Job Performance

RI 62: Recognizing important information

FUTR Tool: 168
PACT: yes

Supplies: None

Explain that the following details are important pieces of information for the identified groups.

1. School-starting time is important information for teachers and students

2. The definition of "sternum" is important information for a student taking a test on the Skeletal System.

Ask volunteers to share other examples of important information at school or in other parts of their lives.

Point out that the number of rocks on a road is not important information. Ask volunteers to share some other examples of unimportant information.

Objective: Student will share examples of important and unimportant information.

Subject: Receptive Literacy **Mode:** Discussion **Training Zone:** [S] Self-Awareness	**Readiness Factor:** [3] Personal/Social **Readiness Factor Category:** [j] Leisure/Desires/Choices

RI 63: Searching for job options

FUTR Tool: 150
PACT: yes

Supplies: None

As a group, brainstorm ways to search for job options. Make sure to include some of these ideas:

1. Read newspapers
2. Talk to friends
3. Talk to people you sort of know
4. Ask at businesses (in-person or on the phone)
5. Call former employers
6. Take out a work-wanted ad in the newspaper
7. Post work-wanted signs

Objective: Student will help make a list of ways to search for job options.

Subject: Receptive Literacy **Mode:** Brainstorming **Training Zone:** [L] Logic	**Readiness Factor:** [1] Career **Readiness Factor Category:** [a] Career Preparation

RI 64: Securing legal documents

FUTR Tool: no
PACT: no

Supplies: Preplan a phone call to the county courthouse so they know you are going to call and that you want to learn about getting copies of legal documents.

Discuss that you should talk with someone at the county courthouse about getting copies of legal documents such as birth certificates, marriage licenses, divorce decrees, death certificates, and adoption papers. Explain that you should listen very carefully and take notes so you can follow the directions you get.

Take a "phone field trip"—Call the county courthouse on a speaker phone and discuss how to get copies of legal documents.

Objective: Student will talk to the county courthouse to find out how to get copies of legal documents.

Subject: Receptive Literacy **Mode:** Hands-On **Training Zone:** [E] Exploration	**Readiness Factor:** [3] Personal/Social **Readiness Factor Category:** [k] Community Involvement and Responsibility

RI 65: Seeing letter and idea sequences

FUTR Tool: no
PACT: yes

Supplies: The items listed below or logical substitutes

Discuss that you can put things in order using different methods. Show students the following examples of sequences:

1. A file or list that is in ABC order
2. A calendar that it is in month order
3. A list of questions that is in numerical order
4. Vitamins on a nutrition label that are in quantity order
5. A school fire drill plan that is in classroom order
6. Test results that are in grade order

Objective: Student will look at and discuss examples of different kinds of sequences.

Subject: Receptive Literacy **Mode:** Hands-On **Training Zone:** [O] Organization	**Readiness Factor:** [2] Daily Living **Readiness Factor Category:** [g] Time and Order

RI 66: Separating fact from fiction

FUTR Tool: no
PACT: yes

Supplies: None

Point out that facts are always true and it's a fact to say "Some apples are red." Add that fiction is not true and it's fiction to say "Some apples weigh 80 pounds." Ask students to pair up with a partner. Give each pair one of the topics below. Ask teams to have one member say a fact about the topic and the other say something fictional about the topic.

forks	hands	pencils	books	flags
pillows	chairs	TVs	trees	dogs
fences	oceans	alligators	pumpkins	daisies
trucks	walls	footballs	shoes	treadmills

Objective: Student will work with a partner to generate two statements—one fact and one fiction.

Subject: Receptive Literacy **Mode:** Oral Response **Training Zone:** [A] Analysis	**Readiness Factor:** [2] Daily Living **Readiness Factor Category:** [h] Transportation/Travel/Worldliness

RI 67: Signing contracts knowledgeably

FUTR Tool: no
PACT: yes

Supplies: None

Discuss that you should never take contracts lightly and nor sign them without reading them. As a group, brainstorm situations where you might have to sign a contract. Make sure to include some of these ideas:

apartment   job   bank   cell phone service   TV service

Discuss what you can do if you can't read the contract, or can't read it fast enough. Some possible answers:

• Ask to take it home to read before signing.

• Ask to have it read and explained to you.

• Make sure you take a reader friend with you.

Objective: Student will discuss situations that require contracts and ways to make sure he knows what the contract says if he can't read it.

Subject: Receptive Literacy **Mode:** Discussion **Training Zone:** [U] Conclusion	**Readiness Factor:** [3] Personal/Social **Readiness Factor Category:** [k] Community Involvement and Responsibility

RI 68: Understanding a lease

FUTR Tool: no
PACT: no

Supplies: A copy of a lease for each student (a simple lease or just the first page of a complex lease)

Pass out copies of a lease and read and discuss it sentence by sentence. When necessary, reword sentences, diagram on the board, and/or turn huge sentences into lists or smaller sentences on the board. Have students underline key information in their copies.

Objective: Student will work through a lease sentence-by-sentence.

Subject: Receptive Literacy **Mode:** Hands-On **Training Zone:** [A] Analysis	**Readiness Factor:** [2] Daily Living **Readiness Factor Category:** [h] Transportation/Travel/Worldliness

RI 69: Understanding a warranty

FUTR Tool: 176
PACT: yes

Supplies: Copies of a warranty (one for each student)

Pass out the warranties and ask students to use them to answer the following questions (or questions of your own choosing):

1. What type and brand of product is this warranty for?

2. For how long is this warranty good?

3. Do you have to send the product somewhere if it has to be repaired?

4. What, if any, kinds of problems are not covered by the warranty?

5. If you need to have the product repaired, what, if anything, do you need to take or send with it?

Objective: Student will read a warranty and answer questions about it.

Subject: Receptive Literacy **Mode:** Hands-On **Training Zone:** [A] Analysis	**Readiness Factor:** [2] Daily Living **Readiness Factor Category:** [d] Household Care and/or Chores

RI 70: Understanding and following your cell phone plan

FUTR Tool: no
PACT: no

Supplies: Copies of a cell phone plan (one for each student)

Pass out copies of a cell phone plan. As you read through it, make bullet points on the board summarizing the important points. On their copies, ask students to put an X in the margin next to the source of each bullet that you put on the board.

Objective: Student will read a cell phone plan and mark the main points.

Subject: Receptive Literacy **Mode:** Hands-On **Training Zone:** [V] Observation	**Readiness Factor:** [2] Daily Living **Readiness Factor Category:** [g] Time and Order

RI 71: Understanding basic cell phone functions

FUTR Tool: 174
PACT: yes

Supplies: A cell phone

Ask volunteers to explain how to do each of the cell phone functions below. If there is a function that no one understands well enough to explain, demonstrate it on your cell phone.

- Placing a call
- Checking to see who your last five calls were from
- Checking your messages
- Adding a name to your address book

- Changing your ringer
- Calling someone in your address book
- Sending a text message

Objective: Student will explain how to perform different cell phone functions.

Subject: Receptive Literacy **Mode:** Demonstration **Training Zone:** [M] Manipulation	**Readiness Factor:** [3] Personal/Social **Readiness Factor Category:** [j] Leisure/Desires/Choices

RI 72: Understanding cooking and baking words

FUTR Tool: no
PACT: yes

Supplies: None

Ask volunteers to act out cooking and baking tasks. Have them identify the "food" they are "preparing" and use words such as the following:

mix	grate	fry	peel	bake	brown the meat
chop	stir	saute	preheat	drain	grease the pan
shred	slice	dice	beat	peel	

Ask volunteers to show the size of each of these baking and cooking measurement items:

cup	teaspoon	tablespoon	pound (of butter)

Objective: Student will role play some cooking and baking tasks and will show sizes of some kitchen measurement items.

Subject: Receptive Literacy **Mode:** Role Play **Training Zone:** [V] Observation	**Readiness Factor:** [2] Daily Living **Readiness Factor Category:** [d] Household Care and/or Chores

RI 73: **Understanding insurance**

FUTR Tool: 153
PACT: yes

Supplies: None

Discuss the four main kinds of insurance and the purpose of each.

1. Life insurance [Covers funeral expenses and can help with expenses a family has after a wage earner dies]

2. Health insurance [Pays for medical expenses]

3. Car insurance [If you are in an accident, pays for damage to you or your car or to a car or person you hit]

4. Home owner or renter insurance [Pays for damage to your home or theft of things in your house]

Objective: Student will discuss kinds of insurance and purposes of each.

Subject: Receptive Literacy **Mode:** Discussion **Training Zone:** [R] Responsibility	**Readiness Factor:** [2] Daily Living **Readiness Factor Category:** [d] Household Care and/or Chores

RI 74: **Understanding job benefits**

FUTR Tool: 180
PACT: yes

Supplies: None

As a group, brainstorm a list of benefits that come with some jobs. Encourage students to think about specific-job benefits (such as a discount on groceries) as well as general benefits (such as health insurance). Make sure their responses include ideas such as these:

1. insurance
2. vacation
3. retirement
4. airline miles to put toward free tickets
5. free food at company meetings
6. company parties
7. incentive awards (non-monetary)
8. bonuses (monetary)
9. clothes with company logo
10. company vehicle

Objective: Student will help make a list of company benefits.

Subject: Receptive Literacy **Mode:** Brainstorming **Training Zone:** [U] Conclusion	**Readiness Factor:** [1] Career **Readiness Factor Category:** [b] Job Performance

RI 75: **Understanding job titles**

FUTR Tool: 147
PACT: yes

Supplies: None

Discuss that the working world has a hierarchy and that understanding job titles is one way to tell who is whose boss. Read the pairs of jobs below. In each case, ask volunteers to assume the two are working together and choose the one that is probably the boss.

1. Assistant Clerk, **Mail room clerk**
2. **President,** Supervisor
3. Summer Help, **Secretary**
4. Manager, **Vice President**
5. **CEO,** Department Head
6. **Team Leader,** Intern

Objective: Student will identify job ranks by job titles.

Subject: Receptive Literacy **Mode:** Oral Response **Training Zone:** [O] Organization	**Readiness Factor:** [1] Career **Readiness Factor Category:** [a] Career Preparation

RI 76: Understanding jokes

FUTR Tool: no
PACT: no

Supplies: Several jokes

Discuss that jokes are often funny because they have an unexpected or silly turn, a play on words, or tricky wording. Read this joke and talk about why it is funny. [Because Tommy is so clueless that he actually thought his dad was talking about the teacher being in trouble]

Teacher: Yes, Tommy?
Tommy: I don't want to scare you, but my dad says someone is going to be in big trouble if my grades do not improve.

One at a time, read other jokes and discuss what it is about them that makes them funny.

Objective: Student will listen to jokes and discuss what makes them funny.

Subject: Receptive Literacy **Mode:** Discussion **Training Zone:** [Z] Socialization	**Readiness Factor:** [3] Personal/Social **Readiness Factor Category:** [j] Leisure/Desires/Choices

RI 77: Understanding nonverbal communication

FUTR Tool: 162
PACT: yes

Supplies: None

Ask volunteers to send the following messages without saying a word:

1. Be quiet.	4. No.	7. I'm thinking.	10. I can't remember.	13. I think that's a great idea.
2. I can't hear you.	5. I'm angry.	8. I'm happy.	11. I'm embarrassed	14. I'm ready to leave.
3. Yes.	6. I'm worried.	9. I'm confused.	12. I'm bored	

Objective: Student will send messages without using words.

Subject: Receptive Literacy **Mode:** Action **Training Zone:** [V] Observation	**Readiness Factor:** [3] Personal/Social **Readiness Factor Category:** [i] Relationships

RI 78: Understanding titles that go with names

FUTR Tool: no
PACT: yes

Supplies: None

Discuss that some titles that go with names explain the type of work a person does and others give personal information about the person. Ask volunteers to tell what these titles mean when used before or after a name:

1. *Rev.* Smith [a minister]

2. *Dr.* Lloyd [a medical doctor, dentist, or university teacher]

3. *Your Honor* [a judge]

4. *General* Rowe [a high-ranking military person]

5. Annie Jones, *DDS* [a dentist]

6. David Shocklee, *JD* [a lawyer]

7. Crystal Jones, *RN* [a nurse]

8. *Miss* Creeger [a single woman]

Objective: Student will tell what some titles mean when used before or after a name.

Subject: Receptive Literacy **Mode:** Oral Response **Training Zone:** [L] Logic	**Readiness Factor:** [3] Personal/Social **Readiness Factor Category:** [k] Community Involvement and Responsibility

RI 79: **Understanding utility bills**

FUTR Tool: no
PACT: no

Supplies: Five copies of each of these three types of utility bills: gas, electric, water

Divide the class into five teams and give each team a copy of three utility bills. Ask questions that they can answer by reading the utility bills. Include questions such as the following:

1. When are each of the bills due?

2. Do any of the bills offer a discount for paying early?

3. What are the customer service phone numbers?

4. Is this month's bill more or less than last month's bill?

5. Besides the actual fee for the amount of utility used, what other fees are included?

6. How or where are you to pay the bill?

Objective: Student will read utility bills and answer questions about them.

Subject: Receptive Literacy **Mode:** Hands-On **Training Zone:** [A] Analysis	**Readiness Factor:** [2] Daily Living **Readiness Factor Category:** [d] Household Care and/or Chores

RI 80: **Using a dictionary**

FUTR Tool: 173
PACT: yes

Supplies: A dictionary for each student

Give each student a dictionary. Ask students to write the answers to these questions:

1. On what page is the word "leaf" located? [will vary]

2. What are the guide words on the page where "leaf" is located? [will vary]

3. How many definitions does "leaf" have? [will vary]

4. How is the plural of "leaf" spelled? [leaves]

5. Which letter in "leaf" is not heard? [a]

6. What is the clue word for the vowel sound in "leaf"? [will vary]

7. On what page is "dinner" located? [will vary]

Objective: Student will use a dictionary to look up words and answer questions.

Subject: Receptive Literacy **Mode:** Hands-On **Training Zone:** [M] Manipulation	**Readiness Factor:** [3] Personal/Social **Readiness Factor Category:** [j] Leisure/Desires/Choices

RI 81: **Using a newspaper**

FUTR Tool: 161
PACT: yes

Supplies: A newspaper for every one or two students (Does not have to be current)

Ask students to find the following parts of the newspaper:

1. Date	5. Job Wanted Ads	9. Obituaries	13. Comics
2. Cost for a single issue	6. A retail advertisement	10. Name of newspaper	14. A letter to the editor
3. Sports section	7. Weather report	11. A main headline	
4. Help Wanted Ads	8. Movie schedule	12. Index	

Objective: Student will find parts of a newspaper as requested.

Subject: Receptive Literacy **Mode:** Hands-On **Training Zone:** [V] Observation	**Readiness Factor:** [3] Personal/Social **Readiness Factor Category:** [j] Leisure/Desires/Choices

RI 82: **Using a phone book**

FUTR Tool: 172
PACT: yes

Supplies: A phone book for every three or four students

Divide the class into teams and pass out the phone books. Ask students to find the following information:

1. A list of companies that sell gravel
2. A list of people who sell houses (realtors)
3. (Insert a local individual's name)'s phone number
4. (Insert a local individual's name)'s address
5. Area codes for other parts of the country
6. Phone numbers for local government agencies

Objective: Student will use the phone book yellow pages and white pages to find specific information.

Subject: Receptive Literacy **Mode:** Hands-On **Training Zone:** [M] Manipulation	**Readiness Factor:** [3] Personal/Social **Readiness Factor Category:** [j] Leisure/Desires/Choices

RI 83: **Using a program to understand an event**

FUTR Tool: no
PACT: yes

Supplies: Copies of a program for an event such as a play, concert, or graduation ceremony

Pass out the programs and ask specific questions that students can answer by reading the program. Include questions such as the following:

1. What event is this program for?
2. What is the first thing that is going to happen at this event?
3. Name a key person taking part in this event.
4. What is one thing about the event that will be more clear because you have a program?
5. What is one thing you could easily have figured out without the program?
6. What is the last thing that is going to happen at this event?

Objective: Student will read an event program to answer questions.

Subject: Receptive Literacy **Mode:** Hands-On **Training Zone:** [A] Analysis	**Readiness Factor:** [3] Personal/Social **Readiness Factor Category:** [j] Leisure/Desires/Choices

RI 84: Using a table of contents

FUTR Tool: no
PACT: yes

Supplies: Several copies of a book with a table of contents OR copies of a table of contents

Pass out the books or copies of tables of contents and ask specific questions that students can answer by reading the tables of contents. Include questions such as the following:

1. About how many pages are in this book?

2. How many chapters are in this book?

3. In what chapter are you most likely to find information about _____?

4. On what page does Chapter 3 start?

5. Are there appendices?

6. On what page would you look to read about _____?

Objective: Student will use a table of contents to answer questions.

Subject: Receptive Literacy **Mode:** Hands-On **Training Zone:** [M] Manipulation	**Readiness Factor:** [3] Personal/Social **Readiness Factor Category:** [j] Leisure/Desires/Choices

RI 85: Using a TV program guide

FUTR Tool: no
PACT: yes

Supplies: Copies of a TV program guide from a newspaper

Divide the class into teams of three or four students. Give each team a copy of the TV program guide. Ask team members to choose three shows the whole team would like to see and to list the times, show titles, and channels. Ask teams to share their choices with the whole class.

Objective: Student will help choose three TV shows to watch.

Subject: Receptive Literacy **Mode:** Hands-On **Training Zone:** [A] Analysis	**Readiness Factor:** [3] Personal/Social **Readiness Factor Category:** [j] Leisure/Desires/Choices

RI 86: Using an ATM machine

FUTR Tool: no
PACT: yes

Supplies: None

Discuss that ATM machines are used to get cash from the bank without having to go into the bank or even have the bank be open. Ask students to brainstorm local ATM locations. Ask a volunteer to list the steps involved in using an ATM. Make sure to include ideas such as the following:

1. Enter your ATM card.

2. Choose whether you want to withdraw form checking or saving.

3. Enter your password.

4. Enter the amount you want to withdraw.

5. Take your money.

6. Take your card.

Objective: Student will discuss how to use an ATM machine.

Subject: Receptive Literacy **Mode:** Discussion **Training Zone:** [M] Manipulation	**Readiness Factor:** [2] Daily Living **Readiness Factor Category:** [e] Safety and Security

RI 87: Using an electronic voting machine

FUTR Tool: no
PACT: yes

Supplies: None

On the board, draw a sample touch-voting screen. (Several names with choice boxes to the left and forward and backward arrows at the bottom) Discuss that electronic voting machines have boxes or circles next to each candidate's names and all you have to do is touch the box or circle next to the name of your choice and a check will show up in the box. Tell students that, when you are finished with a page, you usually have to touch an arrow to go to the next page. Explain that, if you want to go back to a page you have finished, you will usually have a back arrow that you can touch to take you backwards. Point out that you can change your mind by touching a checked box to uncheck it and then touching a different candidate's box to put the check there. Tell students that touch voting is very much like playing some computer games where you make choices by touching the screen.

Objective: Student will discuss how electronic voting machines look and work.

Subject: Receptive Literacy **Mode:** Demonstration **Training Zone:** [M] Manipulation	**Readiness Factor:** [3] Personal/Social **Readiness Factor Category:** [k] Community Involvement and Responsibility

RI 88: Using an index

FUTR Tool: no
PACT: yes

Supplies: Several copies of a book with an index OR copies of an index

Pass out the books or copies of indexes and ask specific questions that students can answer by using the index. Include questions such as the following:

1. Is there anything in this book about ___? (Ask this question with several different items or ideas.)

2. On what page can you find information about ___? (Ask this question with several different items or ideas.)

3. What is one thing that is talked about on more than one page?

Objective: Student will use an index to answer questions.

Subject: Receptive Literacy **Mode:** Hands-On **Training Zone:** [M] Manipulation	**Readiness Factor:** [3] Personal/Social **Readiness Factor Category:** [j] Leisure/Desires/Choices

RI 89: Using manners in meetings

FUTR Tool: no
PACT: yes

Supplies: None

Discuss that going to meetings is sort of like being in class because you have to do these things:

1. sit down

2. be quiet when others are talking

3. be polite when you talk

4. listen to the person in the front of the room

5. sometimes stay longer than you want to

Ask students to brainstorm reasons why manners are important in meetings. [So business can be conducted, so meetings can get over on time, so meetings are not stressful]

Objective: Student will discuss how meetings are like classes and why manners are important in meetings.

Subject: Receptive Literacy **Mode:** Brainstorming **Training Zone:** [C] Conscientiousness	**Readiness Factor:** [1] Career **Readiness Factor Category:** [b] Job Performance

RI 90: Using the Internet for personal needs

FUTR Tool: no
PACT: yes

Supplies: A computer with Internet service

As a group, brainstorm a list of personal uses for the Internet. Then choose one of them to demonstrate by actually going online.

Answer: Some possible personal uses—General shopping, searching for a friend's contact information, reading the news, playing games, talking on chat lines, checking the weather report, buying airline tickets, reading movie reviews, getting health information, watching sports clips, looking for houses for sale, looking for information about a topic of personal interest, selling something, downloading software, reading product reviews

Objective: Student will help make a list of personal uses for the Internet and will then watch a demonstration of one of them.

Subject: Receptive Literacy **Mode:** Demonstration **Training Zone:** [E] Exploration	**Readiness Factor:** [3] Personal/Social **Readiness Factor Category:** [j] Leisure/Desires/Choices

RI 91: Using the Internet to find interview information

FUTR Tool: no
PACT: yes

Supplies: A computer with Internet service

Choose a local company and find the company's website. As a group, make a list of the pieces of information you find on the website that might be useful in an interview. Look for ideas such as the following:

• Products the company sells
• Number of locations and where they are
• Names of company officers
• Company history
• Available jobs

Objective: Student will help make a list of pieces of information on a company's website that might be helpful in an interview.

Subject: Receptive Literacy **Mode:** Hands-On **Training Zone:** [E] Exploration	**Readiness Factor:** [1] Career **Readiness Factor Category:** [a] Career Preparation

RI 92: Watching and reading airport signs and screens

FUTR Tool: no
PACT: no

Supplies: None

Discuss the following signs and screens that might typically be seen at an airport:

1. No one without boarding passes past this point
2. Arrivals
3. Departures
4. Baggage Claim
5. Ground Transportation
6. Terminal 2
7. Gate C

Objective: Student will discuss signs and screens that are typically seen at airports.

Subject: Receptive Literacy **Mode:** Discussion **Training Zone:** [O] Organization	**Readiness Factor:** [2] Daily Living **Readiness Factor Category:** [h] Transportation/Travel/Worldliness

RI 93: **Willingly following instructions**

FUTR Tool: 157
PACT: yes

Supplies: None

Discuss that, when you are in a class, at home, or anywhere else where someone in authority is asking you to do something, one of the most helpful things you can do is to willingly follow directions. Point out that you might not always want to just do as you are told, but that unless you have a serious reason to do otherwise, it makes things easier for everyone if you go along. Explain that the "willingly following instructions" relates to simple things like when the teachers says "Please sit down and be quiet" and more complex things like when your mother says "I will walk you through making the pies while I make the casserole."

Objective: Student will discuss reasons to willingly follow directions.

Subject: Receptive Literacy **Mode:** Discussion **Training Zone:** [F] Flexibility	**Readiness Factor:** [1] Career **Readiness Factor Category:** [b] Job Performance

RI 94: **Zooming in on coupon dates and requirements**

FUTR Tool: no
PACT: no

Supplies: Two or three grocery coupons per student

Pass out two or three coupons to each student. Ask students to circle the following pieces of information on each coupon:

1. The expiration date (if there is one)
2. The purchasing requirements (How much of what you have to buy)
3. The amount you will save.

Objective: Student will find expiration dates, requirements, and benefits on food coupons.

Subject: Receptive Literacy **Mode:** Hands-On **Training Zone:** [V] Observation	**Readiness Factor:** [2] Daily Living **Readiness Factor Category:** [f] Shopping and Eating at Restaurants

About the Author

Dr. Ellen McPeek Glisan received her Ph.D. in Education from the University of Nebraska, her Master's degree from Northern Illinois University, and her Bachelor's degree from Illinois State University. With more than 25 years of experience in the education field, her teaching methods have helped thousands of students and teachers. Her early success with life skill training methods in junior high and high school special education classrooms led also to innovative training methods for the corporate environment. From her Master's thesis work, the life skill writing program *Footsteps* became her first education product, and since then she has developed over 200 educational programs and spoken at many educational conferences.

Her interest and involvement in making education meaningful for her students led her to develop a comprehensive program for teaching life skills and assessing life skill competency. Her *Forecasting and Understanding Transition Readiness* (FUTR) program is a tool that provides training goal information about individual students' life skill abilities. In addition to *Aligning Life Skills to Academics* and other Attainment Company publications (*PACT Life Skill Review, Life Skill Academics Series, Job Ads and Career Paths,* and *Geography Reader*), she is the author of *Real Life Math, Basic Work Skills,* and *Day-to-Day Life Skills Series.* Dr. Glisan can be contacted for training or workshops at eglisan@swbell.net.

The FUTR Tool: *Forecasting and Understanding Transition Readiness*

The 650 transition activities presented in *Life Skill Lessons* are drawn from the FUTR Tool collection of questions and activities for assessing competency in five life skill areas: Math, Social Studies, Science/Health, Expressive Literacy, and Receptive Literacy. The full test presents 180 questions (36 per subject) and is flexibly organized to provide what is most appropriate for each student.
